TOUR DE FORCE

MARK CAVENDISH
TOUR DE FORCE

My history-making Tour de France

sourcebooks

Published by Sourcebooks
P.O. Box 4410, Naperville, Illinois 60567-4410
(630) 961-3900
sourcebooks.com

Originally published in 2021 in Great Britain by Ebury Spotlight, an imprint of Ebury Publishing.

Cataloging-in-Publication Data is on file with the Library of Congress.

Printed and bound in United States of America.
VP 10 9 8 7 6 5 4 3 2 1

To Peta

*For your love and unwavering belief.
Your stories of strength through the last
few years deserve their own book. You set
an example for our kids to aspire to.*

CONTENTS

PART II THE TOUR

PART I
THE RETURN

CHAPTER 1

11 October 2020: Wevelgem, Belgium

You won't find the first Tour de France record I ever set in any history book or almanac. I made my Tour debut in 2007 and it was a decade before I got through a whole edition of cycling's greatest race without at some point shedding tears. I sobbed with joy, wept in sorrow, cried because I couldn't stand the agony of another pedal rev, and cried because I knew that for three weeks of the year it was a pain I also couldn't live – couldn't conceive of life – without.

These tears were different. For one, we were at Gent–Wevelgem – another race I'd dreamed of as a child, but one which as an adult and participant had brought me mainly heartache and frustration. Now I was faced with the prospect of it being my last ever race as a professional bike rider.

I blubbed almost those exact words as I crossed the line and, against my better judgement, pulled up in front of a Belgian TV network's microphone in the mixed zone.

'Mark Cavendish, it was a really hard day for you …'

The interviewer couldn't see the pools of salt water collecting behind my shades, but my body was trembling, like the voice that he was about to hear.

'I can see you're quite emotional. How was your day?'

I pulled off my glasses and wiped my eyes. 'That was perhaps the last race of my career now, so I'm a little bit ...' My throat was closing, more tears welled.

'Do you really think that could be your last race?' the interviewer persisted as I took cover behind my glasses again and made to ride away.

'Maybe ...' I blubbered as I went, leaving his last question hanging in the autumn air.

Until a few hours or certainly a few days earlier, the notion of retirement hadn't remotely entered my head. Yes, I'd turned 35 in May and was now clearly in my twilight years. I had also not won a race since February 2018, not truly looked my old self in races since the summer of 2016, when I won four Tour stages, an Olympic medal and the World Madison Championship with Bradley Wiggins. But I knew, understood, could explain the multitude of reasons for what had been one long, private nightmare. A 2017 season wiped out by Epstein-Barr virus, the realisation in 2018 that I'd never been given time to recover, a team manager I despised, clinical depression – a straight-from-the-cookbook, easy-to-follow recipe for total disintegration.

Those close to me knew about all of this, and there was no one closer to me professionally than Rod Ellingworth. As a young coach at British Cycling, he'd believed in me when others hadn't, principally because we shared the same credo – that the only line that mattered in cycling was the one painted on the road, the finish line, not anything you could see on a graph, plotted with numbers from a test in a lab on a stationary bike. In 2020, after years at Ineos Grenadiers, formerly Team Sky, Rod was untethering himself from the mothership and his own mentor, Dave Brailsford, to take on the top job at another WorldTour team, Bahrain-McLaren. And, naturally, I went with him. It was going to be the hard reset I needed, in an environment and with an entourage that would finally allow me to pick up where I'd lost the thread in 2016. I'd signed a one-year deal, but Rod had also said that it was basically open-ended: I could retire at the end of 2020 and work for the team if that was what I wanted, or I could carry on racing with them for as long as I thought I had something to give.

But, as I said, I hadn't given option one any serious consideration. The victories hadn't flowed, for reasons we'll discuss, and Covid torpedoed four months of the season, but throughout the spring and summer and into the last races of the rejigged season in October, I had no real anxiety or uncertainty about continuing my career in 2021. Or about continuing it with Rod and Bahrain.

Then, the week before Gent–Wevelgem, my agent, Duncan, called. 'Mate, something's going on here. Things aren't as we thought they were. Expect a call from Rod.'

That call duly arrived. It was the day before teams had to submit their provisional rider lists for the following season to the UCI, cycling's governing body.

'Mark, we're not offering you a contract next year.'

After years of setbacks that, one by one, had chipped away at my spirit and also my legacy, this felt like death by the thousandth cut. I was crestfallen, dumbfounded, incandescent. And, above all, totally in limbo, contemplating a retirement I didn't want, hadn't prepared for. Mid-October was late, simply too late to begin the process of sounding out other teams, aligning demands and expectations, laying out why I'd fallen so low and why I was certain, *certain* of what I'd been telling people for the last four years while they nodded sheepishly and their eyes glazed over: 'You don't just lose it overnight. You can't. Can't. You don't go from winning what I did in 2016 to nothing. You might go from ten wins to five, then two, then nothing, but not from best in the world to zero overnight. *Impossible*. Fucking impossible.'

I'd get angry – still get angry now about it – thinking they thought I was lazy, not training, fat, unprofessional, when I'd *always* grafted and was now training harder and better than ever.

The idea that Rod had now defected to the camp of the disbelievers cut deep. But I had no other option than to block it out, try to gather my thoughts and steel myself for the last races of the season – Gent–Wevelgem, the Tour of Flanders, Scheldeprijs. Big races, historic races. Races that had inspired me. Races that my future now, unbelievably, might hinge on.

Gent–Wevelgem has become one of those baffling cycling misnomers in that it now starts in the town of Ypres, 70 kilometres to the west of Gent. The reasons are partly commercial, although the race is also designed as a kind of homage to the victims of the First World War, half a million of whom died in Ypres, which itself was also obliterated in the last of three battles there in 1917. Now it's a beautifully reconstructed but sombre place, particularly on a damp, cold October morning like this one was – in a nearly silent, deserted Grote Markt square.

These 'ghost races' had become the norm, with their vacant roadsides, obligatory PCR tests and the constant, looming threat that a government or organiser would pull the plug at an hour's notice. The third Covid wave was raging through Belgium – and now, on the start line under Ypres's Menin Gate, its Memorial to the Missing, so were the rumours between riders.

The talk was that this could, probably would, be the last race of the season. The Tour of Flanders: cancelled. Scheldeprijs: cancelled. A big red line through the rest of my 2020 programme.

Gent–Wevelgem isn't the same race it was earlier in my career, the so-called sprinters' Classic, as much as some pundits still see it as such, despite some pretty radical route changes. Even on my best day, my chances would be slim, and now, with my head in a spin, my stomach in knots, I decided to at least try to enjoy what might be my last hours as a professional rider. A seven-man break pulled away almost as the flag went down, and, no doubt to most people's amazement, I was in it. Four hours later we were still hammering away at the front, over cobbled *bergs,* across vast fields scattered with thousands of white First World War gravestones, until finally the peloton closed in and swallowed us up with around 65 kilometres to go. At which point there was nothing for us to do except roll in to the finish line.

I was physically spent, and, perhaps because of that, on the long, straight road into Wevelgem, the emotions started to build and eventually spill over. When I crossed the finish line, my defences were breaking.

Then came the question. And inevitably the tears. And finally those nine words that, from panicked thoughts locked in the vault of my distressed mind, I'd now released and thereby given a new, terrifying power: the potential to crystallise into reality.

'That was perhaps the last race of my career.'

CHAPTER 2

12 October: Wevelgem

Patrick Lefevere is a white-haired, honey-voiced team manager who, depending on your point of view, is either one of professional cycling's most brilliant minds or a shameless provocateur with Jurassic and too-readily expressed opinions – or perhaps even both.

To me, Patrick had continued to be a friend after I left his team in 2016, the end of three happy years together. He was also someone whose company I still regularly enjoyed, despite his lack of public diplomacy. I like Patrick because, as well as some antiquated opinions, he also upholds 'old-school' values like loyalty and transparency. You always know where you stand with Patrick. He won't just tell you what you want to hear. He'd rather be straight, and he also expects you to respond in kind. If you cross or bullshit him, you're finished. That's what I never did, and it's why we're still friends: when I was leaving the team I told him my reasons, and he, in turn, told me his for not bending to what could have been my conditions to stay. It may not be what people want to hear, but his principles are the fundamental reason why the team has won more races than any other WorldTour team *every year* for the last decade. Patrick's riders know that, if they give back what they get from him, he'll defend them to the end of the earth.

Patrick is also a noted *bon vivant*, a man of luxurious and impeccable taste, a one-man Michelin guide whether meeting in London or Paris; but the week before Gent–Wevelgem we'd agreed to meet *after* that race not for a fancy lunch or dinner, but in his office in Deceuninck-QuickStep's headquarters. It would be one of our usual, periodic catch-ups. But now, all of a sudden, there was another, unexpected item on my agenda.

It felt like destiny, or at least serendipity: suddenly I didn't have a team for 2021, and the only one I wanted to join, the one I'd ached for since I left, was managed by the man sitting on the other side of the desk. Within minutes of my interview the previous day, after Gent–Wevelgem, the clip had gone viral, cycling Twitter went berserk, and within an hour or two enquiries from team bosses had started to land on my phone. 'How much would you want to ride for us?' 'Can we talk?' From unwanted, doomed, resigned to my fate, suddenly I at least felt seen, if not exactly saved. To each of them I replied with a variation on the same message: I really appreciated them wanting me, but I needed to speak to Patrick. In fact, I realised, whatever soul-searching had taken place over the previous few hours had brought me to a stark conclusion: it was either Patrick and Deceuninck-QuickStep or I stopped racing.

To me it was really that simple. I thought to myself, *I know where I stand at QuickStep. I like how the Belgians race – they're not trying to reinvent the wheel, they just race. Cycling's evolved over 120 years. It's not evolved because some people have said, 'This is the way that racing has to go.' It's evolved because it's the most efficient way of racing, depending on what teams are there. Some teams want to be away for TV camera time, some teams now look for UCI points just to survive. But this team just goes out and tries to win a bike race. That's it. There's nothing more, nothing less.*

The team was also a perfect fit in another sense. Since leaving Patrick's team in 2016, I'd never clicked with a bike the way I did on the Specialized that had been designed around my geometry and which Deceuninck still used, albeit in an updated form. In the case of Bahrain's frame supplier, it certainly wasn't their fault that something never felt right. Their bike was stiff, fast, light – everything I wanted – but the mechanics, the manufacturer and I just couldn't get it to fit me in the way the Specialized had all those years ago.

One of the reasons why I'm a good sprinter is that I'm an odd shape – short legs, stubby arms, narrow shoulders and long torso – which may not ever earn me a modelling contract but is ideal for minimising aerodynamic drag and saving watts. But it also presents a challenge in terms of getting me low yet still comfortable and agile in the saddle. The manufacturer was reluctant to produce a longer, more race-oriented frame, preferring to stick to the more comfortable, consumer-oriented geometry of the bikes they wanted to sell. So throughout 2020 we'd tinkered with the bike's set-up, tried different cockpits and sizes, and eventually settled on a tiny frame with an extra-long stem. All to no avail – or at least I never felt completely 'dialled in'. It was basic physics. Imagine you have a truck with multiple trailers on the back. The longer the trailer, the slower the reaction time at the back end of the truck when you turn – not exactly ideal for a sprinter, or at least not an oddly proportioned sprinter like me.

So there was a magic, beckoning finger, or just another common-sense good reason: at Deceuninck I'd be back on a Specialized.

I studied Patrick's body's language, imagined the cogs in his head turning as I laid it all out, laid myself bare.

'I wanted to look you in the eye and see that you still want to continue,' he said finally, part challenge, part warning, part signal that maybe I was getting somewhere.

'Look, I would have stopped two years ago if I didn't think I was good enough to win,' I picked up. 'Every year that I ride without winning it damages my legacy. It's not about the money now. I just have to prove that it's not my problem. Or that what's happened in the last year has been my problem but not my fault. I can't talk about what's set me back publicly – at least not yet – but put me in an environment where I have no excuses, like it would be here, and I'll win. I promise that I'll win.'

Over the course of my monologue I'd noticed his posture shifting. From friendliness, it had moved first to sympathy, then curiosity and finally a sort of tentative engagement. He leaned forward. 'The problem is, Mark, that I'm at the limit with my budget. I can't …'

'Pay me minimum wage,' I blurted, without letting him finish. 'It's not about the money, because that'll come when I win for you.'

Patrick smiled apologetically. 'Mark, I have one spot in the team … but no money at all. Not even to pay the minimum wage.'

CHAPTER 3

November: Essex, Belgium and Denmark

Heinrich Haussler had always been one of the more exotic beasts on the ark of professional cycling. Born in Australia, raised as a cyclist in his dad's native Germany, Heino had immediately turned heads after arriving in the pro ranks in 2005. In his first season he rode the whole of Paris–Roubaix, the Queen of Classics, listening to his second-gen, five-ounce iPhone 'so as not to get bored'. Then, later that year, he won a stage of his first Vuelta a España a few hours after knocking back red wine in his team hotel until four in the morning. He gave off a punkish, surfer-dude air that clashed with my brand of youthful swagger – and we'd literally clashed, ploughed into each other in a sprint at the Tour de Suisse in 2010. Heino had broken his hip and later told the press that he had 'zero respect' for me as a result.

Relations had thawed over the years – then in 2020 we were suddenly teammates at Bahrain, a pair of old-timers trying in our different ways to roll back the years. Part of Heino's strategy was his diet: in lockdown he'd turned vegan, as he proudly announced when we met up for a training camp in July. At first I mocked him for the repeated monologues about the devastating environmental impact of cattle farming, how it was helping his performance and yada yada.

A few years ago I started to avoid dairy because I'd noticed that it made me feel groggy and sluggish in training, but I told Heino there was no way I'd be joining him in his endeavour; I liked my meat too much, and cutting it out looked like hard work.

This was also our team chef's feeling when Heino arrived at a race later in the year claiming that he'd seen the light. The chef said he now didn't know what to cook for him, so Heino told him to 'improvise'. Soon these plates started coming out of the kitchen for Heino that were giving me serious food envy. A few days later I cracked and asked whether I could just have what Heino was having. I lifted the fork to my mouth and it was like those moments in films or on adverts when the food lands on the tongue, the music stops and the world changes colour. It was incredible, a rhapsody of flavour, aroma, texture.

I was straight on the phone to my wife, Peta, to ask whether she could come up with some recipes. I wanted to try going vegetarian, or at least flexitarian, if not completely vegan. I got home and out went the buffalo chicken wings, in came the buffalo cauliflower. I also devoured the Netflix documentaries that most people have probably seen about the ethical reasons to try a plant-based diet but also the potential benefits for athletes. And, yes, like Heino, I also started to feel better on the bike and off.

Unexpectedly, all of this would become very pertinent in the autumn of 2020, some time after Patrick had informed me, with regret, that he simply couldn't afford to sign me for Deceuninck-QuickStep. Initially, my prospects seemed pretty bleak, for all that a few loyal friends were doing their best to help. The former Danish pro Brian Holm has been one of my longest-serving directeurs sportifs – at Telekom, then HTC and finally in my first stint with Patrick's team, where he'd stayed when I left. Brian was also one of the best men at my wedding.

He now swung into action, trying to persuade Patrick that I'd be a good investment, that I could win again, and also helping me to sound out sponsors about effectively bankrolling my minimum salary. Brian just happened to be a friend of the Danish businessman Jesper Højer. Jesper and I had also met at a team anniversary bash a few years earlier.

I told Jesper my story, why I was in this position, how it had all unravelled, and he was sold; he said I'd be needing a team *and* a film crew, because this was going to be the sporting fairy tale of the century. He asked how much I needed and I gave him a blunt answer – a minimum salary and 'team's' expenses. Fine, he said. Jesper would speak to Patrick about a partnership with Lovingly Made Ingredients, manufacturers of the protein used by his company Meatless Farm, the UK's fastest-growing meat-alternative brand, for whom I would become an ambassador. I wouldn't even need briefing about how to represent and talk about the product, I told him. I could just speak honestly about the positive effects I'd experienced since making the switch to a predominantly plant-based diet.

I was elated. I'd gone from oblivion to my dream solution. Which is not to say that the deal happened immediately, or that they weren't nervous days while I waited for the final OK. Fortunately, I finally got the call to say that, financially, Patrick was happy with the arrangement and that the main issue was therefore out of the way.

The very last stumbling block was my personal sponsors, particularly Nike, who I'd been with since the start of my career.

In other teams I'd been allowed to carry on wearing Nike shoes, but Deceuninck had a deal with Specialized that didn't allow for exceptions. People may scoff and say it's only a product, a brand – a 'swoosh' in this case – but it was still gut-wrenching to not be able to race in Nikes given I'd been associated so closely with them for more than a decade. Other commercial earnings would also suffer, but whenever such thoughts arose I gave myself the same pep talk: 'You'll win and get the money back ... but it's not about the money. Just stop thinking about the fucking money. It's about winning.'

Which in fact was only half right: it was about winning *and* having fun, not that either would exist without the other in my mind's eye. The deal was getting close, we were down to the fine print, and I sat down with the team's technical director, Ricardo Scheidecker, to discuss what my racing programme might finally look like. 'Listen,' I said, 'this is probably going to be my last year, so I want to *race* and I want to have fun. When I left the team for Dimension Data in 2016 it wasn't for money, it was because I wanted to race the Classics and do other things. I was winning but I was bored of being paid to sit in seventh, eighth wheel and just sprint over the line ...'

Some of this, I didn't need to spell out. Everyone in the peloton knows that you don't go to Patrick Lefevere's team to get rich; you go there to get successful, to win. And you win by *racing*, really *racing*, for the ribcage-thumping love of the sport. Riders and, to a lesser extent, staff had come and gone from the team over the years, but what had never changed was the spirit, the passion that also imbued everything about cycling in Belgium.

'Can I race in Belgium as much as possible? I'm craving that,' I told Ricardo. 'Big races, small races – I just want to have fun. Mud, cold, cobbles, the fans – I love it up there. It's just stripped down, no bullshit, number-on-the-back and kick-seven-bells-out-of-each-other. *That's* what I want to do.'

Ricardo nodded, smiling.

On the fifth day of December there was a surprise behind the fifth door of cycling fans' advent calendars: a press release from Deceuninck-QuickStep announcing that I'd rejoined the team after five years away.

CHAPTER 4

Mid-December: Calpe, Spain

The location was a hotel bar in Calpe on Spain's Costa Blanca, but in some ways the scene laid out before me couldn't have been more Belgian. I stood surrounded by familiar faces – the cracked, wind-lashed faces of men who had spent decades of their lives rattling over cobbles and grinding up notorious farm tracks with names like the Wall of Geraardsbergen. There was laughter in the room, an intermittent chorus of deep, approving grunts, but also the sense that the mood could and would become very serious when the conversation turned to the most serious subject of all – the business of winning bike races.

And, of course, there was beer.

All of the other riders went through the same grilling. In my case, the directeurs sportifs and coaches were getting the opportunity, just as Patrick had, 'to look into my eyes and see that I still wanted to continue'. There were also some things that I wanted to say to reassure or even make amends with one or two people. When I left the team in 2015 I'd been outspoken, pretty tactless and actually quite unfair vis-à-vis one of the directeurs sportifs, Wilfried Peeters, particularly in my book *At Speed*. It was important to me now that Wilfried could see and hear my contrition, and also that I was back for the right reasons. I hoped that by explaining to them what had happened over the previous five years, in my own words, I could allay some of their doubts about why I was back and what I could achieve – doubts that anyone would have had observing from afar, without seeing my side of the struggle.

At the end of my monologue you could have heard a bubble burst in one of their Trappist beers. The response was unanimous: 'We'll do everything in our power to help you win. We will give you the opportunities. Everyone's behind you.'

'Everyone' was perhaps stretching things. I could sense that the team physiologist, a young Dutch guy named Koen Pelgrim, who had been on the team when I was last there in 2015, had his doubts. I dutifully met with him to discuss 'my goals for the season', and it felt like a backhanded compliment when he cast his eye over my power files and said something along the lines of, 'These aren't actually too bad.' Patrick had signed me out of sympathy, was the strong vibe I was getting from Koen, but I'd been around too long, had too many sports scientists crumple their brow at my lab test results to let it get to me. The fundamental difference in this team, the reason I was desperate to come back, after all, was that in a sport increasingly overrun by eggheads and laboratory quarterbacks, they recognised that the most important peer-reviewed studies went by names like the 'Tour of Flanders' and 'Paris–Roubaix'.

The team's no-fluff credo didn't begin or end with racing. It's long been an open secret among pros that, to put it impolitely, Deceuninck's training camps are an exercise in kicking seven shades of shit out of each other. Consequently, I was nervous arriving in

Calpe in December, more than ever before at this time of year. Proving people wrong, sticking two fingers up to preconceptions, has been the theme of my career, and the battle has often started at the first training camp of every season. It was the same at Bahrain-Merida in 2020: me clinging on to the wheels of the team's best climbers in the hills, like a dog with his teeth locked on a bone, and them finally getting mildly annoyed but at the same time, I could see, also thinking to themselves, *Shit, well fair play.* And then, months later, being more willing to wait for me in races because they'd seen that I wasn't a lost cause.

Now, at Deceuninck, there were only five 'survivors' from my first stint with the team – Zdeněk Štybar, Julian Alaphilippe, Dries Devenyns, Yves Lampaert and Pieter Serry – and I felt under pressure to demonstrate that I could dig in, work hard, get over a climb and also still sprint. Fortunately, over the years the rides had obviously become a bit more structured, a little bit less like races, and I was able to hold my own. Then when the shouts did go up – 'Sprint to the next sign!' – I'd be going toe to toe, wheel to wheel with the fastest guys – the team's 2020 Tour de France green jersey winner Sam Bennett, his lead-out man Michael Mørkøv, and our young sprinter Fabio Jakobsen, who was recovering from an almost fatal crash at the Tour of Poland earlier in the year. I wasn't winning them all, but I did just enough to show there was still life – a bite as well as a bark – in the old dog yet.

A cacophony of barks, growls and yaps was also coming from one of the team cars following us on our rides. This was another one of the team coaches, Vasilis Anastopoulos, or Vasi for short, born in the Peloponnese village of Megalopolis and with a megaphone for a voice. Brian Holm had suggested that maybe Vasi would be the right guy to coach me, having seen his structured, disciplined and passionate approach to his work. Vasi then suggested we have a meeting and asked me to come to his room. By that time we'd established that he was the same solitary Greek guy that I occasionally ran into at track races when I was younger, whom I invariably beat but never passed without noticing him, partly because of his size and muscularity.

Now I sat on his bed and listened to him explain a little bit more about his career as a rider, the years he'd spent on an Austrian team, how Koen had wanted him at Deceuninck, and what he envisaged for me. 'I've been looking at your files and we need to work on a few things,' he said. 'We need to do more sprinting, more sustained power work – that's where you were always good, but you've neglected it over the last few years. It's going to hurt and I'm going to say a lot of crazy things. You're going to hate me … but you have to trust me. We don't need to focus on leg-speed because you've got that naturally, but there's going to be a lot of work on your top-end power, a lot of capacity … and you'll have to watch your weight, so stay off the sweets and desserts.'

As he spoke, I could hear the echoes of what someone else had been telling me over the previous year. The Australian former British Cycling coach Shane Sutton can be as loud as Vasi – but considerably brasher. Shane had also always observed me and my training through a high-precision lens that others didn't possess. I'd had sporadic contact with Shane for a few years and always tried to check in with him every few months after he left the federation under a cloud, amid allegations of sexism, in 2016. I'd hated Shane at various times, often winced at some of his words and methods, but he had also been great with me and right about what I'd needed. So when Vasi now effectively told me the same things I'd heard from Shane over the past couple of years – as Shane put it, 'They're training you to get over climbs, but what's the fucking point of getting over climbs if you can't sprint on the other side?' – I knew immediately that I'd found my new coach.

Stevie Williams, one of my old teammates at Bahrain, had been coached by Vasi in his amateur days and also gave him a glowing reference. 'Oh, mate,' Stevie said, 'he'll give you these training programmes where he'll tell you to write down your efforts on a piece of paper and then keep that in your pocket. Mad shit like that. And it's super-hard. But he's incredible – you just need to trust the process.'

I heard similar things from others who had worked with Vasi. They told me to focus on retaining the key message and not to be put off by his intensity and constant contact, which simply stem from his passion. That day in his room, I was frank with him. 'I'm nearly 36. I'm not a kid. But what you've told me is exactly what I already thought myself. We're on the same page. And I'll say to you what I say to every coach: you won't have to kick me out on my bike. I'm a professional. I'll do what you tell me.'

Which is not to say I was immediately smitten with his delivery. In fact it reminded me of something Dave Brailsford, Sky's manager, used to tell me: 'Cav, everything you say has a point to it, but people stop listening to you because you're shouting at them. It's not what you say but how you say it that makes them stop listening.'

Finally, a bit later in the winter, I'd realise that it wasn't Vasi being a disciplinarian, trying to impose his authority. He was simply passionate – just like me. In fact he was vicariously doing the effort with me. Later, when he took me to Greece, I'd realise it was also a bit of a national trait: I used to think the southern Italians were noisy, amped up, unnecessarily demonstrative, but then I went to Athens with Vasi …

What was clear from the off was that he was invested in me, and as the days of that December camp ticked by, I felt more and more comfortable, more and more trusted, more and more at home. Outside the hotel window we could see the Mediterranean lapping, but it also felt like I was back in Belgium, which in turn felt a bit like being back on the Isle of Man. Little things just cracked me up. Just the Belgian mentality. It's like going back in time. Nobody's in a rat race. Everybody shops locally. I don't think they have Amazon in Belgium. You need a ladder? You go to see Willem or Brecht or Pim at the local ladder shop. And if you ask for directions in Belgium, it's always 'about an hour'. 'Brussels airport?' About an hour. 'The team headquarters from Antwerp?' About an hour. 'Okay, how about from Brussels?' Quizzical look, little shrug, puff of the cheeks and, 'About an hour.'

It may seem quaint, provincial even, but I love it, and they're the same with cycling. They adore it, but in a matter-of-fact, unshowy way that sort of says, 'Well, yeah, it's great, but we've always known that …' They just get the sport, you really feel it there. Everyone all over the world watches the Tour de France, but the Belgians come out in their thousands for a village race, a kermesse. Why? Because that's just what they do. It's in their veins, but it's also hard to explain or describe.

I'll sometimes get recognised in the UK or somewhere else, and people will ask for a selfie or an autograph, and they also do that in Belgium, but somehow it's different. They're happy but they're not star-struck. They'll smile, say something funny, do this little grunt that's like a Belgian purr, shrug, then shuffle off to wherever it is they're going that's 'about an hour' away. It's like they're having a conversation with someone they've known for years, which is exactly the feeling I get on the Isle of Man. There I'm never 'Mark Cavendish, the Tour de France rider'. I'm just the same old Cav or Mark they've always known.

Even the riders I didn't know had made me feel similarly welcome in the team ... although they also announced that I had to be formally 'sworn in' with an initiation ceremony on the last night of the camp. Josef Černý and Fausto Masnada would be my fellow 'victims', as the other newbies in the team. Young Mauri Vansevenant seemed petrified so was spared. Not that what ensued – involving pink mankinis, an extremely ragged rendition of 'Bohemian Rhapsody' and, yes, some fairly industrial liquor – was anything like the ritual humiliations that these affairs can sometimes turn into.

My other memorable contribution to the same evening was suggesting we hold a 'Fight Club' in the gym where we did yoga and core stability sessions in the mornings. We matched up riders of more or less equivalent height or weight, and I got paired with Yves Lampaert. *Good match-up. Perfect,* I thought.

We squared up on the mat, started stalking and eyeballing each other, then I went to grab him, felt his foot connecting with one of my shins and, *Boom!* I was on my back. Three seconds it had lasted.

I was like, *Huh? OK, let's go again.* So we went again. I'm watching my feet this time, and this time I last … seven seconds. *Boom!* On my back again. Everyone's creasing at this point, but I won't have it. I'm saying, 'Nah, that's not possible. Let's go again.' So we do, for a third time … and for a third time he's just Vinnie Jonesed me and I'm horizontal, staring at the ceiling.

I should have read his bio on the team website, shouldn't I? 'Yves became a cyclist at the age of 17. After 11 years of judo, he earned his black belt and wanted to do something different.'

He was Belgian national champion, for fuck's sake.

CHAPTER 5

Christmas and New Year: Calpe and Essex

After the December camp I rented an apartment in Calpe for a few more days and stayed on to train on my own. I was looking forward to Christmas with the kids, playing Santa, seeing them open their presents, getting stuck into my training again in the UK ... but there was an issue: Peta had caught Covid just after I'd arrived in Spain. I had two choices: go home, run the risk of getting infected, with all the associated dangers – including long Covid – or stay in Calpe, alone in a rented Airbnb, staring at the walls when I wasn't out on my bike. Luckily, by the time I was due to leave, Peta was no longer contagious. I'd also decided that, in the unlikely event that I did get it at home, being sick now was a far lesser evil than it would be later in the season.

It seemed like the smart move ... until I woke up on Boxing Day feeling drained, groggy and unable to train. Straight away I panicked and called the team doctor. He asked whether I'd had a drink on Christmas Day, to which I replied that I'd had a few glasses of wine.

I've never been much of a drinker. Apparently it had been so long that I'd forgotten what it was like to be hungover.

Recovered and relieved, over the next few days I trained mainly with Tao Geoghegan Hart, the recently crowned Giro d'Italia winner who grew up and still lives not far from our Essex home. They were easy enough rides, and it was nice to catch up with Tao. He had stayed and trained at my place in Tuscany a few years earlier and always been polite and respectful. Then it was back to Calpe for another camp, again preceded by a few days on my own before the team arrived, to squeeze in an extra three-day block, just to be totally ready.

The December camp had surprised me a bit by not being quite the smash-fest I'd feared, but there was no chance of January being in any way *tranquillo*. For a Belgian team, the one-day spring Classics are the *sine qua non* of the season, and they come early in the calendar, in March and April. Consequently, everyone has their racing head and legs on from the very start of the year, and some of the sessions at the January camp can look like full-speed, real-life simulations of what's to come in a few weeks' time, albeit with the hills and headlands of a Spanish costa rather than the *bergs* of Flanders as the arena.

During my three years with the team between 2013 and 2016, training rides would end with a race to the boatyard in Calpe. The resort sits underneath a long, thousand-metre-high rocky outcrop that acts as a partition between the bay and everything inland; there aren't too many ways in or out, but one we used regularly passed a big boatyard just as the road sort of rippled up between two round-abouts a few hundred metres apart, just as you came into town. Back in the day a few of us – Tom Boonen, Zdeněk Štybar, Niki Terpstra and Michał Kwiatkowski – would all stick in €50 and have a sprint to the boatyard at the end of our rides.

The custom of 'the boatyard sprint' had evolved in the time I'd been away. There were no longer any bets but the boatyard had become the finish line for all manner of improvised, more or less spontaneous races during or at the very end of rides. The shout would go up, usually from big Tim Declercq – 'Race to the boats!' – and it'd be fucking *on*, whether we had a kilometre to go or 30, whether it was all downhill or over climbs.

These sprints or 'races' now suddenly became important yardsticks. The kick to the boatyard itself was often windy, slightly uphill and a delicate test of timing from the last roundabout, not dissimilar to the old finish line on the Champs-Élysées from the Place de la Concorde in the Tour de France. It was a test of power but also race craft, reading the wind, and a lot of the time I was nailing it. I wasn't necessarily winning every sprint, but with almost every one I was gaining confidence. I could also tell that I was impressing some of the lads.

We were practising lead-outs, sometimes doing 10 or 15 sprints in a training ride, and I was holding my own in those, too. These were also my first chances to sprint with and from behind Michael Mørkøv, the team's ace lead-out man. Morky's one of the world's leading track riders and someone I'd known for over a decade, since we started racing against each other in velodromes at the start of our careers. I'd wanted to bring him into my lead-out train at various times over the years, possibly as the 'third man' to come before Mark Renshaw and me in our train, but Renshaw was never quite as keen and I didn't want to unsettle him.

So Morky and I had remained friends, occasional training partners and mutual admirers. But he'd also found his sweet spot working for others, most recently in 2020 with Deceuninck's green jersey winner Sam Bennett. That pair had become inseparable, a double act like Renshaw and I had once been, so rooming with Morky in Calpe in January looked like being one of our last chances to spend time together before we went our separate ways, he and Sam to a considerably more prestigious 2021 race programme than me.

Even as roommates we seemed to click, despite our very different personalities. I'm loud, Morky's dead quiet; being around me when I'm in a good mood is like trying to wrestle a firehose, whereas Morky's sense of humour is biscuit-dry; we both love cycling but I'm obsessive, romantic, evangelical, whereas he loves it like a neuropathologist loves taking apart people's brains. He's surgical, unsentimental, cool as a polar bear's toenails. Like I said, for some reason we just clicked, and I couldn't help wondering what it would be like if we raced together – while reflecting on the fact that, sadly, I might never find out.

The camp itself abruptly became a lot less enjoyable when one of my teammates tested positive for Covid. Suddenly everyone who hadn't been vaccinated had to isolate for a few days. Even our group rides had to be adapted, and one day Shane Archbold, our Kiwi 'flying mullet', and I were sent off to do 200 kilometres on our own. Vasi and Tom Steels, himself a former Tour de France sprinter, could clearly feel our pain, whereas Koen Pelgrim seemed to find the whole thing mildly amusing. That wound me up, but I bit my tongue and got on with it.

Finally, then, the doc gave us the all-clear to stop isolating and we could 'look forward', if that's the right expression, to another team tradition – the end-of-camp race near Oliva, 40 kilometres or so up the coast from Calpe. In the team this was a major event that the riders and staff had hyped up over the years, creating rituals like the dinner the night before, where the directeurs sportifs draw names out of a hat and divide us into five or six different heats or races. Generally the race will be four kilometres long – three on a long, straight road, a bit that kicks up for 600 metres or so, and then the last 400 metres are totally flat. The format is 'hare and hounds'. There'll be one hare who's generally a good time triallist and sets off 20 seconds or so before the hounds. They then have to judge and time their effort to catch the hare and also beat the other hounds. We all get points for our finishing positions and, after three heats each, the five or six riders with the most points go through to the final.

I was going well: I won two of my three heats and was second in one, so I was in the final. I wasn't just sitting in the wheels, waiting for the sprint, either – I was racing and loving it, just racing on instinct, trying to solve problems, dosing my efforts, working out when to go 'over the top' and counterattack and when to sit tight. In the final there was no 'hare' – it was me, Morky, our world champion Julian Alaphilippe, Sam Bennett, Mikkel Honoré and João Almeida. The first two kilometres into the bottom of the hill were steady but still cagey. No one had made their move.

I'd tried to time it so that I went onto the climb in last position, but suddenly the pace slowed and I found myself in third wheel, with Julian, João and Mikkel, the best climbers out of the five, tucked in behind, ready to jump me. I was a sitting duck … so I took flight, catching everyone except Julian by surprise. Probably the strongest rider on the planet at those punchy, uphill efforts, Julian hit out and

I followed with João, almost clawing my way back. It took his first trademark turbo boost of the year to narrowly beat me on the line.

I'd also gone deep. Slumped over my handlebars, my heart still drumming and my muscles still choking on lactic acid, I saw Tom Steels out of the corner of my eye getting out of the team car and ambling over. 'Seeing that, you'll win this year,' he said. 'I've got no doubt about it. It's there. You'll win. What you'll win, I don't know, but I have total faith that you'll win.'

CHAPTER 6

14 February 2021: Almería, Spain

To win any kind of race, first I'd have to ride one – and that initially proved harder than I'd imagined. Covid was still tearing through Europe and numerous races were being cancelled. I was supposed to start my season at the Volta ao Algarve, but that got postponed until May. I didn't panic because the team had put me down for the Vuelta a Valencia, only for them to then swap me out for another sprinter, the Colombian Álvaro Hodeg. Now I did start to worry. Did they not believe in me?

Vasi told me there was no point fretting about what I couldn't control and just to get my head down. He drew up a training plan for me to follow at home – double days with a normal road ride in the morning and a simulation of track efforts in the afternoon, also on the road. It was less than I'd done the previous year in terms of quantity, but at times it was excruciatingly dense. Every rider hates split days, heading back out after lunch, and these were double-daily helpings of pain. The weather in Essex was also damp, cold, grim. One day I got so cold as I finished my efforts, dripping wet, in the dark, that I didn't think I could get home. I was shaking so much when I did finally swing into the drive that I couldn't pull out my key and had to headbutt the door to get Peta to open up. She had to undress me in the hall, tear off my saturated kit, and I was nearly in tears. In other years I might have said, 'Fuck this,' with two or three efforts to go, but I had to get the set done. Vasi had committed to me, and I had to commit to his plan. There could be no excuses.

Bloody-mindedness was getting me through, but so was my family. One of the dishes on Vasi's à la carte hurt menu was a series of uphill sprints in a low gear, 'torque efforts' – a bit like standing starts on the track. I'd always do them on the same hill a couple of kilometres from home, and Peta would bring the kids to watch and cheer me on. To be honest, she probably didn't have any choice in the matter, because nothing comes between my youngest, Casper, and cycling, whether it's riding or watching – cyclo-cross, road races, anything and everything.

Most kids learn to ride a balance bike when they're two or three; Casper was on his from dawn until dusk when he was 11 months. Not long after, he taught himself to ride a proper bike – I came out of the garage one day and he was doing laps of the drive. Now, at three, he can do things some pros struggle with, like grabbing a bottle. He watches TV and YouTube like all other kids, but for a long time he didn't know who or what *Peppa Pig* is, whereas Wout van Aert … he recognised Van Aert even when he was riding for Belgium in a different kit! He also did indoor sessions with me during lockdown on a baby turbo-trainer I'd hacked together out of a plank of wood and a couple of old shelf brackets I'd found in the garage. He cries when he can't come with me on rides outdoors. So, no, it wasn't difficult for Peta to persuade him to come and join in with my training sessions, as a riding partner or a cheerleader.

At this point in the year I felt as though I needed all the moral support I could get. I was finally going to kick off my season in the Clásica de Almería in southern Spain. It was a race where the sprinter-friendly course would suit me but where I apparently wouldn't be the team leader. We had another fast finisher in our line-up, Hodeg again, and it was made clear in our pre-race briefing that I'd be riding for him. Which was … fine, because no one could begrudge Álvaro anything. So nice, so relaxed, always forgivably late, Álvaro's the prototypical Colombian, loved by everyone in the team. And that left me with a bit of a conundrum: he'd already taken my place in the Vuelta a Valencia and I was the guy who had spent his whole life stepping on toes to get where I needed to go. But I wasn't really in a position to do that now. Suddenly I'm the lowest-ranked rider, lowest-paid rider, and what I've achieved in the past doesn't matter; I have to shut up and do what's demanded of me, while still being curious to see how the directeurs sportifs tackle this.

In Almería I got my answer. Wilfried Peeters, my foe turned friend since I'd rejoined the team, said we were working for Álvaro.

My role in the sprint would be to 'sweep' for Álvaro, meaning I'd stick to his back wheel and thereby stop sprinters from other teams using his slipstream. It was a job I knew how to do, but which also came with its own dilemma: if I could tell that I was faster than him in the sprint and felt he was in danger of getting beaten, should I come around him?

It all turned out to be academic. Almería has two significant climbs early in the race, and on the first one I was getting cut adrift a few hundred metres from the summit. I got on the radio to tell the guys and … nothing. Silence. I tried again: 'Guys, wait, I'm a hundred metres behind the peloton.' But again, no response. Usually, when I was the designated sprinter in this situation the directeur sportif would order the guys to sit up and pace me back on. But Wilfried Peeters said nothing. I wanted to be fuming, but I knew my status here and now and fortunately managed to dig in, join another group and finally make my way back to the rest of the team.

As we came into the closing kilometres our train was all lined out and in position, but Álvaro was losing the wheels. Every time it happened he and I would have to sprint to get back up to the wheel in front. Finally, I decided to move ahead of him. He said nothing, didn't react … then a kilometre or two later Álvaro crashed. The radio crackled, Álvaro announced he'd fallen, and it hit me: *Fuck, I'm sprinting.* The guys were flying – Bert van Lerberghe, Tim Declercq, Stijn Steels, Florian Sénéchal and Jannik Steimle just in total control, me in the stretch limo behind them. *Fuck, imagine if I win my first race …* The thought had barely flickered in my consciousness when I heard a familiar noise: *psssst.* Back-wheel puncture. Fuck. I carried on riding, losing positions and eventually sight of the bunch. Finally the team car arrived and we changed the wheel, but it was too late. I rolled in well behind the winner, Giacomo Nizzolo, who had narrowly beaten our emergency sprinter, Sénéchal.

In the hour or two after the finish I noticed something strange: for the first time in more than a year I felt disappointed not to have sprinted, not to have won. Last year, whether it was because I was older, mellower, a family man – or whether I knew that I was pissing in the wind anyway – I was never really that bothered when I lost.

This was the first time I'd thought, *Fuck!* I was a bit gutted by it.

For every sign that things were moving in the right direction there was also something that made me wonder whether my luck was just fucked forever. The next race was Le Samyn, a one-day 'semi-Classic' in Belgium. I was looking forward to it, having not ridden Le Samyn since my first season as a pro. The course had changed significantly, got harder and hillier like pretty much every other pro race over the last 20 years, but it was still going to be typical blood-and-thunder Belgian racing – second-division teams on the start line, fighting for every corner, attacks all over the place, no one looking at their power meter, no pattern to the racing. And so it proved. The plan was the same as in Almería: 'We ride for Álvaro.' Fine, so we hit the final circuit, breaks are going and it's just as I imagined it, just as I hoped it'd be. Mayhem. Álvaro gets dropped, I'm following these moves, up climbs, over cobbles. In races like this the attacks are different from attacks in a mountain stage of, say, the Vuelta: there, guys are all just looking at their power meters because they know exactly what number they can sustain, whereas in a race that's broadly flat but with wind, it's a different type of game; you can let one guy go, then another guy will go and then three guys will go, then another two and all of a sudden you've got a ten-man group up the road, so there's always a decision to be made about who you go with. You might think, *Oh, shit, that's one too many.* Then you've got to go with it, you've got to close it because the wind is coming from the side. You need to get there before the elastic snaps.

Finally, I found myself in a move that looked as though it would go all the way to the finish, but suddenly no one would ride with me. Again, it was a feeling or realisation that had once been familiar, but which I'd nearly forgotten: they were scared of me. And I loved it.

The first and second groups eventually came together. We were heading for a sprint. This was it. With two kilometres to go we were on the front, just floating, everyone in position. They all bury themselves then pull off – one by one, Tim, Bert, then finally it's me and Florian Sénéchal. There's one last cobbled section. I'm just waiting now, but Florian attacks. What the fuck? The professional thing to do is let his wheel go, leave a gap, so I do … but I'm also wondering what he's playing at. Then guys started passing me and my head was exploding. Needless to say, Flo didn't win and I rolled in without even sprinting.

I got back to the bus with steam coming out of my ears. I didn't know Florian well, hadn't raced with him before, and the lads told me I shouldn't take it personally: he was from just over the French border, it was one of his local races, and above all, no, we didn't know each other. That was when it dawned on me: some of the guys in the team and the peloton had only known me when I'd been – to put it bluntly – a bit shit. They hadn't been around when I was winning. It was an obstacle that I hadn't foreseen but which would be a theme of the early season.

And it was one that, sooner or later, I needed to find a way to overcome.

CHAPTER 7

March: Belgium

It had now been three years since my last win. There was a time in my career when three weeks without a bouquet would have felt like and been described by the press as a crisis – especially if it was in a major tour – but between Le Samyn, which we've already established I didn't win, and the last time I crossed a finish line with my arms aloft, in stage three of the 2018 Dubai Tour, it was, to be precise, 3 years and 22 days. To be even more precise, 1,118 days or 26,832 hours.

For that last win in the Gulf, I'd had an unfamiliar lead-out man. To be honest, I didn't even know his name, and he wasn't even in my team. I'd also never really given it a second thought, until one of my new Deceuninck teammates, Bert van Lerberghe, introduced himself: 'Hey, you know I led you out for your last win, don't you?' Of course, at the time he was riding for Cofidis and was supposed to be leading out Nacer Bouhanni – only it was me who got onto his wheel.

Now I immediately twigged: 'Oh, that was you!'

Throughout the winter it became a running joke: Bert had led me out to my last win and he was going to lead me out to my next one.

The GP Monseré presented itself as the perfect opportunity. Bert was in the team and it was the kind of race I'd insisted on riding when we drew up my programme – narrow roads, twists and turns and not a second to look at a power meter. It was also a special race for the team, as the route passed Deceuninck's headquarters.

We were in great shape coming into the final, too, with me initially on the Alpecin-Fenix sprinter Tim Merlier's wheel before letting Bert into the line and taking his. But, again, we fluffed it – or to be precise, one of the Arkéa team swung into the line, meaning Bert had to swerve then brake, as he found himself in a cul-de-sac. Merlier saw it and reacted in a flash, launching his sprint way earlier than he normally would and instantly opening up an irreparable gap. I sprinted anyway, just to get an idea of my speed compared to Merlier's and the other sprinters in the race, but crossed the line in a very distant second place.

Now the joke on the bus was that Bert had let Merlier go on purpose. They are best mates, after all.

Again, I was frustrated, but this was another important milepost simply because I noticed another subtle change in the way I'd reacted. This time I was disappointed not because I thought I could have won, but because I should have.

At least I was proving my fitness, that I could be competitive, but my race programme also presented a challenge. I was mainly doing one-day races, which put a premium on freshness, but you also have to be careful your condition doesn't deteriorate when you rest between the races. With this in mind I did a solid week of training back in the UK before going back to Belgium for my next 'semi-Classic', Nokere Koerse. I was looking forward to this because it was a race I'd never done but which would often end in some kind of bunch sprint. I knew exactly how it usually went – a fast descent into a cobbled section where balls counted more than skills, then the road kicks up for the last couple of hundred metres. I'd visualised it, pictured the perfect sprint. I even spoke to Adam Blythe, a former runner-up, who confirmed exactly what I already knew – the downhill into that last cobbled section was key.

So I felt fit, motivated, ready to win … then I opened the roadbook on the eve of the race and realised that the course had been completely overhauled. It was unrecognisable from the Nokere Koerse I thought I was going to be racing.

I'd like to be able to say this was the reason why, with eight kilometres to go the following day, I was lying on wet cobblestones like a beetle on its back, my feet still clipped into my pedals and my bike somewhere above my head. There are painful crashes, frightening crashes – and crashes that are plain embarrassing. Here I'd made an absolute fool of myself with an amateur mistake: not lifting my front wheel high enough as I came out of a gutter and onto the cobbles, hence whacking the lip of the road and doing a spot of schoolboy gymnastics. Fortunately, I was unhurt – unlike my teammate, Jannik Steimle, whom I passed as I rolled in, just motionless on the side of the road. It was a massive relief to find out at the finish that Jannik had 'only' injured his shoulder. At moments like these you feel almost brutalised, that the sport itself is just primeval, barbaric. When I'd ridden past him, prone at the roadside, I had no idea if Jannik was going to get up, but I had to just press on to the finish line.

There was no time, never is, to dwell, reflect, question what the fuck I was doing, still trying to prove myself at age 35. It was straight onto the next race, the next Belgian one-dayer, the next chance at the Handzame Classic. It was also more of the same – cobbles, wind, crashes, riders doing crazy, stupid stunts. One example, just one: when wind's hitting the bunch from the side and echelons start to form – basically little groups fanning across the width of the road, as everyone tries to shelter – some rogue thinks that he can ride on his own from one of these echelons to the one in front. Even Eddy Merckx isn't closing the gap; you're much better off working together. The animal kingdom tells us that – the tribe is always stronger than the individual. But these guys think they can do it better alone. It's like the cycling equivalent of Brexit. They think they're strong enough to do it on their own, but they're just going to fuck everyone, especially themselves. You're going to end up in a worse situation than where you started from.

So that was Handzame – crosswinds, mayhem and, finally, a group of riders, including my teammates Florian Sénéchal and Josef Černý, getting away and racing for the win. Meanwhile, I was marooned in the second group with Shane Archbold, we thought just cruising in until, for reasons I still can't understand, teams started getting into their trains, clearly intent on sprinting for thirtieth place. At first I was annoyed – which is also why, when Archie sort of shrugged and asked me, 'Do you want to sprint?' I replied, 'All right, fuck 'em, let's do it.' I suppose it was a power trip, but also valuable practice – and a message to the team that, although the win hadn't come yet, I was making progress. I already felt that I was on the bottom rung of the team's ladder of sprinters, and I knew that it was only by winning sprints – even for thirtieth place, which I duly got – that I stood any chance of moving up.

Unfortunately, that wasn't going to happen any time soon. After a few days training together in Belgium, Archie, the American Ian Garrison, and I flew to Italy to take our place in what can only be described as a mishmash of a team for the Coppi e Bartali stage race on the Adriatic coast of Italy. The description may sound disrespectful or at the very least self-deprecating, but none of us were under any illusions; while all eyes were on our world champion Julian Alaphilippe and the Belgian core that was expected, like every year, to dominate the spring Classics, or on Remco Evenepoel's Giro d'Italia preparation, our odds and sods had been sent to Italy in what, that week, even we began referring to, with gallows humour, as the 'C Team'.

In most stage races you start with seven or eight riders. Here we had five, but we made a little go a long way. The first day of racing consisted of two stages – a format that's now almost extinct and which all riders bar none absolutely detest. The morning stage was pretty much certain to end in a sprint. Again, hopefully I'm not being disrespectful when I say the field was pretty modest, or at least that a team like Deceuninck would be expected to win or come very close. But, yet again, I bottled it, or at least got unlucky: Ethan Hayter, the Ineos rider, waited for ever to launch his sprint, with me on his wheel, while Jakub Mareczko blasted down the other side of the road to win. I got second but was raging: Mareczko is quick on his day, but he rides for a second-division team, which we, the 'C Team' of the world's number-one ranked team, really ought to have dispatched.

By now, maybe some other riders would have been getting disheartened. Don't get me wrong, I was annoyed, angry even, but the previous three years had thrown so much disappointment, so many setbacks my way that I'd become bloody-minded or desen- sitised or maybe just more determined. I was also loving the camaraderie between the guys – a sort of mongrel, underdog spirit that came from a recognition of our status, and which also reflected what I'd been at the start of my career and where I found myself now. In Italy the laughs were also assured by our directeurs spor- tifs, Davide Bramati and Brian Holm: Brama the self-styled 'cycling Mourinho', with his booming broken English and flailing hand gestures; Brian with his very dry humour and weird fixation with British cultural stereotypes like tea-drinking and fry-ups. Together they're a comic duo to rival Morecambe and Wise, Laurel and Hardy, Statler and Waldorf. They're also master strategists when it comes to bike racing.

So our C Team was purring on the bike and rocking off it. The chemistry now carried over into the afternoon team time trial, where we finished third, just two seconds behind a victorious Israel Start-Up Nation team with two more riders than us and stacked with good time triallists. We might have rued another near miss ... but I'd taken the leader's jersey. It wasn't a win as such, but it was the first time I'd been on a podium for three years. A little, big moment.

There's a warm glow, a sort of snug feeling that comes with the prestige of a leader's jersey, but also more tangible benefits. Suddenly I had something to race for, to hold on to. Suddenly we could go out and control the race, and, in all honesty, feel like somebody. Do you want to go somewhere in the peloton? Well, now I'd be able to go wherever I wanted to go. It was partly a result of being in a strong team, but it was also the jersey. And it was so refreshing, so empowering to have that feeling that I'd started to lose way back when I was at Dimension Data – of being able to move around the peloton at will, partly because the strength of our unit allowed me to do that, and partly because other riders see the leader's jersey and say, 'After you.'

Coppi e Bartali is a hilly race, with most stages heading from the coast into the Apennine Mountains, so I only lasted one day on top of the general classification. But the week continued in the same positive vein and, most importantly, on the same upward trajectory: it had been years since I'd got better every day in a stage race, but that was what was happening here. Vasi was analysing my power files every night and kept telling me, 'Wow, you're going well,' and my legs agreed: on the climbs, on the flat, everywhere, they were absolutely singing.

The whole team also finished on a high. On the last morning Brian sat us down in the bus and delivered his pre-stage briefing: 'You've got nothing to lose. Just race and have fun today. Just look after each other and race.' With one lap of a hilly circuit to go the whole team was still in the front group, en masse, and Mikkel Honoré went on to win the stage. The C Team, the misfits, the unselectables, had put on a clinic.

My win drought now stretched to 1,143 days but, unbeknown to anyone outside the team, I was ending the week with an armful of moral victories. The Training Peaks software we use in the team has logged every ride I've done, going back years, and awards 'medals' for personal bests. That week the medals came one after the other – best one-minute power, five-minute power, ten-minute, hour …

I should have told Vasi I was breaking records like plates in a Greek taverna.

CHAPTER 8

7 April: Scheldeprijs

'How are you getting to the airport?'

The voice at the end of the phone was totally unfamiliar, its owner someone I'd never met, yet somehow the whole weird scenario seemed in keeping with my season to date, and certainly the previous few days.

It had started with me asking – again – to be sent to a race for which I hadn't originally been selected. Now here I was taking a cold call from some random dude who insisted he could drive me from Lugano in Switzerland to Milan Malpensa Airport. A few hours later I was getting into his car and then we were bombing down the A8.

In truth 'random' may be a bit misleading. After Coppi e Bartali, on seeing the state of the weather forecast in the UK, I'd headed to Switzerland for a mini warm-weather – or at least *warmer* – training camp, and it was Mikkel Honoré who had now turned travel agent and arranged my emergency transport to Malpensa. 'I have a mate …' was how he presented the idea. There were no trains, the team had already dropped me in it by calling me up at a moment's notice, and frankly there was no other option. Fortunately, he was a nice guy, a fan of mine and a decent driver.

I said the team had dropped me in it. In reality, Covid was throwing up all sorts of complications, the latest being that, having initially gone to Lugano for the weather, I suddenly had a major issue: if I went back to the UK, I wouldn't then be able to go to the Tour of Turkey, where the team had promised me a full lead-out train, because of travel restrictions. Geert Coeman, the team's financial officer, said the team would fly my family over to Switzerland or Italy so I could see them, but that didn't work, either, because they simply couldn't travel anywhere from the UK. I was basically resigned to the fact that I wouldn't be able to see them for five weeks. The only alternative was to pull me out of Turkey, which would basically have been akin to raising the white flag over my season, my comeback, my career.

Rik van Slycke was going to be my directeur sportif in Turkey, and he was the latest to propose a different plan – that I would go to Belgium for a few days to train with some of my teammates up there. I didn't fancy it – riding on climbs in Switzerland, you can still work on your strength and explosive power while using different muscle groups from the ones you're training on the flat. But then I also had an idea, a suggestion that I put to Rik: I could come up to Belgium if they put me in Scheldeprijs, the one-day Classic that had been my first ever pro win in 2007. I knew the 'A Team' was going to Scheldeprijs, with our A Team sprinter, Sam Bennett, but I made what I thought was a convincing, sincere pitch: 'Look, if I come to Belgium, maybe I'll come now and do some training, do Scheldeprijs, go to Turkey. I'll work for Sam, go and get bottles, but at least I can race. I like Scheldeprijs, it's probably my last Scheldeprijs, as I'm retiring this year. It would be nice to do

Scheldeprijs, my first win, in my last year.'

Rik said he'd see. Then he called back. 'Sorry, Mark, not possible. No Scheldeprijs.'

I was pissed off – that the team maybe doubted my motives, thought that I might undermine Sam. I also suspected that Sam himself had put his foot down. The call with Rik ended and I vented to Mikkel: 'Why does no one believe that I want to do a fucking job? I know my status in the team, that he's a fucking green jersey winner and there's no one who has more respect for the current king of sprints than me. You do not challenge a green jersey winner. He's the reigning green jersey winner for a year, that's how I see it. I was it once, I know my status.'

So that had been that. I carried on training in Switzerland. Vasi had also wound me up by setting Mikkel and me brutal and totally incompatible training plans, meaning we could hardly ride together. He got a piece of my mind, too, but he was steadfast: 'No, you do what I've set.' I knew deep down he was also probably right. Vasi's a nutter but he's also my nutter. A fucking genius as far as I'm concerned.

We got to Monday and I was leaving for Turkey on Thursday. My phone rings. Wilfried Peeters, 'Fitte'. 'Mark, how would you feel about doing Scheldeprijs?'

'We've already spoken about it and it was a no,' I answered.

And Fitte's like, 'I know, but we've seen the weather now and it's due to be rain, wind, maybe snow, and we know you can deal with that.'

I didn't know whether to feel flattered or offended. Either they thought I was some knucklehead they could send out into monsoons and hurricanes, who would just smile and say, 'Thanks,' or it was actually a mark of respect.

The bottom line was that of course I wanted to do Scheldeprijs. I just had to get there. Which is where Mikkel's random mate came in.

Usually we travel to races two days in advance, but now I got to the hotel on the Tuesday afternoon, with the race on the Wednesday, and immediately jumped on the turbo trainer for a quick tune-up. The atmosphere that night at dinner was good, buoyant. No issues. We had a crack team for what, despite changes to the route over the years, was still likely to be a sprint finish. Sam was there, obviously, and we had Morky, his lead-out man, Bert van Lerberghe, Iljo Keisse, Florian Sénéchal and one fellow C Teamer who'd been flying at Coppi e Bartali – Shane Archbold.

I didn't immediately pick up on any tension from Sam, but then he's a hard guy to read. Nice guy, super-nice, quiet, but I wouldn't necessarily say introverted; he likes a joke, a bit of banter, and is good in a group. We're just different, certainly in terms of self-belief. I'd heard that he'd had misgivings about me joining the team at the start of the year, and that was indicative of his propensity for self-doubt generally. He'd won two stages of the Tour and the green jersey the previous year, yet still talked about needing to gain confidence. Whereas faith in my own ability had never been something I'd lacked.

The weather on the morning of the race was bleak; outside the bus window we could see trees at the roadside bent over, rain turning to sleet and then snow. But inside it was rocking; Tom Steels had put on a video from the Tomorrowland dance festival and the music was pumping out of our bus as we drove into the start area. The tactics were arguably less important than the clothing choices on a day like that, and I'd gone for a windproof gilet under my jersey, with just arm warmers, while nearly everyone else was in a rain cape. On a day like that, a course like Scheldeprijs, it was all about staying warm, dry and aero. Scheldeprijs is one of a few races sometimes referred to as 'the sprinters' world championship' – another being the final stage of the Tour de France on the Champs-Élysées – and it was our firm intention that this edition would live up to that tradition, with our top sprinter, Sam, winning. To help him, it had been decided, he'd keep his usual lead-out man, Morky, whose style and reflexes he knew, while I'd give him the additional insurance of sweeping on his back wheel – basically sitting on it to make sure that no rival sprinter could use his slipstream.

Four kilometres into the race, your day can be over on the new Scheldeprijs course. You go over a bridge, the wind hits you from the side and, *Boom!* The whole race can be in pieces. It nearly happened again here but we stayed alert, led onto the bridge and set the tone for a pretty faultless performance, at least until the last kilometre. At one point we had Sam and Morky in a small front group, and Bert, Sénéchal and me in a slightly bigger one behind, meaning that Sam and Morky could do nothing, with the excuse that we were coming back to join them. Consequently, they got an armchair ride and we made it across, giving us five strong riders coming into the final in Schoten.

With two kilometres to go we had the situation under control – until an attack went and Bert panicked, immediately upping the pace. Now, suddenly, we were going to burn men too early, which would mean losing speed in Sam's train and getting swamped by other teams. I wondered whether I should go around Sam to give him an extra man in the train, but, no, Sam's used to Morky, so should I jump in front of Morky? This is all happening in my head quicker than I can describe it … and then, before I can do anything, Bert's pulled off, Morky's suddenly in the wind and he has to back off. Inevitably, other teams can now move up around us, and I'm thinking that I should perhaps just launch. But then Morky's left a gap up on the left side for Sam to come up on the barriers, while the Alpecin-Fenix sprinter Jasper Philipsen's going on the right. My instinct tells me to jump onto Philipsen's wheel and sprint from there – but that means abandoning Sam, abandoning my sworn duty and running the risk of … winning.

So I let Philipsen go and wait for Sam to jump across onto his wheel or go up the barrier, where Morky's left the gap. Sam does neither. He finally moves onto Philipsen's wheel when it's too late, and I stay on Sam's wheel like a good dog.

We get second and third. After the finish, Sam says nothing to anybody. We both stand on the podium, smiling, either side of Philipsen, but the mood on the bus afterwards couldn't contrast more sharply with the noise and laughter of the morning.

That night Sam goes home, while I'm in the team hotel with the lads who'll be travelling to Turkey. I keep playing those last few hundred metres back in my head, arguing with myself about what I could have done differently. *Fuck, we're a team, and I know I did the right thing, but we came to win … and we didn't win,* I say to myself. I couldn't sleep, couldn't make peace with myself.

The next day I was still stewing, so I messaged Tom Steels.

'Tom, can we talk?' He told me to call him, so I did and verbalised everything that had been going through my head for the last few hours. Tom was one of the best sprinters in the world in the 1990s, so I was confident that he'd understand my dilemma. I admitted to him that I was angry at myself for not taking the chance when it presented itself, jumping onto Philipsen's wheel. That's what a younger me would have done – so had I lost my killer instinct, and if so what did that mean?

Tom is fair but upfront; I knew he wouldn't just tell me what I wanted to hear. He listened silently to my monologue, then finally gave his verdict.

'Listen, Cav, we probably fucked up by putting you both in that situation. But if we did the race again tomorrow, we'd do the same again.'

CHAPTER 9

11–12 April: Tour of Turkey

Once upon a time, if you'd said the name Mark Cavendish to a cycling fan the image that would have immediately come to mind would be the world's best sprinter winning on the Champs-Élysées, in front of the Arc de Triomphe.

Now, in April 2021, I hadn't won anything for three years and I was racing for … the Golden Arches. We hadn't eaten all day, Covid had shut down the whole of Turkey, including every restaurant and fast-food joint in Istanbul Airport bar one, and that was where our first sprint train of the week was heading. 'French fries all round, please.' Not exactly what Vasi had meant when he'd told me a few months earlier that watching my diet would be key to me regaining my best form and, yes, at some point winning a race.

To be honest, at this point we were having second thoughts about even going to Turkey. Morky had missed out – or dodged the bullet – because of travel restrictions from Denmark, and that left us with a team of six. I'd won seven stages in Turkey in 2014 and 2015, there'd be plenty of chances this year, and the whole team would be riding for me. It was also a race where the organisers always rolled out the red carpet, with great hotels and business-class flights on Turkish Airlines ... or at least that was my memory. Already, a few hours into the trip, I could see things had changed as we examined our boarding passes. Now we were flying with some kind of budget subsidiary of Turkish Airlines, and forget business class, most of us were in the Covid seats – 27C, 18E – squeezed in between two punters.

We all gulped, but we hoped the plane would at least be fairly empty. It was rammed. Like the Tube in rush hour.

We had a few hours' layover in Istanbul before a connecting flight to Ankara – plenty of time for a burger and fries, although it's fair to say we weren't, ahem, 'Lovin' it'. The collective mood improved somewhat when, while the other guys were eating, I took myself off to see if I could find us some entertainment and managed to find a shop selling Uno playing cards. That kept the whole gang amused – riders, mechanics, press officer – until it was time to board the next plane. Then, finally, at the other end, we had a two-hour bus journey to get to the team hotel. It was gone midnight when we arrived; we were hungry again and were told that either the organisation or the hotel had left us packed lunches.

I opened up one of the bags, pulled out a warm sandwich, took one bite and put what was left straight back in. 'No fucking chance.' Fabio Jakobsen was either hungrier than me or less picky. He paid for it by vomiting all night and having to skip our training session the following morning.

Another reason to do the Tour of Turkey usually was the weather. Generally, we'd spend most of the week at the coast, under blue skies. But now, near Nevşehir in the middle of the country, we woke to freezing fog. We finally headed out into the gloom for training that would also serve as a recon of the next day's finish, and it started off raining, then sleeting and hailing. Suddenly, just going up a gentle, steady climb became a scene from *The Revenant*, and we were all swinging, almost whimpering on the bikes.

Before the blizzard, I'd at least done something we rarely get time or have the energy for at bike races: take in our surroundings. We rode past the Kaymakli Underground City near Nevşehir and I was mesmerised. In fact, I stopped and told the guys I'd catch them up later. They didn't seem that interested, were even taking the piss out of me – but I didn't care. I was blown away just being there, even though I wasn't allowed in because of Covid. The tunnels were apparently cut out of the rock in the eighth and seventh centuries BC, and ended up being used in various ways, by various civilisations, from the original Phrygian inhabitants to Christians hiding from Mongolian invaders in the fourteenth century, then right up to the 1920s by local people that the Ottoman Turks knew and persecuted as 'Eastern Romans'.

Back in the present day, our build-up to the race continued to be less than ideal. Everything had been chaos since we'd got here – and now there was more. More snow was forecast for the following day, so stage one was going to be cancelled. We'd suddenly have to pile into minibuses and get driven to Konya, where stage two was supposed to start and finish. That now became stage one, albeit a shortened version – only 70 kilometres. In the morning we trained on the circuit and I surprised myself with how good I felt, particularly when we did a sprint effort. I then looked at my power meter: I'd hit my highest peak power in over a year ... by a considerable distance.

So later that afternoon we're coming into the finish, nice and smooth, dynamite in my legs, ready to launch … but Stijn Steels jumps way too early, with seven kilometres to go. After that it's just a shitshow, with other teams swamping us, people dive-bombing underneath each other coming into the corners, someone nearly putting Álvaro Hodeg into the barriers, but Álvaro managing to save himself with a little pirouette on his front wheel – all the normal chaos of a bunch sprint. Then it was a now-familiar story – me left chasing crumbs, sprinting for a minor place. I 'won' it to get fourth and knew instinctively that it would also have been a stage-winning sprint had the split not occurred. I also knew instinctively that, with that speed, this could finally be the moment, my week.

On to the next day. Again, it's Konya to Konya, exact same finish, but this time a 'proper' stage length – 144 kilometres – and also some climbs. And again, the stage starts and I feel great, I'm pinging, especially going uphill. Don't get me wrong, I'm still not Nairo Quintana, but I can measure how well I'm going just from the information on my radio about how many riders are getting dropped.

That morning we'd talked about not making the same mistake as the previous day, not going too early, not making our move on the big road as we went into the final, which gave other teams too much room to come around. So the race is all together, we hit the big road … and it's a fucking carbon copy of the previous day: we've gone early again, we're getting dive-bombed, crowded out, swamped.

We somehow find a way through, and this time Álvaro gets me to the last corner but peels off so I can find my own line. I'm about five back. Alpecin-Fenix are winding it up, but Israel Start-Up Nation and their sprinter, my old teammate turned rival André Greipel, are also there.

Rick Zabel, André's lead-out man, goes, and Rick's a fucking menace. When he's done his lead-out, he'll just hang there like a Christmas bauble, making it impossible for anyone to come around, which is exactly what he does now.

But Alpecin-Fenix and their sprinter, Jasper Philipsen, have got the jump on Greipel, so now he's got no Rick and five metres to close. Another sprinter would wait for someone else to come around and use him, but I know André. André will try to close it himself.

So I follow André. Follow, then pass him on his right.

Eighty metres to go. Seventy metres. Still five metres between me and Philipsen.

I'm coming on his right, gaining, but I know the wind's coming from the right.

Sixty metres. Fifty metres.

Fuck it. Left. I'll go left. Half a second of shelter could give me three, four kilometres an hour.

The line's coming – coming fucking quick now.

My front wheel's level with his back one.

Twenty metres.

I don't look. Just see the line.

The line. The line. The fucking line …

Ten metres.

Five.

The line.

A sort of silence hits me, then confusion, then disbelief, then the elation.

The relief. It fucking hits and engulfs and overwhelms me.

It's fucking over. I've won a fucking race.

CHAPTER 10

13–18 April: Tour of Turkey

The first thing I did was call Peta. The first thing once I'd got to my phone, that is, and that took a while. There's always a whole happy rigmarole that comes with winning, some aspects of it more formal than others, from hugging and thanking your teammates to anti-doping and the podium ceremony.

But here the first few minutes were consumed with something I'd never experienced, not to this extent, after any of my previous 146 wins – a procession of riders from other teams coming to congratulate me. Riders I didn't know, riders I did know, riders I got on with, riders I didn't get on with. Fuck, I'd even have hugged Peter Sagan that day. I don't remember all of them, but I do remember most. And if I wasn't already emotional enough, seeing fellow riders so happy for me – and a sort of unspoken recognition in them of what I'd been through – completely broke the dam.

For years, in every one of my wins there'd always been an under-lying element of 'fuck you' – real or just perceived. From me to my doubters, from critics that had the hump that I'd won again, from rivals towards me or me towards them.

This was completely different. I felt it immediately. Everyone seemed thrilled, for themselves because it was an inspiring or just mildly heart-warming story, but also, genuinely, for me. I'd stopped doomscrolling through social media years ago, when I first suffered from depression and started realising that it was poison for my mind. But now, suddenly, I could open up Twitter or Instagram and appreciate people's generosity and the realisation of how much they'd cared and admired my resilience, even if they didn't know *exactly* what I'd overcome. The messages on WhatsApp were in some cases from people who *did* know, but I realised almost immediately that I couldn't reply to even a fraction of them. There were hundreds, literally hundreds of them.

A call from Fitte, who was in Belgium. Brama in Italy. Patrick, the boss, who I answered with a question – 'Are you proud of me?' – to which he responded in his usual way, usual tone, same octave, just, 'Yes, I am,' and a smile that I couldn't see but could picture. The doc, Yvan Vanmol, who never cries, fighting back tears. And Vasi, on a video call, not fighting them back at all, just letting them rain down his cheeks, setting me off again. 'Thank you so much. You got me here,' I told him. These were just the guys who weren't there. After dinner, the whole team on the race and the staff all went up to the rooftop bar of our hotel and we toasted again.

Then Peta and the kids – before, after, and once more when they were going to bed. Delilah had grown up around races, in some of my best years, celebrated her first birthday on the QuickStep bus at Scheldeprijs. Even Frey had seen me win. But Casper hadn't even been born the last time. Just reflecting on that, that he now wouldn't just know Dad as a former winner, an old and no-longer champion, was super-nice.

It was all overwhelming, unforgettable, unrepeatable. Only I did repeat it – I won stage three as well. And stage four. And stage eight. This after we'd almost gone home, jacked the whole race in, after win number two.

It wasn't the bananas, although they nearly sent me over the edge too: it was tradition that the winner in Alanya was always given a big bunch on the podium. And here's the thing – I fucking hate bananas. I'd won there in 2015 and just stood there, holding this enormous bunch of them, pretending to smile and trying not to gag. But I've got a phobia of bananas and apparently it's not uncommon. In their skin, they're OK – I can touch a banana, although I don't really want to – but an open banana or someone eating one gives me goose-bumps. Even thinking about it makes me gag. I don't mind banana bread, banana milkshake. It's not the flavour, I like them. It's just the bananas themselves, the stringy bits on them, if that makes sense.

And now here I was for the second time in six years, holding the world's biggest bunch on a podium and trying not to puke. But, as I said, that wasn't why we wanted to go home.

The second win itself was as routine as the second in two days after three years of nothing can be. I was in the leader's jersey, the guys got me in position – albeit a little far back – and I went long, at over 200 metres, knowing that it was downhill and I could hold the speed. Once I'd launched, I didn't look left or right, just ripped straight down the middle of the road and was never threatened.

Again, we were all overjoyed, until we went down to dinner in the hotel that night. We were now on the south coast, there were tourists everywhere – and, again, the buffet was a Covid cluster waiting to happen. It was rammed, with riders, team staff, tourists, the organisers' bus drivers. People were coughing, not even keeping 20 centimetres apart, let alone a metre. Some of the staff from another team kindly pointed us to a table they'd saved outside, but we all knew we couldn't go through the week like this. We took pictures and put them on the group chat for the guys who hadn't been down to dinner. The team doctor, Yvan, saw them and immediately called a meeting. 'Guys, listen, let's look at obvious solutions,' Yvan said, once we'd all crowded into one of the rooms. He laid them out for us. Then I spoke. 'First, is it ideal? No, it's not. From a selfish point of view, we're winning here and it's an opportunity for us to win. So we've got to look at opportunities to stay. But if we can't find any, then we go home. The sponsor wants us here, but, if it's going to cost money to make us safe, they have to take that on.'

Then Yvan called Patrick, who told him, 'Do whatever you need to do, whatever it costs.'

We considered all the options. Booking into our own hotels, rather than the ones allocated by the organisers, which is usually against UCI rules. Eating in restaurants. Not leaving our rooms. Going home – which was the solution a number of my teammates preferred.

Finally, we settled on a compromise whereby a member of staff would call ahead to all of the hotels and organise a private dining area, with our own food, drink and everything we needed. Then in the mornings it went like this: the soigneurs used one of the bedrooms to set up an improvised breakfast table for the whole team, with cereals, coffee, fruits, everything we needed. They'd even got hold of a little stove to warm up pancakes for us. They were getting up in the early hours to set it all up – which, again, was just more evidence of the passion that drives everything in this team. The soigneurs, who usually only prepare the food we eat when racing, just live for it, love it. I can promise you that just witnessing it has a tangible effect on the riders' performance.

So we stayed. And yes, carried on winning. I knew the stage four finish in Kemer, or at least had won there before – but weirdly I had no recollection of it when we discussed the final that morning in the briefing. When we then came into the last kilometre in the afternoon I was a little too far back again, but I saw Philipsen kick and reacted instantly. I could almost hear him groan as I passed – 'Aghh, arghh …' – beating him for the third time.

But within seconds of crossing the line, as I turned to hug my teammates, my delight had turned to horror. When I had drawn alongside Philipsen, before the sprint had really opened up, I heard a sudden, crunching noise behind me – the sound of metal on metal, bodies on barriers. A huge crash a few hundred metres from the line. Now, panicking, I scanned the waves of riders rolling over the line, some of them with ripped and bloodied shorts and jerseys, and couldn't see Fabio Jakobsen.

A year prior to this Fabio had been the fastest, most exciting young sprinter in the world. Then, at the Tour of Poland in August 2020, his life had turned, in fact nearly ended, when another Dutch sprinter, Dylan Groenewegen, deviated in the final metres of a sprint and put Fabio into the barriers. Fabio had half-somersaulted through the air before smashing into the finish-line gantry and coming to rest a few metres away, unconscious and with his face unrecognisable. For a few hours the cycling world held its breath, before the hospital where he was being treated confirmed that he'd survive, but that his injuries were extensive: a brain contusion, hairline fractures in the skull, a broken palate, ten lost teeth, chunks out of his upper and lower jawbone, cuts to the face, a broken thumb, damage to the nerves of the vocal cords and a lung contusion.

That he was making his comeback here in Turkey was already a miracle. Now, as I looked for him, I feared the unthinkable, worst-case, repeat scenario. The very notion was so harrowing that I started to cry.

It was a few seconds, but they felt like hours. Then his silhouette appeared in my field of vision, and the relief was like nothing I'd ever felt, not even anything like two days earlier.

'Fucking hell, Fabio …' It turned out he hadn't even crashed. He'd just stopped to check that someone who had was OK.

It had also been the first stage that he'd ridden in our sprint train, just the next step as he eased his way back. I'd sat on his wheel, watching the way he surfed and swayed through the corners and gaps. *Yep, he's a sprinter, all right. This is easy,* I thought to myself. It was like riding a magic carpet.

Fabio will probably become the dominant sprinter of his generation, but Jasper Philipsen also impressed me hugely in Turkey, both on and off the bike. We got to the last stage with my victory tally still on three and Jasper now on two after wins on stages six and seven. In the last 200 metres, he had me exactly where he needed me, against the barriers with nowhere to go, but he moved to give me just a few inches more space. Had he not done that I could, probably would have crashed. It also meant that I ultimately came around him on the line for the fourth time in a week.

A lot of guys would have been seething, but all week he'd been gracious in defeat. He's 23, I was about to turn 36 – we were from different eras, but the respect between us was clearly mutual. 'I remember watching you, I remember buying the first Cavendish signature Oakleys,' he said to me.

They'd brought out those glasses at a time when I was passing so many landmarks that, in most cases, journalists would quote a number or record to me and I'd just nod, like, 'Oh, that's nice ...' But now it had been five years since I'd last won four stages in a single race, at the 2016 Tour de France. As we left Turkey, I thought about how quickly it had all flown by – even the days in the last few years that had seemed like the longest of my life. I'd got my hundredth pro win in my first spell with QuickStep, way back in 2013. The maths was easy yet baffling: a hundred wins in the first five and a bit years of my career ... and just under fifty in almost a decade since then.

I shook my head as I tried to process it all. 'From hero to zero and back again: Cavendish goes full circle,' I kept hearing and reading that week – or words and headlines to that effect.

Where had the fucking time gone?

CHAPTER 11

Late April: Essex

In Turkey, the Screen Time graph on my phone app looked like the profile of a Tour de France summit finish. Having built barriers over several years, learned the hard way that social media could be toxic for my mental health, I spent a few days luxuriating in an outpouring of affection that seemed to span every platform, every corner of the cycling public and media, and reach much further and more broadly than that.

Again, it was gratifying and surprising, partly because of the contrast with what had been my experience for so long. And it made me reflect, particularly on the fickleness of it all. Even now, it didn't take long before little pockets of people online or in the traditional media, on seeing the tidal wave of support, felt the need to temper it with criticism or nitpicking. It's like Newton's third law of motion – every force in one direction has to be met by a force in the other direction, in this case meaning that it couldn't all be praise, not for more than a few hours or days. I guess there's just something in human nature – I'm not sure what exactly – which compels us to piss on people's parade, to rejoice in their hardship. If Tadej Pogačar doesn't win the next Tour de France you can guarantee there'll be people saying, 'He's lost it.' At age 23. The same way that, now, they felt the need to belittle what I'd done in Turkey, argue that I'd beaten 'no one', that it had been low-hanging fruit.

I don't know if it's just modern culture or it's somehow programmed into our DNA that when things are good, you don't really say they're good, you just take that for granted. It's when things are bad that people speak up. I tell some of the young guys, when we talk about social media, to remember that if they post or something happens, out of a hundred people who are fans of our sport, forty won't even have heard, forty won't give a fuck, and twenty will react but only half of those will express that. It's fine when something's positive, but it also works like that when they perceive you to have done something negative. They're the only people you'll hear because they're the only ones who, firstly, have heard, secondly, give a fuck, and thirdly, are sad enough to need to externalise that.

This is why I rarely ever log on to Twitter now. It's become such a negative place, and it's a shame because it's ruined for the people who want to say or read the positive or just objective, interesting or compassionate stuff that is on there. I don't actually look at my mentions because, although maybe 90 per cent are good, I can't respond to or just be grateful for even one positive comment because I know it'll be catnip for someone who wants a fight, an argument, to make themselves feel better by making others feel worse. So I end up logging off again. Just not wanting to unleash something – but also, unfortunately, not engaging either.

Nonetheless, after Turkey there were times when I got lured back into the vortex, the echo chamber. Predictably, for every person who said they were four easy wins in Turkey, there was someone else wondering if I could now get picked for the Tour. Even I thought that was a fanciful notion – although not so fanciful that I didn't wonder if, maybe, somehow, let's say in an emergency, suddenly something went wrong …

I called our technical director, Ricardo Scheidecker. 'Ricardo, I've got something to ask you. What's the plan if Sam doesn't do the Tour?'

Silence at the other end. Or at least a hesitation.

I carried on. 'I mean, I know it's a long shot, thinking four wins in Turkey means I could do the Tour, but I reckon that, if you needed me … I'm not trying to compete with Sam or challenge him. Not at all. That's not it. I just want to know what we'd do if something happened to Sam, whether it's worth me getting ready *as if* I was doing the Tour. Or if the contingency plan's Fabio …'

'I don't know if Fabio will be ready,' Ricardo said flatly.

'I mean, I've got the Tour of Belgium in my programme,' I picked up, babbling now. 'I've also got the Ruta del Sol, but I've got nothing else. I think I need to at least go to the Dauphiné or Tour de Suisse and prepare in the mountains. I know you've got an altitude camp at Sierra Nevada. Would it be worth missing the Ruta and going to the altitude camp? I'm prepared to do whatever. Doesn't matter if I need to go to the Suisse to try and win a stage. If there are no sprints, it doesn't matter. I think maybe I should just go and prepare for the Tour just as a back-up plan …'

Ricardo didn't say yes, didn't say no. He just let me talk myself out, let the monologue fade away. And the conversation die. Ricardo had supported me this year. But I knew he'd have a job presenting this as logic and not sentiment. Anybody would!

Cavendish to the Tour? No one in the team mentioned it again. Not to me, anyway. Not for a while.

CHAPTER 12

4–12 May: Athens, Greece

By early May, I had an ambition, a dream even, and it was about to come true: as promised, as I'd requested when Vasi said we should just train *as though* I was going to the Tour and he'd invited me to Greece to do just that, we were on our way to the Acropolis.

In fact here I was, looking up in awe at the 46 outer columns of the Parthenon that had been standing on the same hill above Athens for two and a half millennia.

Prior to this trip I'd always been fascinated by ancient history – history rather than mythology, which was why I'd always been a bit hungrier for knowledge about Ancient Rome than Ancient Greece. I've been to Rome and loved diving into Roman history, which is basically what you do just by entering the city. Whereas the line between history and mythology had always struck me as being a bit blurry with Greece. Nonetheless, I'd always wanted to go, especially to the Acropolis, and now Vasi had said he'd see to it that I got the chance. I also had no idea what Athens was going to be like beyond the famous monuments, and I was fascinated to find out.

I did know for sure that we'd be busy in Greece, because Vasi puts his heart and soul into everything he does. He'd shown that just in the planning. I was having to cover my own costs because it wasn't strictly a team camp, but Vasi was already calling in the favours: from a mate at the Ministry of Sport, getting us free track time; from the tourist board so that I could get my guided tour of the Acropolis, even though it was quiet because of Covid. Nothing was too much trouble for him.

Leaving home is always a wrench, with the saving grace usually that you're going to see the boys and it'll be a laugh. In Greece it was just going to be Vasi and me – and I knew it was going to be hard. Hard but necessary. When you're at a camp there's structure, an inherent discipline. You know you're not going to sit around for another half an hour to have an extra cappuccino. There are fewer distractions, you sleep well, recover well. Vasi said that, with this one in Greece, a decent block of power training and some long rides would take me to another level.

When I landed I had to get a Covid test in the airport. While I waited in the queue, I had my first revelation of the trip. Everyone was just screaming at each other. I said to Vasi, 'Everyone's shouting.' And it suddenly dawned on me that Vasi's not loud, he's just Greek. They're like the southern Italians on speed.

It was all new and exciting – the landscape, the road signs, the alphabet that Vasi was explaining to me as we drove to the hotel. The next morning, we kicked off with an easy ride behind the scooter and some track work to finish off. The roads were like Italy – poorly maintained but with a millionaire's backdrop of coastline, mountains and whitewashed hilltop villages. Vasi paced me on his scooter and it was just beautiful. Then we got to the velodrome and I immediately got out my phone, took a picture and sent it to Brad Wiggins. 'Look where I am.' As a teenager I won a schoolboy national title on the track but initially wasn't really into it, but by the time Brad was winning gold in Athens, the next Olympics in Beijing had become an actual goal. So it was amazing being there but also weird; I can remember watching Brad's ride, the thumping atmosphere, yet now here we were and it was silent, eerily so. There's something romantic even in that, and just generally in going onto an empty track, with no one in the stands and the only noises being your wheels on the board or the echo of whatever your coach is barking at you. It's Rocky running up the Philly Art Museum steps, Ali at Deer Lake.

The image is an appealing one, but fuck, was it hard. On the second day we really got stuck into the first block on the track. Oh, my life! It was all based around riding behind the motorbike to work on leg speed. Vasi had prepared everything – track bike, all set up perfectly so I didn't have to travel with mine, everything perfectly sponsor-compliant just in case anyone took a photo. It had been a huge effort on his part, and now it was my turn. He explained that the session would be pretty much like a points race in that it would have sprints every five or ten laps and a total distance of around forty kilometres. I got just over halfway and we had to abort because I couldn't hold the bike any more; I'd gone too deep. I tried to stand up but the velodrome was spinning around my head. The last time I'd gone that deep with a track effort was the 2016 Olympics. I eventually stopped trying to stand up and just lay in the track centre, staring at the ceiling, thinking, *What the fuck?* And that I might not last a week without killing Vasi.

But we'd only just started. There were even harder days later. Sessions where I was retching, sessions where I could taste blood in my mouth, sessions where Vasi had to catch me as I fell off my bike. Then, the worst of all, this 'pyramid' workout on the last day where

Vasi was the 'hare' on his scooter, and I'd either be following or chasing him, with shorter and shorter intervals to recover between the efforts. After that one, I couldn't walk for two days. I could barely make it onto the plane to get home.

It was horrific, but phenomenal for my fitness – and incredible because of what I saw. On every road ride Vasi made sure we passed some kind of landmark, just to satisfy my curiosity, and on the first day it was Marathon, where the first marathon started in the modern Olympics in 1896. There's a statue of the goddess Nike there. And you could see the starting line of that race. For any sports fan, it's quite a special place, the birthplace of perhaps the most iconic running discipline on the planet. You think of Pheidippides running from the battle and collapsing dead, having delivered the news of the Greek victory over the Persians. But is that history or mythology? Whatever it is, it was great to learn all about it.

Then, the night before my first rest day, Vasi told me, 'Make sure you've got sun cream on tomorrow,' but didn't say why. He'd arranged a tour of Athens on Bromptons, which he also said could be my 'recovery ride'. We went to see everything, the original modern Olympic Stadium and of course the Acropolis, as he'd promised. Everything was closed because of Covid, but Vasi knew a guy, I think he was a journalist, and he'd fixed it for us to get in. Usually it's packed, but in the photos it's just me, like I've been superimposed on a postcard. For every second of that tour, I felt like one of the luckiest people who'd ever visited Athens. It was incredible. There were no people, no queues, plus Vasi had got me a tour guide who took us around on the bike and explained everything. It was hands down the best rest day I've ever had, finished off with a late lunch in one of Vasi's favourite restaurants.

I was going home shattered, but emotionally and culturally invigorated and inspired. I also had an idea of how to show Vasi my gratitude – but it might have to wait a couple of months and didn't entirely depend on me.

The odyssey continued.

CHAPTER 13

20 May: Villarrodrigo, Spain

Between the villages painted brilliant white, the olive groves on the mountains and the neon-blue sky, I could still have been in Greece, only it wasn't just my location but also my mood that had shifted almost the width of a continent.

Now I was in Andalusia, not Greece. I was also sitting in a team car, not on the saddle of my Specialized. It was two weeks since the end of Vasi's savagery retreat. After my four wins in Turkey, the camp was supposed to make me even stronger, even quicker, even more ready for any eventuality should the team need me – even the Tour. Yet now here I was, a fortnight later, having just abandoned the Ruta del Sol midway through the third stage, empty and unable to carry on.

I was horrified. Confused. On stage one my legs had already felt numb, lifeless, in the neutralised zone. Then we'd gone up a drag – not a climb, a drag – and I'd been dropped immediately. We were still a hundred kilometres from the finish and I'd ridden them alone, in the scorching heat, sweating like a pig in a butcher's.

Day two was more of the same. This time at least I wasn't alone: my American teammate, Ian Garrison, was also struggling. We rode the last 60 kilometres together, way off the back of the bunch, last and second-last in the race.

I thought all of the training would finally kick in on the third day, that I'd suddenly find my legs, but it was even worse. There was a power cut in my legs. At that point I flagged down our team and climbed in. I told our directeur sportif, Rik van Slycke, that my hips were sore, my legs like jelly. I was panicking. This was the first time since the start of the year that I'd taken a significant backward step. I also knew that all the naysayers – the 'it's only the Tour of Turkey' brigade – would be watching and feeling vindicated.

If I was fretting, Vasi didn't sound particularly alarmed. He simply told me to take a good few days off. No efforts, no rides, no meetings, nothing. 'Trust me, trust me,' he said. So I did.

I'd forgotten three things. One, this always used to happen to me after big training blocks. When I was younger, in my best years, I'd always taken days off whenever I felt fucked, but over the last few years I'd never felt I could afford it. Fundamentally, I'd also forgotten another thing that a lot of novices and fans don't understand, namely that it's not the training that makes you better but the recovery. So what is training? Particularly when it's power training, it's damaging your muscles so that they are more durable when they repair themselves, and therefore stronger. That's what it is. And if you don't let them recover enough this is what happens.

I'd also just raced a kermesse in Belgium two days previous. Shit weather, aggressive racing and the travel on top of that – Greece to London to Belgium to Spain and then assorted other bus and car journeys. These days off were the first time I'd really rested, allowed that muscle-repair process to really do its work. And, sure enough, after a week I was back on the bike and my numbers were off the charts.

My next races were a pair of one-dayers in Belgium over a weekend at the start of June. The first one, Dwars door het Hageland, had some cobbled sections, some gravel sections, and we'd gone in with about five potential winners, all better suited to the course than me. I sacrificed myself early for the team, climbed off before the end and made my way back to the bus. As I approached, I could see a cameraman with his lens trained on me. *For fuck's sake,* I thought to myself. This had happened a few times in 2020 in similar circumstances, when I'd only been there to work for my team, but it had been spun or flagged up in the media as another dramatic Cavendish failure. I should have just ignored it, but I found myself circling the team bus, trying to shake him off.

Our best finisher in Hageland, Yves Lampaert, had 'only' finished third, so the pressure was on us the next day in the Elfstedenronde, as it always is in Belgium. I was also feeling it because I was finally going to be racing with Michael Mørkøv – aka Mr Midas, the lead-out man who made sprinters' dreams come true. He'd been supposed to come with us to Turkey but couldn't make it because of travel restrictions. In his absence, our C Team had cleaned up – to the point that Fabio had jokingly asked me whether I was going to buy all my teammates commemorative watches. My response had been 'No' – in fact it had been 'Fuck off!' But it also led to a conversation, and an idea about what we could do. We all ended up going on the Nike website and getting trainers custom-designed for all of us, with first names embroidered on one shoe and 'C Team' on the other.

The lads loved it, but it was just as well Morky wasn't there. When he heard about the trainers he wasn't impressed. 'You've got to stop with this shit about the C Team,' he said to me at one point, deadly serious. 'It's condescending to the other riders.'

I told him it was our in-joke, that he needed to chill out. But, in fact, Morky's coolness was one of his biggest virtues, especially on the bike. He also had a good sense of humour, but it could be dry, different to mine, although we'd generally always got on. As partners in races, I thought we'd now be a perfect match.

If you'd asked me with five kilometres of Elfstedenronde to go, I might have revised that opinion. There were crashes, carnage, and I wasn't so sure how I was following Morky, but he was moving through the peloton like a track rider. I was like, *Woah! Some of those gaps are a little bit …* He clearly knew what *he* was doing but I wasn't so sure. I gripped the bars a bit harder and winced as I started to see Morky's backside disappear further ahead in the sea of riders. *Change of plan, I'm on my own.* Thankfully, with 500 metres to go, I was in prime real estate, on Pascal Ackermann's wheel. The German sprinter was someone who had really emerged as a prolific winner in the last couple of years, when I'd been missing in action, so I didn't really know how he moved. Here, he seemed to be waiting, waiting, way too long – and, finally, I decided I had to go it alone and just find my own way. By now the line was coming, I was eight or ten positions back and it was game over. Tim Merlier won; I was coming fast behind him but could only get second.

Basically, we'd fluffed it. I'd been telling myself all year that getting led out by Morky pretty much guaranteed victory, and I'd proven myself wrong. Not only that, but I'd nourished what had become a prevailing narrative: I'd become a flat-track bully, a collector of cheap wins and sympathy votes.

We watched the replay on the bus, and I turned to Morky. 'Mate, that was a bit different to how Renshaw used to lead me out …'

The issue wasn't that Morky had got out of position. He was at the front, where he was supposed to be. The problem was that I hadn't wriggled through the gaps that he'd created, mainly out of fear that I'd have to lean on riders with my head, which would get me disqualified. With me it was morphological – my shoulders are so narrow that if I lean on riders alongside me it looks like and can be classed as a headbutt, even though it's the safest way to just ease a guy to one side. That had been taken out of my repertoire, so sometimes I saw the kind of keyhole that Morky had gone through and thought twice or backed off. I could see it now, watching the video back: this one was on me; it was me who had to adapt.

'You're right,' I said to him finally. 'You did your job. Let's think about how we make this work.'

The good news was that I'd felt fast when I sprinted – easily fast enough to win. That night I had dinner with Patrick, and admitted I was frustrated that it'd be weeks before I could make amends. My legs were on fire, the work in Greece had paid off … but my race programme for the next few weeks was bare. The Tour of Belgium was a few days away, but Sam was coming back for that and the rest of the team had already been picked, without me in it. An idea popped into my head – Zdeněk Štybar had crashed the previous day in Hageland and hurt his elbow. Might he have to pull out of Belgium? Should I stay in Belgium a day or two longer, just in case?

Patrick shrugged apologetically. The doctors thought Štybie should be OK. He said I'd be better off just going home.

This disappointment aside, we had a good meal and talked about the rest of the season. Patrick asked what I wanted to do next year.

I said, 'Look, I obviously wanted to stop this year, but I'm going that well that I want to carry on. Already at the beginning of the year

I wanted to carry on because I was enjoying it. But now it's not just about enjoying it, I know I'm still going to win.'

We agreed we'd talk about it again properly, perhaps with a contract, the next time we met. And that was that both for the evening and the first half of my season. The next day I was getting the train back to London while the A Team arrived for the Tour of Belgium.

CHAPTER 14

7–9 June: Belgium and Essex

I never thought the Tour of Belgium would be the defining race of my career, especially as it had been pulled from my programme a week or so before I was due to start there.

The original plan had been for me to ride Hageland and Elfstedenronde, then stay on in Belgium for the five-day national tour. But the week before those two races, I found out that I wasn't going to be needed for Belgium. Sam had said he'd like to do it because he wanted to do more sprints before the Tour. So, as had been the case with Algarve a couple of weeks earlier, he was in and I was out. In that first instance, I'd been switched to the Ruta del Sol, but this time there wasn't another race where I could be slotted in. I just had the two one-day races and then faced the prospect of two months off. *What the fuck can I do?* I thought. *After all, he's going to the Tour, so he should get everything he feels he needs.*

I asked the team whether it would be worth it for me to stay on until the start of the Tour of Belgium, just in case someone had to drop out at the last minute, but they said no. So, the morning after Elfstedenronde, just as some of the guys were starting to arrive at our hotel for Belgium, I made my way to the station and the train home.

I mentally switched into holiday mode. I was still going out on the bike, but also doing the school run with Peta, chilling out with the kids. On my second evening back in the UK, we collected them from school and went out for dinner. I was just starting my first portion of French fries in a long time when Peta said, 'Patrick's just messaged me saying get Mark to call me.' I looked at my phone and I had three missed calls from Patrick and three more from Ricardo.

My initial reaction was, *Fuck! What have I done now?* I figured I'd messed up in some way. Why else would they be calling me? I went outside and called Patrick.

He said, 'Listen, you're gonna hate me.'

I thought, *God, what's he going to say? Is he going to make me go and do a sponsor event in some faraway land?*

'Mr Bennett's arrived in Belgium with a sore knee,' he told me. Sam had apparently arrived not long after I'd left the day before and hadn't told anyone about his knee. This was now the evening before the Tour of Belgium started. 'He can't race Belgium. Can you get here?'

I thought for a few moments. 'There are no flights this evening and France's borders with the UK are currently closed because of the Covid restrictions, so I can't even drive.'

'Listen,' he said, 'do you want me to send a helicopter over?'

'That might work,' I told him. 'Do you want me to look at helicopters and jets in the meantime?'

'Yeah, the team will pay for it, whatever it costs. You have to get over here tonight.'

Here we go, I thought, although I'll admit that Peta did it all. She got straight onto any jet or helicopter broker she could find. As she was waiting for the replies, Patrick called and said that he'd organised for a helicopter to come from Belgium, and he gave me the details. 'Cancel everything,' I told Peta, who was already getting quotes in from the brokers. We went home and I started packing my suitcase, ready to leave the instant I got confirmation from the guy in Belgium on where and when he could pick me up.

It was early evening and I didn't hear anything for a while. I was getting anxious because it was obviously an hour later in Belgium. I called the helicopter company and asked them where I needed to go. The guy told me that they were still looking at places where they could land in the UK.

'What? You haven't left yet?' I told him there was an airfield just down the road from me and that would probably be the best option. Another half-hour passed and I heard nothing. I called again.

'Anything happening?' He said they hadn't found anywhere yet and that they'd keep me posted. I was beginning to think that it was getting too late for them to fly to Essex and back again. Another 30 minutes went by. Then a call.

'We need to give an airfield two hours' notice.'

'You knew two hours ago!' I told him. I called Patrick, who was pissed with the helicopter company and majorly stressing. 'Boss, listen, don't get wound up. We'll sort it, I'll be there.'

Peta was immediately back onto the flight brokers. She told them that we'd been messed around and that I still needed to get to Belgium. One of them said they could do it, but not until first thing in the morning. Which was a bit late, but by that point we had no choice. Peta kept calling people until almost midnight, but they all said the same thing. Nothing going that night.

That meant making the trip as early as possible on the Wednesday, as the first stage began in Beveren, just south of Antwerp, at 12.40. One option was a jet at 8am, but if it got delayed for any reason I'd be cutting it fine to make the start. Then Peta found a helicopter company who said they'd do it at 6.30 or soon after. It was more expensive than the flight, so I called Patrick. 'Whatever it takes,' he said. 'Just make sure you're here ...'

The next morning, I got up early, went to Stansted and took a helicopter over to Antwerp. I got picked up at the airport and arrived at the team hotel near the start about 90 minutes before the race got underway. It was straight out the car, onto the bus, to the start, and then race. I was a bit fucked, to say the least, but managed to do what was asked of me to help Remco Evenepoel, our designated leader for the week, who finished second that afternoon.

The next day was a shortish time trial. I managed a good performance, Remco won it and took the overall lead, and Yves Lampaert was second, so Patrick was happy. He'd arrived at the race that day, and after my time trial I was telling him and a few of the staff about the helicopter saga, all of us laughing at the craziness of the situation. While we were talking, Patrick said to me, 'If you win here this week, we'll take you to the Tour.' Those were his exact words. I don't know if it was a promise, a test or merely a clever way to motivate me, but I snatched that sentence like the music was about to stop on the last layer of paper during a kids' game of pass the parcel.

A little later I was talking to Tom Steels and telling him about how nervous I now felt. *Fuck, I could be going to the Tour de France.* I hadn't thought about it, hadn't trained for it, I didn't even know where it started or what the route was like. 'Mate,' I said to Tom. 'I never thought the Tour of Belgium could perhaps be the most defining race of my career.'

CHAPTER 15

13 June: Tour of Belgium, stage 5, Turnhout–Beringen

After the time trial on the second day, there were two more clear opportunities for me to sprint, the first of them arriving the next day. I knew I was going well, but it takes time for a sprinter and his lead-out to gel, and the finish into Scherpenheuvel-Zichem highlighted that very clearly.

Coming into the finish on a long, wide road, I was on Morky's wheel, but I was further back in the peloton than I'd have liked. I was in a panic, fully aware that if one thing went slightly awry my opportunity to sprint would disappear. Things began to unravel thanks to a bus stop or parking bay that suddenly emerged on one side. As we went past, Trek sprinter Matteo Moschetti swerved into it and came dive-bombing back out in a bid to move up the line. If I hadn't let him in, he'd have taken out half of the peloton. Doing that meant I lost Morky. That's what happens when you're too far back. At the front, shit can still happen, but there are fewer people around to cause shit to happen.

I rolled in way back, but Morky had got through and accelerated, and I thought, *Fuck, he's done it again*. Once we'd analysed the sprint, though, I realised that I had to speak to him. Morky's a really good guy and super-intelligent. I don't profess to being the next president of MENSA, but I do have the capacity to think my way around a bunch sprint. I said to him, 'I know what I'm doing. If we're in a vulnerable position, you don't have to just get me to 150 metres to go, we have to use you earlier. I'm not Sam who just has to be delivered at 150 or 200 to go and powers away, because then there's a chance that we won't win. I don't want to win seven out of ten times, I want to win ten out of ten times. So we've got to work out something we're both comfortable with. If we've got to commit, we commit, and I'll find my way after. But we can't do that again.'

Morky was fine with it. 'We've only sprinted with each other a couple of times and it's going to take a bit of time to work things out,' he said.

The pair of us spent the next day controlling the peloton through the Ardennes because we had Remco in the jersey, which just left the final stage into Beringen to try to capitalise on Patrick's promise. In the team meeting beforehand, I was more vocal than I'd been all year about what I wanted and how I wanted it. I'd been a bit timid before, firstly because this was the latest in a series of moments when I felt I was having to prove myself. And secondly, this was the A Team, and I hadn't raced with these guys this year, which made me wary of asserting what I wanted. But now I didn't hold back. I told them, 'This is what we do, this is where I want to be.'

It was a point-to-point stage with a finishing circuit, which was really technical, especially on the run-in to the finish, where there were roundabouts, narrow sections, ups and downs and some tight turns. We talked it through, decided which side of the roundabouts we needed to take, and emphasised that we shouldn't hit the front too soon, but stay just behind and all together, using our advantage in horsepower to move up in the closing moments.

The plan worked to order until the peloton crossed a wide bridge with a couple of kilometres left and we got ambushed, totally fucking swamped. As we went into Beringen, we were scattered all over the place – one of us up at the front, then five guys, then another Deceuninck, then five guys, then one of us … And I was the furthest one back, trying to move up on my own as we got further into the town, gaining two or three positions through each corner.

Suddenly, I found Remco, resplendent in his blue leader's jersey. He should have been further ahead, but luckily for me he wasn't. I yelled, 'Go!' and he went to the outside of the group, opened the throttle, passed ten guys and dropped me in on Morky's wheel. By that point, Morky, Yves and Davide Ballerini, known to everyone as 'Ballero', had found each other and, after Remco had done his bit, they took over. We hit the first roundabout, where Lotto were up there taking it on for Caleb Ewan. 'Go!' Yves went, did a good pull, then swung off.

We still had a kilometre to go. If you're a lead-out man, the instinctive thing to do is to go full gas and hold on for as long as you possibly can, but that's not the key to getting it right, because you need to be thinking of your teammates behind you who have to accelerate when you've reached your maximum speed. If you go full-on and then die, other riders can close up on your lead-out, so you need to start at the pace they're going and steadily wind it up, dragstripping them, always trying to remain just ahead. As you reach your top speed, the next guy can take over and wind it up a touch more.

We were just behind Lotto and Ballero went. He was going so fucking fast past these Lotto guys, close enough that we could see the panic on their faces, that *What the fuck?* tilt of the head and scrunch of the nose.

The panic elbows came out, the three of us bouncing off each one as Morky was screaming, 'Easy! Easy!' with me sat on his wheel. When Ballero swung off, the finish was still a little bit too far away for Morky to go flat out, so he wound it down for an instant, taking the tempo down just a touch, then started to build up again, building and building, faster, faster, faster, faster, faster …

Just before he hit his optimum speed, I saw Alpecin's Tim Merlier jump on the right-hand side of the road. Where Merlier is good is that, unlike some guys, once he's accelerated like that, he's got this sustainability to his effort that's hard to match. He's a dragstrip sprinter. He doesn't die at the end but keeps going all the way to the line. It means that he can go from a longer distance out than most sprinters and maintain a very high speed. The antidote to this sustained power is the surging acceleration that the likes of Caleb can deliver. They can jump no matter what the speed is, producing the quick burst of acceleration that Merlier-style sprinters can't match. I used to be like Caleb. Was I still?

As Merlier made his move, I thought, *I have to go now.* I jumped past Morky on the left and it was then a flat-out race between me and Merlier up opposite sides of the road. When I jumped, I had so much speed initially that I passed him; then he overtook me. As I glanced right, teeth grimaced, I double-kicked, unleashing that second burst of acceleration that I was once so renowned for. *Boom!* I passed him again. I'd won!

I screamed when I went across the line, not just because I'd won, but because of the significance of that win. Dylan Groenewegen was there, Merlier, Caleb, Pascal Ackermann, Nacer Bouhanni, too.

We'd nailed the lead-out, Remco had won the general classification (GC) and, to top it all off, I was going to the Tour de France. It was the most significant point in my recent memory.

It had been so long since I'd had a double-kick, even before 2016, when I last tasted success at the Tour. It had been years and years back, when I was at my very best, when I used to train on the track. All of a sudden everything with Vasi in Greece had paid off. That was what those double days and torturous track sessions were for.

It was all smiles after the finish and in the press tent. When I got back to the bus everyone was celebrating. Patrick wasn't there and I went a bit quiet, unsure where this left me. I said to Tom Steels, 'Does this mean I go to the Tour?' He couldn't tell me. 'What should I do now? If I'm going to the Tour, I need to go to Italy, I need to train in some mountains for a bit. I've got a couple of kilos I need to lose.' Tom shrugged and told me, 'Yeah, train as if you're going to the Tour.'

I called Vasi, who offered the same advice. He asked me if I'd spoken to Patrick and I told him I hadn't yet.

There was no clear news either way on the Tour. I was told that they were picking the team the next day and I should wait by my phone for a confirmation call. I went back home to the UK and didn't hear anything all that day. I called to see if there was any news, and was told there wasn't any update yet, although it seemed that Sam's knee issue hadn't improved. I was getting frantic, wanting to know whether I needed to organise that trip to Italy to get some Tour prep in.

Eventually, Brian Holm rang. They'd asked my best friend to break the news. 'Don't go to Italy,' he said. 'You're not going to the Tour …'

CHAPTER 16

16–18 June: Quarrata, Italy

Movistar directeur sportif Max Sciandri was pumping up my tyres for me. I'd flown to Bologna that morning and he'd offered to come and pick me up at the airport and take me back to his home in Quarrata, 20 or so kilometres north-west of Florence. I've got a house in the same town, a big old place that's built for a family, too big for me when I'm on my own. What's more, when I haven't been there for a long time, even though somebody does look after the place, there's always something wrong – the heating needs fixing, the electrics have blown, there's been a leak …

When I called Max, who's been a good friend for years, to say that I was coming to Italy, I told him, 'Here's the situation …' Once I'd explained it all to him, he instantly invited me to come and stay at his house, which is just a couple of kilometres away from mine. 'You can stay in the guest room,' he told me, adding that Valentina, his wife, would get whatever I needed to eat so that I wouldn't have to think about anything. I could just concentrate on my bike.

'You know what, I'll do that,' I told him. 'It's so kind of you. Thank you!'

The decision to stick with the plan of a few days' training in Italy had been taken not long after I'd spoken to Brian two evenings before. I called Vasi afterwards.

'Look, Cav,' he said, 'go to Italy and just train. I know it's hard. But you've got to be professional, show them that you're doing what it takes.' It was what I needed to hear. I booked my flight to go, two days later.

I spent the Tuesday with the kids because there was still a remote possibility that I might not see them again for a month if I did get called up to the Tour. I didn't know quite how to break that to them, as in all likelihood I'd only be gone for a week, but it could well be four or five. That wasn't easy to explain. I also spent a lot of time that day packing because there's so much shit that you need for a Grand Tour – clothing for every kind of weather, countless spare shorts in case of crashes, all of it packed in square packing bags so that everything's in order and fits neatly in the suitcase. When I'd finished my suitcase, I packed a little trolley holdall with a couple of pairs of shorts, a couple of jerseys, the minimum I could survive on for a week's training in Italy.

As soon as I arrived at Max's house, I put my stuff in the spare room and got changed into my kit. When I came out my bike was just about ready to go. Max might have been a directeur sportif for years, but he still thinks like a rider. With the tyres fully pumped, I headed out for three hours, getting straight into the training programme Vasi had worked out for me. When I got back, Valentina asked what she could make me for dinner. She's an incredible cook and you know what the Italians are like: 'Eat, eat, eat.' She'd always looked after me when I'd been in Quarrata on my own. I was always up at Max's, always.

'I'm not being impolite, but I don't want much. I need to lose weight,' I told her. So she cooked light risottos. 'Do you want more? Do you want more?' she'd always ask. 'I'm OK, I'm OK, thank you,' would be my reply. The truth was that I was fucking hungry, but I was being exact with the calories I was burning and consuming.

I'd seen stories in the press about Patrick saying Sam would be going to the Tour, but nothing had been said officially about the team's line-up. That evening I rang Vasi again – I called him all the time because I either needed a kick up the arse or reassurance. He's like a sounding board for me, like Rod Ellingworth had always been in former years. 'Ignore it,' he told me. 'We'll carry on with what we're doing. If you don't go to the Tour, it's a good training camp. We'll go to Livigno, blah, blah, blah …'

Vasi's optimism swept me along, and I tried to put all thoughts of what Patrick and the team might be discussing out of my mind as I stuck to the training plan. I did five hours on the Thursday with Fabio Sabatini, who rides for Cofidis. He's been a good mate since we were at QuickStep together in my first spell with the team. The following day, Vasi's instructions were to go out in the climbs and just ride for six hours. Fabio had said he'd join me again, but he had to call off that morning when something else came up. 'Listen,' he said, 'if you want I'll come and pick you up on the scooter and then in the afternoon we can do part of it motor-pacing.' I told him that'd be great and went off on a five-hour loop in the hills around Lucca. As I descended off the Apennine Mountains into his home town of Montecatini, I called him to say I'd soon be there. 'Mate, give me 30 minutes more because I'm going to do another climb,' I told him. When you're motivated, you often add another climb like this, and as I got to the top Fabio was waiting for me on his scooter.

I was fucking cooked by this point. 'Straight back to yours?' he asked. 'No, we'll go and do Carmignano.' That was another climb. 'Just do a bit more, just do a bit more, hold on,' I was saying to myself. When I got back to Max and Valentina's, after seven hours and 200 kilometres, I was absolutely finished. You feel proud of yourself when you do something like that. Even now, even though it's my job to ride a bike, when you do a ride like that you always feel like you've accomplished something.

I slumped down on the bed and noticed a missed call from Wilfried Peeters – Fitte – on my phone. My heart sank.

CHAPTER 17

18 June: Quarrata, Italy

Sitting on the bed in Max and Valentina's spare room, I was numb. It was like the feeling I had when I suffered my bouts of depression, but the thing is it's not a feeling. It's quite the opposite. It's no feeling. I didn't feel anything. I wasn't happy, anxious, bewildered. Nothing. Just nothing.

It was karma that I got depression because I used to be one of those people, like Piers Morgan, who just thinks it's an excuse. I was the last person on earth who thought they'd get it. My attitude towards people who had it was, *You're just weak in the head!* But the illness, injuries and other issues that set me back from 2017 resulted in crippling depression, which made me realise that it could affect anybody. None of us are immune. Anyone who's in that position also needs consistent support, understanding and compassion. Even believing that you can come back from it is difficult, and managing to achieve that is fucking hard. I don't want this to be taken as bravado, but I showed it's doable, and I honestly hope that others who are in the same position can look at me and see that.

I hadn't even got out of my kit before I rang Fitte. They always call all of the riders on the long list for the Tour de France to say they're not going to the race – as well as the ones who are. As he picked up, I was waiting for the inevitable. 'Got some good news for you, *maat*,' he said, using the Flemish word for 'mate'. 'You're coming to the Tour de France.'

I was just quiet. I wasn't excited or even bemused. I can still feel it now. I was just … OK. I was just giving one-word answers to Fitte, while he was buzzing about it. When I put the phone down I didn't feel anything. I called Peta and told her, but I don't remember anything about the call. I was still numb. Nothing was getting through. Not because I expected to be going, quite the opposite, in fact. All I can think of now is that those few minutes – coming in after having ridden myself almost to my physical limit, seeing the missed call from Fitte, then hearing why he'd been calling – had left me in shock, because the next day I was fucking bouncing.

I had a recovery day the next day, two hours' easy riding. I went out with Max and I was euphoric. I couldn't say anything until the news had been released by the team, which didn't happen until the following Monday. But by then the whole rigmarole had started – when and how I was travelling, where I was meeting the team, plans for the days leading up to it. I started looking at the route, which I only knew quite vaguely. If you'd have asked me ten days before the Tour de France where it was starting that year, I wouldn't have had a clue, although if you'd said that the Tour was starting in Brittany, I'd have said, 'Yeah, that's right.'

I had all of the motivation I could have needed to finish my week in Italy, getting myself as well prepared physiologically as I possibly could for the Tour de France, while also steeling myself for the shit-storm in the media that was going to blow up when the news that I was riding was released. Whether it would be positive or negative, I didn't know …

CHAPTER 18

21 June: Quarrata, Italy

I was caught in two minds about whether to contact Sam after the Tour team had been announced. I wanted to wish him the best with his knee problem. At the same time, I was fully aware that I might well be the last person he'd want to hear from after the news about the Tour had been released. I simply didn't know Sam well enough to be sure about what I should do.

My uncertainty was fuelled by a couple of conversations I'd had in the previous week or two. The first was at the Tour of Belgium with Caleb Ewan, who's Sam's best mate. I honestly don't get that because they're sprint rivals. I'd class Caleb as a mate, I really like him, but I'm not going to start hugging him after a finish. They do all that shit and it leaves me shaking my head in bewilderment. Anyway, Caleb and I were chatting in Belgium, where I'd obviously been called up as the last-minute replacement for Sam.

'What's up with Sam?' Caleb asked me.

'You're his best mate, you tell me,' I said. 'Look, I want to stay out of it.' But I did want to ask Caleb something. 'Listen, does Sam have a problem with me? Turning up in Belgium when you can't race … I took that a bit personally, like he'd rather race injured than let me race. I never wanted to be a threat to him. I want to support him, but he's like ...'

Caleb either didn't know or wouldn't say, and that was as far as we went with it.

No one seemed to know what was going on. No one had heard from him. He changed his WhatsApp and Instagram pictures to non-team kit when it was all going on. It was fucking weird. When you asked guys on the team, 'Has anyone spoken to Sam?' everyone was like, 'No, but he's behaving really strangely.' They weren't slagging him off but, like me, they'd rather not know what was going on.

The issue was complicated by the fact that it was widely known that Sam was leaving the team to rejoin Bora, although UCI regulations meant the news couldn't be made official until 1 August. The QuickStep mentality is always to go with their best team, so I don't think this altered any decision that had been made about selection for the Tour, although it may not have done him any favours.

All I can say about his decision to leave is that I could understand why he'd made it. Although Sam had had some tough years at Bora before coming to QuickStep, he'd decided to go back there for his own reasons, whatever they were, and I don't blame him for that. He's a brilliant bike rider, although shyness will never give him the charisma of a superstar. But I think it's important that he makes as much out of his racing career as he can. After all, we're a short time in this game.

In the end I didn't call or message him. He had his reasons for behaving the way he did, and I had no idea what they were.

Ultimately, I've never had an issue with Sam and never wanted anything from him. I didn't want to be a threat to him. All I wanted to do was get my career back on track. When I managed that, I never heard a thing from him. Not a dicky bird. Maybe that was the best thing for both of us.

CHAPTER 19

21 June: Quarrata, Italy

I was a bit nervous about how the news of my selection for the Tour would be received, and even more so about how I would react to the massive response that I was certain it would trigger. Would it put pressure on me? Would I suddenly be scared of failing? I didn't really know at all. When I was younger, I didn't really think about this kind of thing because I didn't care. I was winning, so I was always guaranteed a place at the Tour and didn't give a monkey's what anyone thought about it. Then, as I got older and the wins didn't come as often, I did care. Then the victories dried up completely and there was a phase when there was never anything about me in the media, apart from the occasional story suggesting that I'd be best off retiring.

In situations like this I need reassurance, and I turned to Vasi for it first. After a big day on the Sunday, a double day with sprint intervals, I checked in with him and he confirmed that I was in good shape from a performance-based perspective. Then I spoke to Ricardo Scheidecker and Tom Steels, who both stressed that the team weren't putting any pressure on me. 'If we didn't think you could do anything, we wouldn't take you. We just wouldn't. But there isn't any pressure on you. There's nothing to lose if you don't do anything. There's no pressure on you to get to Paris, there's just a load of sprints in the first week. We need to take a sprinter and we know you're in good shape,' they said.

I didn't have any preconceptions about whether I would reach Paris or not. I didn't really think about any of that. I knew it would be difficult, purely because I hadn't trained properly for the Tour. I was ready for the sprints, but I hadn't trained for the Tour specifically. Normally, I'd have done quite a long training camp at altitude as a fundamental part of my prep, but everything had happened too quickly for that. I'd trained a bit for the mountains in Italy, but you're limited in what you can do in a week.

Despite the nerves, though, I was buzzing about the prospect of being back at the Tour de France. After three years away from it, you forget what it's like, that it's on another level. The standard's really high in the WorldTour, at the Classics and other major stage races like the Giro and the Vuelta, but the Tour's up another level again, out on its own in absolutely every way. It's a different style of racing. The speed's always faster because it's the best riders competing in peak condition at some of the most iconic places in bike racing, watched by the biggest crowds of the season. Nothing else compares with it.

After the big day I had on Sunday, I cut my training short on Monday because I felt tired and didn't want to overdo it. When I got back to Max's house, I checked my weight and realised that I'd dropped a little more than a kilo during that week, so the training and Valentina's cooking had had the desired effect. Meanwhile, my phone had just blown up. There were too many messages for me to read, let alone respond to. Dozens and dozens of them. I sat in the spare room scrolling through them, then looked at the articles that were being posted about my selection. The reaction seemed mostly positive. In fact, I can't recall reading anything negative about it at all.

On Tuesday morning I got up super-early to do a final short ride. Then I packed my bag and my bike, and headed for the airport. My next stop would be Brittany for the Grand Départ.

CHAPTER 20

22 June: Charles de Gaulle Airport, Paris

I flew to Paris Charles de Gaulle Airport, where I had a long layover before my onward flight to Brest, and bumped into Michael Matthews as I was coming out of the toilets. He's another green jersey, a sprint rival, but I've always got on really well with him. He's always upbeat and happy, a good guy to hang out with. We got some lunch at YO! Sushi and talked about all kinds of shit, but mainly the Tour: what we thought we were going to do there, our form, our teams.

It felt a bit weird because I hadn't done a WorldTour race all year, so I hadn't been racing against people like Michael very often. I'd seen a few of the biggest names in some of the races I'd done, but the enormity of what lay ahead was striking. When we got to the gate for the flight to Brest, I saw some of my teammates, including Julian Alaphilippe, who'd sent me a voice message a couple of days before, having heard who was on the Tour team: 'Mark, I'm so 'appy for you, it's so nice. I'm very 'appy about zis, Loulou.' That was super-nice and I was buzzing to see him. Yves Lampaert was there too and, suddenly, as we waited at the gate, I was like a kid again. Being with the boys made it feel real for the first time: we were going to the Tour de France.

When we arrived, some of the team staff were waiting to take us to the hotel, where I was rooming with Mattia Cattaneo. I don't think I'd seen him since the January training camp and I couldn't remember if I'd even spoken to him then. I didn't know the first thing about him, nothing in fact beyond the fact that he's Italian. *Fucking hell,* I thought, *a month away with someone and I don't know what they're like.* When we got up to the room, we started talking, and almost instantly we clicked. He's soft-spoken and super-friendly, with an infectious Cheshire cat smile. Over the next three weeks we spoke in a mixture of Italian and English, with no kind of rhyme or reason to which we were using, chopping and changing language in mid-conversation. He was making his Tour debut, and that first afternoon I talked at him full gas for about an hour about the race, what it is, how it is, how it differs from the Giro and Vuelta, which he had ridden a few times already.

I was surprised to find out that he was 30, which is pretty old for a Tour debutant, and he filled me in on his career, which was some fucking story. It turned out that he was one of the biggest things on the under-23 scene in 2011, winning that edition of the Baby Giro and finishing third in the Tour de l'Avenir, which was won by Colombian climber Esteban Chaves. He'd eventually turned pro in 2013 with Lampre, but his career almost immediately went off the rails. He was out training one day that year and passed out on his bike. He wasn't too badly hurt, just had to take a few days off, but then he went out again and the same thing happened. This time he bashed himself up pretty badly and got taken to hospital, where he was diagnosed with a heart problem. It took a while for that to be sorted and it set his career back a good bit. He ended up stepping down a level to join Androni in 2017, and Deceuninck noticed him when he was top ten in a time trial at the 2019 Giro with, as far as professional standards go, a botched-together TT bike with exposed cables everywhere. He joined the team in 2020 and has been a real find: never gets tired, super-strong. Off the bike, he's a really chilled guy, always happy, and getting to know him was a cracking start to the whole Tour experience. I knew we'd be all right together.

The next day we went training and did three or four hours as a team, including a recon of the closing kilometres of the first stage. This felt like the next big step towards the reality of the Tour. That evening, the atmosphere was great at dinner. I was really buzzing, getting the banter going, cracking jokes, but a bit too close to the mark at times. Everyone was laughing, though. I felt like I was in exactly the right place – at the Tour de France with Deceuninck-QuickStep.

We had a press conference over Zoom the next day. It was the same as usual, journalists trying to outdo each other with their questions, often giving the answer in the question they asked, rather than just asking something simple and getting a good answer. On the upside, they didn't ask me about the Merckx record, although some of them might have been put off that subject already. I'd done an Instagram post, a *Star Wars* meme where you could change the writing on the opening text crawl. Mine said something like:

I'm going to the Tour.

Journalists: And you're going for the Merckx record, right?

It was a fucking good meme and I was dead proud of myself for managing to put it together. I think it spooked people into not asking about it, although there was one question. As I've said so many times, it's never been a goal. I guess it was first asked in an attempt to put into context what I was doing, because at the time – in 2008, 09, 10, 11, when I was winning loads – I'd always get the question: if you can win six stages why aren't you winning the Tour de France? I think it was talked about then just to put into perspective what Eddy had achieved and what I was doing. Ultimately, it's fucking hard to win a stage of the Tour de France. If you do win a stage, you've got another stage the next day and it's your job to focus again. That sounds easy, but think how many riders win one big race and that's it.

What drives me on much more is the thought of legacy. You read books that talk about the exploits of Eddy Merckx, Gino Bartali and Freddy Maertens, the greats of the sport, and I've always wanted to be written about like that, to feature in those books with those guys. I don't know if it's egotistical to think that I would have been there if I'd stopped in 2016, but the years after have kind of erased my standing – and each year that I was going off would undermine it a little more. What kept me going was that I knew I'd be back. I knew there was a reason why I wasn't winning, but nobody else believed it. As I've said over and over, you don't go from winning what I won to winning nothing in one year. It doesn't happen.

I also know there's no one with a fucking work ethic like me. Maybe in the past it looked like I wasn't professional, but like Lewis Hamilton or Valentino Rossi, the secret to making something look easy is by not having an easy life. The people who make it look easy are the ones who work harder when no one is watching. When I won, it was because I grafted all the time behind the scenes. I always focused on sprinting, even though I had dreamed of doing more, because sprinting set me apart. Here was my chance to do that again.

CHAPTER 21

24–25 June: Brest

On the Thursday evening before the Grand Départ, we had the team presentation down by the docks in Brest, in the same place they'd held it before my second Tour de France, in 2008. Before that, we all went to the riders' briefing, where they talk to you about throwing litter, safety, the rules and regulations. Walking into it, I was struck by the number of people who came up to say they were pleased to see me back in the race. Half of them might have been saying it just to be polite, but it's still nice, though, especially as I could see how many people genuinely meant it. It wasn't just riders either, but directeurs sportifs and staff on other teams, people at the Tour organisers ASO.

Once again, I was reminded just how much I'd missed the Tour. French riders aside, I truly believe that there's no other rider who views the Tour de France like I do. It blows my mind that someone would want to go to the Giro or Vuelta instead of the Tour. It's the fucking Tour de France. It's not a cycling event, it's a sporting event, and I've always shown it the respect it deserves by being properly prepared for it. I love it and wear on my sleeve how much the race means to me.

After we'd been given the required talking to about what was expected of us, we went to the presentation. With Julian Alaphilippe in our team, the reception we got was fucking crazy – France's world champion, the darling of French cycling, of the Tour de France. It was actually quite nice that I could follow in his slipstream and not have to make eye contact with people, especially when we got to the media mixed zone, where they all wanted to speak to him and no one was really that bothered about me. I know that part of my job as a bike rider is media relations, but you don't want to do it if you don't have to, and it's quite a relief when that's the case. I stopped to do a couple of interviews, but I was happy to sneak past and let Julian have the limelight there.

Part of my reluctance to spend too much time speaking is that, like everything at the Tour, the media pool is far bigger than at any other race, maybe 50 times bigger than most. And it's not just the cycling media asking you questions, the journalists who are clued in to the sport. You get journalists in the media corps who don't give a fuck about the sport, who have no idea about it and are told what to ask. There's often no research behind their questions. When I was younger, I'd be like, *What the fuck are you saying?* It was actually Chris Boardman who said to me once, 'Don't think of it as talking to a journalist, but that you're talking to the people that journalists are projecting to. That's what you've got to think about.' That's always stuck with me. Combined with that is the fact that the Tour is not just cycling news, it's sometimes not even only sports news: it's news full stop, all over the world.

That evening was the first time I got a good idea of what the interaction with the media would be like at the Tour in the Covid era. Before, the press would be outside the bus and they'd want to speak to you when you were in the middle of a team meeting, when you were having a shit, when you were getting yourself together. They'd come and say, 'We've got to do it now because we're interviewing Peter Sagan at the Bora bus in five minutes.' So you'd get into kit, go out and do the interview, then get back on the bus and undress again. At the 2021 Tour, though, the media were corralled into individual pens and you went to them one by one, either just before or just after you signed on to race at the podium – that's the traditional ceremony that gives the public time to see each team before the start, like a ring walk but with less flames and glitter. It was a lot easier, less chaotic – there was a logic to it. You went along the line and actually spoke to more people.

One other thing I noticed was how often I was using the line, 'We'll have to see how it goes ...', or, worse still, 'We'll take it day by day.' This is the biggest bullshit line in cycling and every GC rider uses it. 'We'll take it day by day.' Fuck off, you're paid €5 million! Just tell us: are you going to fucking win the thing or not? I really despise it. I know it's all about taking the pressure off, and that was something I was keen to do going into the Tour, but I hated myself every time I used it. It did take the pressure off, but at the same time it's the Tour de France, so of course I want to fucking win.

Overall, though, I felt like I was quite calm this year with the media and all of the other things that happen around the race. If there were any stupid questions, I let them wash over me. I was just happy to be there, and, I have to admit, I'd missed stuff like that. All that shit that I didn't like, I'd missed it. Every time I talked, it wasn't with a fake smile. I was buzzing to be there.

I'd missed everything that makes the Tour what it is, the power of what that race does. It's so much more than just the TV images of someone crossing the finish line. It's how journalists portray it, how they show the emotion of it. You don't see that very clearly when you're a part of it, but when you're not there it stands out, and I was so much more aware of that this year. The press are the reason the Tour de France goes on, not the TV images, not the bike riders. Go to the Critérium du Dauphiné and it's the same bike riders, the Tour of Croatia and it's the same bike riders. But there's no media at those races, because they're not the Tour de France.

The next day, we had a team meeting, not to discuss tactics, because that would happen on the bus in the briefing immediately before the start of the first stage; this meeting was about the Tour and the grand scheme of what we were doing. Tom did this incredible presentation, going through each of the riders and staff, telling a little story about them, a funny anecdote, and also what was expected from each rider during the race, almost like rules for the team. For instance, he told us that we had to be specific about what drink we wanted at the end of a stage. He said if we asked for a specific drink, then that's what we'd get; we couldn't say that we'd asked for something else.

Towards the end of it, he said to me, 'Cav, you do it better than anyone. Can you just explain to the new guys [it was Davide Ballerini's first Tour as well as Catta's] what to expect from the Tour?' And I just went off ...

'I just fucking love it. Guys, you cannot imagine. This race will change your life. After these three weeks, cycling will never, ever be the same for you. You'll never look at another race in the same way – ever! Because no other race comes anywhere near as close. It's shit, it's horrible, it's the hardest thing you'll ever do, it's suffering. You'll get to Paris and you'll say, "I'm never doing that again." On the Wednesday after you'll be like, "I can't wait for next year." It's like a rollercoaster: when the big dipper goes up you're scared to go down, but then all of a sudden you get that amazing rush – that's the Tour. If you win a stage at the Giro, it will change your career: you'll get more money and a change in your career. If you win a stage of the Tour, it will change your fucking life. It's not cycling, it's bigger than cycling.'

I looked at the lads and half of them appeared to be in shock and the other half were laughing. I get so passionate about it. I don't know what it is. I don't know if it's an obsession, but I do know what this race has given me. Maybe it stems from the fact that it was the only thing I knew about growing up. I didn't come from a cycling background, so the only thing I heard about when I was growing up was the Tour de France, the yellow jersey and Chris Boardman at the Olympic Games. I live for it, I've always lived for it, and thinking about it had, I know, helped in my rejuvenation.

The Tour is everything – it's just everything. It's more than cycling. Of course I know who won Flanders or Roubaix, the riders and the battles, but the Tour is something else. It's not even about its history – it's more about how unique it is as an annual sporting event. There's nothing else like it. It's not a one-off game, it's not the Super Bowl. It's three weeks. It's the hardest sporting event on the planet. I know what you have to put in just to be there. There's so much to it, especially as a sprinter. You not only have to be able to sprint, you have to be able to survive in the mountains and conserve your energy so that you'll be able to sprint again. The consequences of winning and losing are just massive. They're life-changing. I love it, *love it*. It's fucking brilliant.

PART II
THE TOUR

STAGE 1

26 June: Brest–Landerneau, 197.8km

The old adage is that you can't win the Tour in the first week, but you can lose it. Since Christian Prudhomme took over as the director of the Tour de France in 2007, GC leaders and their team directors have been trotting this line out with increasing frequency. The reason for this is simple – Prudhomme and his organising team, headed by route director Thierry Gouvenou, have tossed out the long-standing template in which the opening week barely featured a classified climb and the domination of the sprinters was almost total. In a bid to make the action more dynamic and spectacular, as well as to force the GC leaders out of the shadows where they always preferred to hide until the first stages in the mountains, they've packed them with potential ambushes – short but steep climbs, narrow roads, technical descents. Yet the one thing this has done for sure is to make the first week a ludicrously nervous affair.

The opening stage typified this. The small town of Landerneau, where we would finish, is just 30 kilometres east of the start in Brest, but to reach it we'd be racing for close to 200 kilometres on a huge loop that twisted to the south and back again, and featured no fewer than six categorised climbs, the final one, the Côte de la Fosse aux

Loups, coming right at the end, rising for almost three kilometres to the finish line. In other words, it wasn't a stage for me.

Following our training-ride recon, our directeur sportif Tom Steels had worked out a simple plan. It was, he told us during the pre-stage briefing on the team bus, all about getting Julian positioned so that he could attack on the final climb. Tim Declercq would naturally do most of the riding behind the break. His smile-like grimace had become synonymous with the camera shot of the front of the peloton. Pulling for kilometre after kilometre, chewing up and spitting out every workhorse from another team that tried to help him, he'd earned the nickname 'El Tractor'. My job was to get Julian and the other riders well placed for the tight descent into Landerneau. That was, Tom told us, one of four pinch points where the whole team, ideally, had to be at the front. We knew that the eight riders on each of the other 22 team buses parked close to the docks in Brest were likely to be getting almost exactly the same briefing. You didn't need to be a tactical genius to realise that it was going to be carnage all day.

The Tour's always a nervous affair anyway because almost every leading name is on the start line and every one of the 184 riders is at the peak of their form. They've been preparing for this moment since the winter, building up steadily through training camps, altitude camps and racing, initially in smaller events, the level rising all the time until July, or in this case in order to avoid a clash with the Olympics, the end of June. The sense of expectation was palpable as we all began to gather on the start line.

We rolled away in the neutralised section, which leads away from the obstacles in the centre of the start town to a safer official start point on the outskirts. With the front line of riders right on the bumper of Christian Prudhomme's scarlet Skoda, I found myself rubbing shoulders with Israel Start-Up Nation's André Greipel, a teammate from long ago in my Columbia-HTC days who became one of my biggest sprint rivals. 'Who'd have thought we'd be here?' I said to him. 'Here we go, another lap around France. We've done enough of these to know what it's going to be like.'

Traditionally, once the peloton arrives at kilometre zero at the end of the neutralised section, it stops for an official start ceremony. But, just like crowds around the team buses, posing with fans for photos and talking to the media outside the closely policed mixed-zone areas, Covid had ended this ritual. Instead, standing through the sunroof of his car, Prudhomme waved a flag to signal the start of hostilities.

As soon as we passed kilometre zero, it was warp speed. The peloton was in one line, as attacks went and came back again. For about 15 kilometres, as we bobbed up and down these little kickers, the terrain never flat, I did nothing more than look at the wheel in front. *What the fuck have I got myself into?* I thought to myself. Had I just forgotten what it was like? Had it got even faster? Or was it simply that I wasn't ready? I had no idea. All I did know was that I was hanging on and hoping the speed would ease up soon.

Finally, after about 20 kilometres, four riders got some daylight, another two jumped across to join them, and the peloton throttled back. At any other race there would be a five-minute lull before the peloton started its initial pursuit of the breakaway group, allowing them to build up a lead of a couple of minutes. But at the Tour there's barely a pause. Within a couple of minutes of the breakaways scampering away, the chase started up. The aim's not to catch them, but to ensure that they're always within easy reach.

There are other battles going on too. From the off, the stronger teams, the likes of Movistar, Jumbo, UAE and Ineos, want to impose their authority, and there's an unwritten rule that whoever rides first gets to choose where they go, sitting with all of their riders together in the sweet spot of the snake-like peloton. Too far forward, you're using energy by taking too much wind in your face. Too far back, you're at a bigger risk of being behind a crash or split in the bunch. The sweet-spot would perhaps be the jugular of the snake. Essentially, though, it's a dick-swinging exercise that makes the peloton even more nervous, results in more crashes and leaves me wanting to yell at them, 'Just grow up!' But as the peloton settled down and Tim began to work with the help of two or three domestiques from other teams, I just focused on trying to stay well placed and out of trouble until the intermediate sprint, three-quarters of the way through the stage.

Since they changed the rules about the intermediate sprints in 2011, making it one big sprint per stage rather than three individual ones, I've always approached them in the same way. I usually go for them, but without making an all-out effort that might cost me in the bunch sprint at the finish. My thinking is that you can't win the green jersey on the intermediates, but you can lose it by not going for them, and there's mathematical reasoning behind it.

The winner of the finish sprint on a 'flat' stage earns 50 points, the runner-up 30, the third-placed rider 20, the next 18, and so on. Whereas, at an intermediate sprint, the first rider gets 20 points, then 17, 15, 13 and down to 1 point for fifteenth place. The hitch, though, is that you can't win the big points at an intermediate sprint if a breakaway goes through it first, so why would you go all out to win the sprint for, say, seventh place at an intermediate when you only get three more points than you do for being tenth? So my strategy has always been that I don't over-exert myself if there's a breakaway. If there isn't, you have to go full gas because you can get useful points.

We'd looked at the intermediate sprint at Brasparts during our stage-one training-ride recon. It was uphill for almost two kilometres at 4–5 per cent. Beyond it, the hill carried on and at the top of that climb there was a pinch point, one of the four corners where we had to be at the front. That would ensure the GC riders would be right on our heels as we went through it. What's more, on the Tour's first day every sprinter goes for the intermediate, all of us looking for points but also hoping to score a psychological blow on our rivals. Some teams will even do a full lead-out like it's a bunch sprint for a stage win.

We'd talked about it in the briefing. I'd been asked how I wanted to play it. 'Don't worry about giving me a lead-out,' I said. 'Morky, just drop me off. Don't worry about killing yourself because you need to be there just after.'

As it turned out, the breakaway group was reeled in before the intermediate sprint, which gave it extra significance. The guys brought me up towards the front with a kilometre to go. Soon after, the road kicked to the right around this house with its edge sticking out like they often do in France. I took a quick glance back as we approached this little kink, and as I did so, Nacer Bouhanni chopped into me from the left. I either had to brake or hit the house. By the time I got some speed up again, the little sprint group had gone clear and Caleb Ewan and Peter Sagan were fighting it out for second place behind the lone breakaway, Ide Schelling.

Seeing that I wasn't going to get close to them, I looked back again and realised that the sprinters had got a little gap. If I'd exerted myself I might have been able to get another point or two but, seeing as I had that cushion over the pack behind, I just rolled through the intermediate, still pedalling, but ready to accelerate when the bunch closed and the frantic rush to the pinch point began.

Morky was still close to me and we sensed the bunch coming up the hill towards us. As expected, everyone had the same idea about wanting to get to that corner first. And then I was swamped. As the bunch engulfed me, I was hanging on up this climb and couldn't find a way through. The corner was coming and Tom was saying on the radio, 'Three k to the corner … two k to the corner …' and I couldn't move up. Then came a small crash. *Phew! I wasn't in it.* Then a gap. *Shit, I can't get into it.* The lactic acid was making my legs feel like I was riding through sand. The left-hand bend came, accompanied by the screech of brakes, and I could see my team at the front. *I've fucked up here,* I thought. *I'm not with the guys.*

Thankfully, the mayhem calmed down on the narrow road, because once you reach a point like that the road is effectively blocked and everyone's stuck wherever they are in the bunch. We then rolled along and it felt relatively calm for a few kilometres before we hit a couple of 1.5-kilometre climbs. Once again, there's no chance of moving forwards, but you can't afford to slip back, so you just grit your teeth and hang on, the bunch stretching as it goes over the top of them, forcing you in the drops to accelerate and hold your position.

It's a bit like riding a rollercoaster. If you sit at the front you can see where you're going, and a lot of people prefer to be in that position. But if you sit in the back seat, instead of going over the top of the big dipper and dropping, you actually get dragged by the momentum of the front cars over the top with even more of a kick. The tops of these little climbs are like that. They're quite hard, and really tough going over the top. That's where the line snaps, because the guys at the front are accelerating before you even reach the top, and each rider in line behind them has to accelerate a little bit more.

So if the front guys accelerate at, say, 400 watts to get back up to speed, the riders in the next rank have to do an extra 40 watts going over the top, the next line another, and if you're 40 back like I was, you really have to sprint to hang in and not let the wheel go. And that's usually where snaps happen, because guys just can't hold the wheel. If you're right behind someone who lets the wheel go, you can maybe sling around them and close the gap. But if you're two behind and the guy immediately in front of you doesn't move, the split happens and the group ahead has gone. Before you know it they're five seconds ahead, ten seconds ahead, twenty seconds ahead, because they're on the motorbike, sitting in its slipstream, and you're not. It opens super-quick, and it kept doing that. Then the pace at the front would ease a little, and the bunch would close up again.

Boom! One moment we were hurtling along this narrow road, the next there was a massive clatter of bikes and a sea of bodies on the road ahead. *Shiiit!* Your natural instinct is to pull on the brakes and hope that you finish up short of it, which you're more likely to do nowadays using disc brakes. You'd imagine this would bring a sense of relief, but the flip side of disc brakes is that you never think, *Phew! I'm lucky that I stopped before hitting the pile,* because you know that there's likely to be some dozy fucker behind who hasn't reacted as quickly and is going to plough into the back of you. You're actually waiting to get smashed from behind, and, sure enough, someone ploughed right into the back of me. I was lucky that I didn't come off – I just got a cut on the back of my leg and my bike wasn't damaged.

Ahead of me it was carnage, though. You rarely know why a crash happens when almost the whole peloton's involved, and we had no idea then that this crash had been caused by a fan stepping into the road to send a message to her grandparents. You're oblivious to how it's happened; you just want to find a way to get out of it. You start to look for a way through, climbing over bodies and bikes. The race is speeding away up the road and your sole aim is to get back into it.

I was picking my way forwards when I noticed a white jersey at the bottom of the pile. It was Julian. Holding my bike in one hand, I lifted bikes off him and helped him back to his feet. 'Are you all right?' I said. 'Do you want my bike?'

He told me his bike was OK and he got on it and went. I chased after him, saying on the radio, 'Julian has crashed. Stop pulling! Stop pulling!' As is usually the case with Julian, Dries Devenyns, whose job is to shadow him in all of the big races, was close by as well. Our only thought was to get Julian back up to the front. Fired up by adrenaline, I went into full panic mode as I started pulling, desperate to get him back up there. As I was pulling, Dries came up alongside and yelled at me, 'Slow down, Mark! They're waiting, they're waiting. Calm down!' The riders who had avoided the mayhem had slowed to allow the peloton to regroup.

We got back up to the front group pretty quickly, but I was spent. It was the first day of the Tour and I was spent. It was relentless, up and down, that rollercoaster drawing on my last reserves. I'd slide back on the climbs, struggle to get back into the line, then wait for the next one to come. Before too long, I'd slid back so far that I was the last wheel.

Even then I was thinking, *I need to find a way to get back to the front.* Landerneau was fast approaching and I wanted to give the other guys whatever help I could. Even pulling for a few seconds might make a difference. The descent into the town offered an opportunity to do this. It was wide, which meant that the peloton was likely to squash up more into a bunch than a long line.

As we came onto the descent, with ten kilometres to go, that's exactly what happened. Having been stretched out, the peloton concertinaed together. I had an opportunity, but as the peloton's speed increased I felt uneasy. We were moving so quickly. In order to get back to the front I needed to find a big gap rather than a small opening, and then I saw one emerging wide on the left. I started to go for it, and as I did there was a crash on the right and the bunch slammed left.

I was on the brakes, expecting an impact from behind but more concerned by what was happening to the right of me, the bunch sweeping across the road like a tidal wave, moving so fast I couldn't escape it.

'Aaargh, fuuuck!'

But just before it swept me up, the wave stopped and I squeezed through the little gap that remained on the left. Ahead of me, the peloton had exploded into lots of small parts and there was no way to the front. With just 500 metres left before we hit the town, I eased off and soon collected Tim and Morky. They had led into the town. We rode through Landerneau, hit the climb and just span our way up it.

Suddenly on the radio I could hear Tom shouting, 'Go! Go! Go! Go on, Julian!' We had no idea what was going on. Was he going after someone who'd jumped away? Was he away? You're often totally clueless in these situations, when all you can hear is a bit of what's going on in your ear. Then the convoy started to come past and the team car came up to me.

Tom pulled the wing mirror in so I could look at what was happening on the TV. Inside the car they were shouting, 'He's away! He's away!' I could see he was a few seconds clear, before the car accelerated away and we kept riding up, listening to the screaming in the radio, saying to each other, 'No, no, surely he can't ...?'

When we got to the line it was mayhem. As we weaved through, Julian came in the opposite direction, but he was mobbed and we couldn't get to him. So we carried on to the bus, where the staff were already celebrating. We got on the bus and the replays of the finish were still going. 'What a ride!' I said to the boys.

As well as Julian's winning attack on the Fosse aux Loups climb, two other performances really impressed us. First of all, Mattia Cattaneo's. His job was to get Julian first into the last climb, and that's exactly what he did. He did such a good job and continued to do so every time something was asked of him during the Tour. That was the first moment that I realised just how good he is. After 'Catta' had done his job, Julian was a little bit back, and at that moment Dries appeared at his side and gave him a nod, telling him, 'This is it, mate, we're off!' What Dries did then sums up what this team is about. It wasn't quite what we'd planned to do, but he improvised, told his leader, 'Come with me,' then emptied himself so that Julian could launch, and the result was the yellow jersey.

I have my routines at races, and one of them is that almost the first thing I do when I finish is call Peta. I tend to call her last thing before I start as well, but she always wants to hear from me at the finish, just to be sure that I'm OK. I usually get a shower first, then call her when I'm still in my towel. She was with the kids and Casper came in, and he'd been watching with her.

Gent-Wevelgem, October 2020, after which I was quoted saying 'that's perhaps the last race of my career'. © SWpix.com

Michael 'Morky' Mørkøv and Wilfried 'Fitte' Peeters at the Calpe training camp, December 2020. © Mark Cavendish

The aftermath of one of Vasi's interval sessions in Calpe, January 2021. © Mark Cavendish

Greece, May 2021.
Main pic: In the Athens Olympic Velodrome
Below: outside Athens in Malakasa.
© *Nassos Triantafyllou*

Morky at QuickStep's training camp,
January 2021.
© *Mark Cavendish*

With Julian Alaphilippe, Dries
Devenyns and Florian Sénéchal
during the Calpe training camp,
January 2021. © *Mark Cavendish*

In recovery mode after a track session with Vasi in Athens, May 2021.
© Mark Cavendish

Rest day in Athens visiting the Acropolis, May 2021.
© Mark Cavendish

A range of emotions after winning stage 4 of the 2021 Tour at Fougères, in June.
This was my 31st Tour de France stage win, and my first stage victory in the race since 2016.

© Guillaume Horcajuelo – Pool / Pool and Tim de Waele / Staff via Getty Images

With Patrick Lefevere in
Fougères after my first
stage win.
© Tim de Waele / Staff via Getty
Images

In time trial mode on stage 5 at Laval
having stitched my skinsuit back together
just before the start.
© SWpix.com

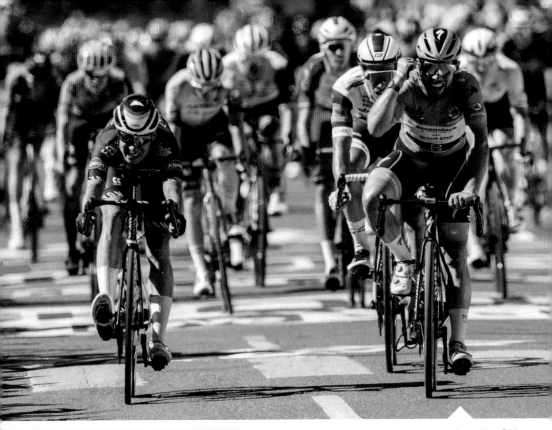

Winning stage 13 at Carcassonne and equalling Eddy Merckx's record of 34 stage wins, July 2021.
© SWpix.com

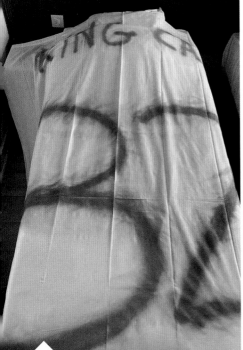

My bedsheet had a makeover from the team's soigneurs after my win at Châteauroux, July 2021.
© Mark Cavendish

Fitte fulfilling his promise that he'd get in the ice bath if I won four stages.
© Mark Cavendish

Having got trapped against the barriers there was no way through for me to challenge Wout van Aert for victory on the Champs-Élysées in the final stage of the 2021 Tour.

© Michael Steele / Staff via Getty Images

With Slovenia's Tadej Pogačar, who also had a great Tour successfully defending his title, July 2021.

© Tim de Waele / Staff via Getty Images

With my kids Casper, Frey and Delilah, marking my second green jersey win on the Champs Élysées, July 2021.

© Jean Catuffe / Contributor via Getty Images

'Loulou won! Loulou won and he's in the yellow jersey!' said Casper, using Julian's nickname.

'I know, mate, I know ...'

It's quite weird when the team's had a victory like that, because you're buzzing but it doesn't change what you do of a night. You go and get your massage, see the physio and go to dinner, because you've a job to do the next day. At dinner, we always have a beer or a glass of wine or champagne when we win, although I only had half a glass of beer. I was still following Vasi's strict regime and not eating any dessert or anything that might mean I'd put on a little bit of weight. Sometimes you can actually gain weight at a Grand Tour if you're fuelling yourself but not actually expending that many calories coasting along in the bunch. I probably could have treated myself that day, though, because it had been so frantic.

Patrick made a speech and then Julian got up and said a few words. 'Guys, we're really good today. My team has zees yellow jersey. It's really nice.' He didn't need to say any more than that. We'd got exactly the result we'd wanted. I guess I'd done little personally to assist the lads, but still, everyone loves it when a plan comes together.

I went up to bed, spoke to Peta again and then chatted to Catta. I felt really good. It was a long time since I'd savoured the emotion of winning something at the Tour de France, five years in fact. I felt buoyed by the success, the atmosphere in the team, and even by my performance, racing at warp-factor speed through almost ceaseless pandemonium.

STAGE 2

27 June: Perros-Guirec–Mûr-de-Bretagne, Guerlédan, 183.5km

Based on past experience of racing in Brittany during the opening days of the Tour de France, I knew that the racing on the second stage was likely to be just as frantic and fraught as it had been on day one. The roads are grippy, the weather is unpredictable and although there aren't any mountains, the terrain is rugged. It reminds me a bit of the countryside around my mum's home in Yorkshire, and you don't have to ride there long to understand why this region's produced so many great racers, Tour winners such as Louison Bobet and Bernard Hinault, as well as a large number of the current members of the French peloton, including Warren Barguil and David Gaudu.

The second stage was almost a mirror image of the first. It started by the sea, this time on the English Channel coast at the picturesque harbour town of Perros-Guirec, stuck to the coast for a good while, then went inland over a series of one- and two-kilometre climbs to reach a circuit at Mûr-de-Bretagne, where the finish was located on the climb above the village. Consequently, the pre-stage briefing was almost the same as it had been the day before, with Julian our protected rider once again. The big difference was him being in the yellow jersey, which would enable us to hold a position close to or right at the front of the bunch and avoid the jostling and turmoil further back. Like the day before, I was given the job of leading Julian and his band of climbers into Mûr-de-Bretagne the first time.

Once Christian Prudhomme had waved his flag to get us going, the racing followed the same pattern as 24 hours earlier. It was warp speed till the break went, although it did go pretty early. It was always up and down, although not as hard as the first day. Thankfully, the climbs were a lot more forgiving. You could ride them in the group rather than having to give everything just to hang on, which meant there wasn't that same drag effect over the top of them.

After sitting safe in the pack for 50 kilometres or so, my first big moment came at the intermediate sprint. With six riders in the break, we were only going for the minor placings as the road dragged up into the town of Plouha. We approached it about ten back, and Morky set me up in what would become familiar fashion, surging past everyone, but as I went to go on his left, Jasper Philipsen jumped and just blocked me, so I had to stall and go to the right. As I began to move that way, Caleb swept past me and I ended up crossing the line just behind him.

I was happy with that, though, because I hadn't really exerted myself in the end. If I'd got through where I'd wanted to on the left, I would have made a much bigger effort and claimed just one more point if I'd beaten Caleb. More significantly, I had a flavour of Morky's prowess. He'd just wowed me, leading out past guys like they were standing still. They were easy points for me.

The back end of the stage was punctuated with some short, sharp kicking climbs, and we moved up for that. I felt really nervous, but super-good. You know you're going well when riders who are probably better climbers and stronger than you are, which for me is pretty much everyone, are slipping backwards and you're just passing them. You get a good vibe off it. Don't get me wrong, it was hard. I wouldn't have been able to smoke a cigarette while doing it. But I never lost position. I was always there.

Up at the very front, Tim had been doing the pulling and he was spent – we weren't getting any help at all. The break was strong, really strong, and at one point Tim came on the radio and said, 'I don't know how much longer I can do this. Guys, I'm struggling.' People eventually came from other teams and helped him, but riding at that same tempo meant he wouldn't get as deep into the stage, because he wouldn't be able to adjust to the sudden increases in pace that were guaranteed to happen.

When you ride on the front all day, your body adapts to a one-power mode, in just a day. You're in tractor mode and can't then start surging. Once people start kicking and the pace goes up, you've had it. You can, however, carry on at the same pace you've been pulling at the front. It's weird, but if you were sitting on the wheel doing that power, you'd get dropped. If someone's pulling and then it's punchy at the end, the riders like Tim who are tasked with keeping the break within range always lose a lot of time. But if someone has been pulling all day and it's not punchy at the end, there's more of a gradual acceleration, on torque power; the rider who's been pulling will go deeper into the race and won't lose as much time. It's a weird phenomenon. Just like a tractor, they can keep trundling on for ever.

That day, though, we'd used Tim earlier than we wanted because the pace suddenly rose. The difference between the Tour and other races is that riders start lining up for the key moments, the pinch points or those other places where riders have been told they need to be near the front, much earlier. At most races, the battle for position usually starts 5–10 kilometres before the crunch points, and this used to be the case at the Tour. Now teams start trying to get their leaders in position 20-odd kilometres before them. The difference is more pronounced for the bunch sprints. It used to be 40 or 50 kilometres out that you lined up for a bunch sprint, and that was it, your position was where you were. This year it was as much as 75–80 kilometres out when that battle for position started.

Coming towards Mûr-de-Bretagne, the route was up and down on small roads, then the closer we got the more draggy they became. Morky was pulling and I was helping him out when I could, the two of us swapping off. That wasn't easy to do because the peloton was just one line across the front. There's a misconception when it's like that. It might look like we're taking it easy on TV, but that's when it's the hardest because there are half a dozen or more teams drag-stripping each other – which is where teams are lined out next to each other, trying to outpace one another in an attempt to control the front of the peloton – and if you don't match the others you end up swamped and in fiftieth position.

You have to stay there, you have to stay wheel to wheel, and if someone is going a little bit faster you have to match them. It's so stupid because if everyone just went easy, we'd still be in the same positions. All those same people could be at the front and riding 5 watts instead of 455. It was doing my head in hurtling along like that, and I was screaming at everyone, 'Fucking ease up!' But they don't. They just keep on dragstripping and I can't maintain power like that on grippy Breton roads. I was flicking my elbow for Morky to come through and he was like, 'I can't.' I can go hard and fast, but to stay at that pace requires one hell of an effort.

I surprised myself a little because I did manage it for longer than I expected. I could feel the lactic acid burning, but I was thinking, *We've got the yellow jersey. Keep going! Keep going! Keep going! Not far to the climb, I need to get to that roundabout first …*

I just about managed it and then all but stopped pedalling. As I eased off, riders started firing past me, and as they were flashing by I noticed that the peloton had fragmented. I was like, *Fuck, I wasn't going too bad …*

Morky and I dropped back into the gruppetto and just rode round the finishing circuit, soon so far behind the leaders that we couldn't hear anything about what was going on at the front. We were hoping that Julian might have been able to repeat his performance on the first day by jumping clear on the climb up to the finish. But as we crossed the line we could see the replays on the big screens and the name of the rider who'd won on the digital display above the finish: Mathieu van der Poel. The Dutch phenomenon had taken the yellow jersey too, riding the whole 25-kilometre finishing circuit on his own, then having enough power left on the final hill to hold off not only Julian, but Primož Roglič and Tadej Pogačar.

Because the team buses were back down the hill on the other side of Mûr-de-Bretagne, we stopped with the soigneur and were given a little silver whistle in a box. It had the words 'Tour de France' engraved on it, which is about the most cycling thing ever. If there'd been more room, they could have added, 'Congratulations for making it to the finish, here's a whistle for when you go risking your life, dodging fans going downhill to a bus that's parked five kilometres away.' We would end up using them a few times on the

Tour, and when we reached Paris I put mine in my case with the idea of giving it to Casper. But when I got home and started unpacking I thought to myself, *This is the most ridiculous idea ever, giving a three-year-old a whistle.* One day he'll get one of his own …

We got back to the hotel and Julian came in a good while later, after the podium ceremony and his media commitments. He felt he'd let us down a bit. 'Guys, I'm sorry, I'm sorry,' he was saying to us. We were like, 'Don't worry about it, Loulou. You've got the green jersey. We've seen the replay, and it's not as if you didn't give it everything. There was nothing anyone could do there.' What can you do when Mathieu van der Poel does that? Just admire it, that's all.

STAGE 3

Three days in and we get to the first sprint stage. Once again it started on the coast, this time on the southern side of Brittany at Lorient, looking out over the Atlantic. There were just a couple of climbs, but once again there were some pinch points that we had to be ready for, particularly in the closing kilometres, where there was a descent coming down into Pontivy and two really tight bends.

It was nervy right from the start, with little crashes. We'd done about 35 kilometres when we hit the coast road heading through Carnac, where there are all these huge prehistoric stones running across the countryside, like a French Stonehenge. We hit the modern equivalent of that going through the town, with speed bumps and road furniture all over the place. The speed bumps weren't big, but you've always got to be ready for them when you're in the peloton, just in case someone else isn't.

Sure enough, the bunch reached one and some riders went down next to me, creating a wave of bikes and bodies in my line. As they went down, I swerved right and had these plastic bollards coming towards me, but I somehow managed to weave between them. As I got back into the bunch, I could see an Ineos rider on the ground and realised it was Geraint Thomas. You don't like to see anyone crashing, but when it's your mate it's not nice. Robert Gesink came down in that crash and I was so lucky. It was like someone was looking down on me because I didn't hit the bollards.

Luke Rowe came up to me shortly afterwards and I asked him how G was. 'He's not good – he's not on his bike yet.' You feel gutted for someone when that happens. You know how much they've committed so that they're at their best at the Tour, and I know all too well how devastating it is when all that preparation comes to nothing.

Luke and I have had this joke about G crashing since we were kids. He just crashes, he always has, and it's always like, 'I dunno what happened.' That's what he always says. Before the Qatar Worlds in 2016, we were out training and doing a team time-trial effort on the road bikes. I was towards the back of this line of maybe seven, and all of a sudden they flicked sideways and I twatted something in the middle of the road. My front tyre was blown out and I was in mid-air, on my side in a tabletop position. Then, *Bam!* I landed really hard with Scott Thwaites clattering over the top of me like we were a couple of trapeze artists wowing a crowd at the Cirque du Soleil.

I got up and there was a huge rock in the road. I was fuming. We went into this little hut at the side of the road and my whole back's off, three days before the world road race. I was raging because I'd seen this rock.

'Who was on the front?'

'G.'

'What the fuck, G. Why didn't you point it out?'

'What rock?'

And the joke came from that. When he crashed in the Giro in 2020, Luke sent me a message: 'What bidon?' It's a running joke.

That day it was, 'What speed bump?' We didn't know then that this was just the start of another day of carnage.

Things were OK until we got past the intermediate sprint, with about 60 kilometres left. That was another interesting one because a kilometre beyond it there was a left-hander into small roads with potential crosswinds, so it was a pinch point again.

Morky did the lead-out again, and, same again, he passed six people in the last couple of hundred metres, setting me up perfectly. But I was lazy. I was trying to wait as late as possible and I got rolled by Caleb. He came by and I couldn't get back to him, but I didn't have the time to say sorry to Morky for not making the most of the work he'd done because as soon as we went through the sprint we had this plan to keep pressing on, because we couldn't lose that much speed before the pinch point on the corner.

We'd talked about it before the stage and I'd said, 'Guys, be on the left-hand side and we'll go to that side after the sprint. If you pass me just give me a little push to get me in the line, to get me back on.' Someone pointed out, 'We can't touch you – you know what the commissaires are like.' Morky and I would just have to keep the pressure hard on the pedals beyond the sprint, looking back as the peloton came up to us, hoping we'd spot a gap that we could get into. It was going to be like one of those efforts I'd done on the track in Athens to get back in behind Vasi on the motorbike.

They passed us about 300 metres before the corner. There was a little bit of crosswind but there were too many teams there for the peloton to split, the speed was too high. People – including a good number of riders in the bunch – think that as soon as there's any kind of crosswind it's going to split. But if the wind is cross-head, it's not splitting because it's a headwind. You can't go fast enough to split it. It's not always the case it will split if the wind is crosstail, either. That's largely because we have reached almost terminal velocity in those situations, so unless you put a massive gear on, a 60 x 11 or 12, say, or a 65, you can't accelerate enough to produce a split. If you're already doing 55 or even 60km/h, it's almost impossible to accelerate. If you're doing 55km/h and you try to accelerate, you're going to get up to 57, and that extra 2km/h isn't enough to force a split.

You create an echelon by going 10km/h quicker than someone. And if you're in an echelon and someone's dangling off the back, you can go 5–10km/h quicker than them for the same effort. That's why the echelon forms and goes. It's simply down to physics. It's the change of pace that causes it.

I don't get why it's so complicated, why some riders can't grasp that. They'll be hammering away at the front when it's not going to happen and you'll think, *What are you doing?* It's always those same guys who are naturally very strong that are up there in those situations. I guess that they've never had to learn how to race on their wits, because all they've ever had to do when they're in a bad position is to make a big effort. Whereas I was always a runt in a bike race – as a schoolboy and as a junior. I had to find my way to survive and compete. That's how you learn to race.

One other thing to remember about echelons is that if there are no blue jerseys at the front – and I say this deadly seriously and without any arrogance – it's not splitting. That's not because we're always the ones that force it, but because it's our bread and butter. If there's any chance that it could split, there's always Deceuninck blue jerseys all over the front of the line. It was always the tactic I used when I wasn't on the team.

So, it didn't split, but the surge that had led into and followed that intermediate sprint meant that we were getting close to the breakaway group. All of a sudden, though, the break's advantage went up by 30 or 40 seconds, which produced a bit of a panic and another surge. Everyone was fighting for the front, desperate to be in a good position, but nobody was actually thinking about the break and trying to take control. We began to panic then too because we were starting to think we weren't going to catch the break at all. Tim was trying to get through. I could just see his head shaking from side to side as he shouted at the guys around him, trying to get back up to the front, but no one would let him past. I don't get that mentality. I was told by one of my coaches as a junior that you're not in the race until you're in the race. But this is often the way in modern cycling, particularly stage races. No nuance to actually cross the line first. But I could write a whole other chapter on how my brain hurts trying to understand tactics – or lack thereof, nowadays.

By this point we were on a small road that weaved left and right and bumped up and down almost all the way to the finish. I was locked on to Morky's wheel, but we were in this area about 20 or 25 back where shit happens. Guys were getting tired, and in that situation you either want to be further forward or just sitting at the back not giving a monkey's. We were in the shit zone. I was a little bit panicked, but I was thinking, *Trust him! Trust him! Trust him!*

It was really sketchy. You were on your brakes, left then right, guys bashing into each other. One moment I was next to Fred Wright, who's a super-nice kid, but too nice to give an elbow back. It was his first Tour and he was like a rabbit in the headlights, this little kid on Bahrain, his eyes almost popping out, getting bashed around, riders around him thinking, *Who the fuck is this? Just get out of my way!* He's such a nice guy, a really good bike rider, but he won't fight back.

Soon after, as we were cresting the brow of this hill and on a road so narrow that you were stuck in whatever position you happened to find yourself in, there was a surge. Morky went with it and I was late to react. *Crunch.* His rear mech went into my spokes, ripping them out like Queen Boudica's wheel-shredding chariot. With rim brakes you'd just grind to a halt in that situation because the misshaped rim jams against the brakes. But with disc brakes the wheel just starts to wobble. I slowed down, thinking, *Someone's going to hit me,* and put my hand up, but kept pedalling because we were only 15 or 20 kilometres from the end and I knew that there'd been a crash not long ago and the cars were behind it. I knew my only chance of contesting the sprint was to try to stay with this group until the cars came back and I could get my spare bike.

But with my wheel wobbling disconcertingly, I steadily lost ground, going through one group coming back from the crash, then another, then another. Then my car came. Off the bike. Change. Back on the spare. As I got going I was thinking, *The other cars are going to go past and I'll able to get in among them and make my way back to the groups ahead.* But three of them shot past and that was it. The rest didn't come. They'd obviously been barraged by the commissaires, who prevent team cars from going alongside or ahead of riders who've been dropped, ensuring those riders can't benefit from the slipstream and regain the ground they've lost. So I was in no man's land, chasing.

'How far am I behind?' I said into the radio. Nothing. I kept going and pretty quickly I was passing guys who had been leading out and had swung over. Then I saw the cars just ahead and thought

I might be able to get back on. But as I got closer, I realised that the reason I was making up ground on them so rapidly was because they'd stopped. That's never a good sign. I reached them, weaving through at a 5kph tiptoe, like I was in Central London at rush hour. A crash, bikes, ripped shorts, wonky helmets everywhere. That was it. I knew, setting off again, that I was never going to get back to the front, so I started riding easy, my first chance to sprint now completely gone.

Five hundred metres later, there was a body on the ground, guys getting up, teammates helping them to change the wheels or put the chain on. A kilometre later, there was another one with more guys. I caught a guy, cut up, who was riding in on his own. The sense of turmoil remained as I started the downhill towards the final pinch point and found myself in a now-familiar scene of sheer and utter chaos.

There was a little narrowing, with a house on the left, then bushes running away from it and a bank, with cars stopped next to it. Jumbo were there tending to Tony Martin, who was on the ground. Bahrain had stopped as well – for Jack Haig, I found out later. I worked my way through and then rode down to the final flat section running into Pontivy, where I caught up with Qhubeka's Simon Clarke.

'What the fuck happened there?' I asked him.

'Oh, mate, it's just gone to shit.'

We rode in easy along the river, turned sharp right over a bridge and then right again back down the far bank, just as Tom Steels had described it in the briefing that morning. Then there was a sharp left onto the finish straight. We knew it was going to be a tight corner, because Tom had highlighted how vital positioning was going into it. But seeing it for myself I said to Clarkey, 'Thank fuck we aren't doing a bunch sprint into this corner.'

Beyond the corner the road straightened out for just over a kilometre into the finish. As I approached the line I saw Caleb in the road with his teammates gathered round him. I stopped next to them just as he was just getting up.

'Are you all right, mate?' I asked him. He was in shock and didn't respond. Then to his teammates, 'Is he OK?'

One of them said, 'His shoulder, collarbone.'

I felt gutted for Caleb, who'd gone down really hard with Peter Sagan when the sprint opened up. I know how bad it is as a sprinter when you've hurt your shoulder like that in the Tour de France. This is your time to shine, and before you've had a chance to do that you're going home. I was relieved, too. If the stage had gone to plan I'd have been coming into that final sprint with Morky and we'd have been on the outside of Caleb and Sagan, coming around the left-hand side where they wiped out. If I'd have been in that final alone I would've been on Caleb's wheel and I would likely have been wiped out there as well. So mostly I was relieved. I know that's selfish, but it felt like there was a reason that my teammates and I weren't there. I called Peta from the bus and she said the same. 'I'm so relieved you weren't there!'

That's all I could get from that stage, really. I finished. To say I didn't feel disappointed isn't true. Of course I would've liked to have sprinted, and it was one fewer opportunity from the seven or eight that we had. At the same time, I wasn't disappointed that I wasn't there. At least I had another chance.

And then it all started to kick off about rider safety. I was kind of on the fence about it. I'm not in any CPA (Cyclistes Professionnels

Associés) chats or anything like that. In all honesty I understand the union, the point of it, but I don't want to be unified with some of the riders in the peloton. Everyone has their own agenda, so we're not unified. It gets my back up that there'll be a big protest about a sprint stage, but not one about a mountain stage. When those guys are riding stupid watts up a climb with a motorbike just ahead of them helping them to do that, do they know what we have to do on a descent just to stay in the race? We have to take bigger risks than they do in a sprint. The GC riders have got their own agenda. They don't want to do a sprint because they don't want the stress of it, but it's the same leading into a climb.

Another thing about saying how dangerous it was is that we all knew that beforehand. In the past we'd have eased up. There would have been a fight for position on the narrow road at the top of the climb because everyone knew that tricky descent was coming; you'd have the odd clown who would try to come underneath and cut a load of guys up going into the corner in the mad hope of gaining a few positions, but the majority would have taken it easy. Anyone who did try to go underneath would have been grabbed by the collar and told they were racing like an arsehole.

I can remember Filippo Pozzato doing exactly that to me in 2007 at the Volta a Catalunya, where I won my first two WorldTour stages. It was the day I took the first of those wins. We were coming down this descent into the town where we'd finish, through a lot of hairpins, and I came underneath him on a tight corner with my back wheel fully locked up. At the bottom we went up this Alaphilippe-style climb hill to the line. He grabbed me just beyond the line, but I didn't grasp what I'd done. Thinking back, I had been fairly reckless there, totally in the wrong.

Now I feel like I'm Pozzato, like I need to grab a few people by the jersey collar. No one's going easy on the descents. They should have that day, and they would have been thankful for it when they could start racing again with three kilometres to go. We'd all be showing more respect for each other if we did that.

So when they started talking about a protest the next day I was like, 'What's a protest going to do? Stop, and then what? What exactly are we protesting about? What will it achieve? Can't we wait until a mountain day and protest?' I was dead against it; I even argued with my teammates about it. It was bullshit.

Perhaps it's because I'm getting older and I see things differently to when I first came into racing, when I was quite reckless. When I was younger I didn't really think about it, but every time we go off to race we're risking our lives. I've seen enough fatalities in my career. This isn't just me being, 'Oh, these youngsters ...', but everyone who rode a bike in the past as a pro was a bike racer, they'd grown up racing bikes; there was none of this hiring guys just because they're strong. And although we were competitors, we were colleagues. People had families, so everyone looked after each other. You would point out holes in the road, you would point out the obstacles, and if it was chaotic like it was on those first days at the Tour, you wouldn't take stupid risks. You wouldn't try to bunch the peloton up at pinch points; you would stay on one side of the road so that everyone got through them OK. Now it's not even a case of people not pointing things out. I've seen cases of people riding towards hazards in the road and swerving at the last minute, so they gain an advantage if somebody crashes. It's absolutely crazy.

I honestly believe that if we'd raced into that descent a decade ago, the peloton would've slowed down. But now they don't, and then they complain about it afterwards. After my wheel smashed and I'd given up the chase, my overwhelming feeling as soon as crash after crash began was, *What on earth is going on?* I can't remember that many previous instances of relief at not being able to sprint, but that day, especially when I got to that left-hand corner going into the descent, my only thought was, *Thank fuck I wasn't there.* I never used to be like that. In hindsight, maybe the fact that I was held up was down to the gods looking down on me, especially bearing in mind what then happened with Peter and Caleb in the final. I didn't know it then, but everything had played out right.

STAGE 4

I was nervous that morning. Not as nervous as I used to get for sprint stages, but just enough so that I was super-focused. I felt like I was really dialled in that day for the first time, more so than the day before, which we'd thought was going to be a sprint. I had a different sensation that morning, not confidence exactly, but eagerness.

Fougères was the site of my last Tour de France win for QuickStep during my first spell with the team, so I knew the finish and was able to describe it when we were going through the race plan in the briefing. I think the main difference was that last time we didn't do any small roads in the final bit of the race. This time, instead of being on a big road for the whole run-in, we were on narrow roads until about ten kilometres out.

I felt sorry for Caleb that morning, and I messaged him to see if he was all right. He had been my biggest threat at the Tour de France, the guy I believed I had to beat. I knew Jasper Philipsen would be good as well, but Caleb was the sprinter who stood out. With all of the others, you can make your own tactics and just do the best you can. But when it came to Caleb and his Lotto-Soudal team, we knew that we would have to factor them into our tactics, to try to work out what they were going to do and make our plans based on that insight. But with Caleb gone, it made things a lot easier for us because we could focus on planning what we were going to do and not trying to second-guess another team.

We rolled out. I hadn't heard that much about the protest that had been arranged for that morning at kilometre zero. There'd been some talk about it the night before, but I was so focused on the stage ahead of us that I was bit surprised when we finished the neutral section and the peloton stopped. I was quite near the back, and as we stood there I was thinking, *What are we gaining out of this?* I was standing next to Mathieu van der Poel, in the yellow jersey, and I said to him, 'Do you want to stop?'

'No, I want to race.'

'Well, go to the front and start riding. I'll come with you.'

Luke Rowe, who's one of my best mates, saw me starting to move forwards and said, 'Where are you going?'

'To ride.'

'But we all agreed on this,' he told me.

'I fucking didn't.'

'Your team did.'

'I haven't spoken about it with my team.'

I still didn't understand what we'd get from stopping. I just wanted to ride, and I still think there are better ways to protest. If we all wanted to be unified, we could have just done a go-slow in the dangerous parts, which would have made more sense.

I'd barely started to move forwards with Van der Poel when the peloton got going anyway. The break went straight away and only had two guys in it, Caleb's Lotto teammate Brent van Moer and Pierre-Luc Périchon from Cofidis. That was perfect for us. Everyone knew it was going to be a sprint and there's never much of a fight for the breakaway on a day like that. Tim set to work pace-making on the front, with Alpecin helping out as well for Philipsen and Tim Merlier, who'd won the day before.

It was pretty uneventful most of the day: the break went out and then we started to wind it back in again, like an angler reeling in their catch. Morky led me out for the intermediate sprint at Vitré with about 40 kilometres left, and I took third there behind the breakaway.

We went onto narrow roads coming out of the town as the route turned north towards Fougères. At times the road was just three or four riders wide, and all of the GC teams were fighting to get in there first. Once again, they passed Tim but didn't ride, and Tim couldn't get through to keep the chase going.

The gap started to go up again, edging past two minutes with 25 kilometres to go. I started to stress a bit. It was just as well that I didn't know Van Moer was the guy who had held off the bunch to win the opening stage of the Dauphiné just a few weeks before, or full panic would have set in. Once again, the calls of 'Stay at the front' through the GC teams' radios were evident as waves of climbers appeared at the front, baulking the movement of the peloton.

Eventually, Tim managed to work his way back to the front, like an Ent in a battle scene from *The Lord of the Rings* moving through the armies of orcs, and started pulling. We got within about 30 seconds of them, then the gap went out to a minute again after Van Moer dropped Périchon and went solo. By then we were on the main road into Fougères, and I knew from my victory in 2015 that the final kilometre would play in our favour as we chased Van Moer down. You're on wide roads till the kilometre banner, where you turn sharp right into the town centre. It narrows a bit, then starts dragging up, getting gradually steeper in the last 300 to 400 metres, all the way to the line.

Once we were on the main road ten kilometres out, everyone was jostling for position, which was winding the speed up, but no one really had control. Dries started pulling up a drag, trying to impose some order, and as we switched to the left there was a touch of wheels and Davide Ballerini had his spokes ripped out. Ballero was instantly done for the day, and he was important because he was supposed to be the guy in front of Morky in the lead-out, the rider who was set to lead us through the two roundabouts in the last kilometre. With him out, the textbook is ripped up and the adaptation manual is pulled out of your jersey pocket.

That left me with just Morky ahead of me. We were isolated, sitting on the side of the peloton with no one really chasing Van Moer. Teams were setting up their sprinters, but waiting for someone else to take it up. His lead was still the thick end of a minute and there was nothing Morky and I could do on our own.

Approaching the final kilometre, the gap was still 20 seconds. Suddenly, almost with a touch of Napoleonic fanfare, there was a blur of green. Julian. He slotted in front of Morky and just started pulling. He could have been looking after the green jersey or his GC chances, but it showed his racing mentality and the dedication that he thought, *I've got to get this break back.*

Ideally, the lead-out rider and his sprinter don't want to be in second and third position more than a kilometre out because, although you've got someone in front of you, you're still pushing more wind than if you're in the bunch, especially as Julian's not very big. On the other hand, as I'd explained to Morky in Belgium, I'd always rather be in a position at the front and able to analyse the situation and see what's going on around us than having to react from behind.

Having got us in that position, Julian pulled full gas into the final kilometre, with Van Moer still a dozen seconds ahead. As he swung off, the rest of the group took over and we slotted into it. We hit the first roundabout, the road narrowing approaching it. The road went right coming out of it so everyone wanted to be on the right-hand side, and as we were coming into it Bouhanni came underneath me, going too straight. He was right on me and I nearly crashed, but I managed to stay upright even though he banged into me.

The fastest line was around the right-hand side. As the liquid movement of the peloton bottlenecked, I used a feathery finger to dab the brakes, my handlebars wobbling as Bouhanni positioned his front wheel on the slice of tarmac my front wheel was about to arrive on. I briefly lost Morky, but a brief, albeit unwanted, push of watts on the pedals rectified it. Alpecin and DSM now had numbers at the front, and we were a little bit too far back, ninth or tenth position perhaps. With 600 to 700 metres left, it was still too far out for him to lead me out, but I needed to be closer to the front, so he surfed up the outside from there with me on his wheel. I don't think he'd have done that with Sam, but it showed that we were now working well together, that he'd taken in what I'd spoken to him about during the Tour of Belgium. He went through the left-hand corner, then flicked his elbow because he'd done his thing, and I had to look for a wheel to get on.

Trek were taking it up for Mads Pedersen and I saw a space. I was in it without hesitation. Alpecin came by with their lead-out and that was the moment, the sprint was about to open up. We still hadn't caught Van Moer yet, but we could see him as the sprint opened up. I knew instantly what was going to happen. DSM's Cees Bol was there, Alpecin's Jasper Philipsen was there, and I knew they'd give the guy coming backwards a wide berth as they went past him. I thought, *It's going to open here, it's going to be tight but I need to use Van Moer to accelerate now.*

When I took my first ever Tour win in Châteauroux in 2008, I used Nicolas Vogondy as my lead-out that day. He was the French champion and had been in the break, and we caught him right at the death. I used his slipstream to accelerate, and a very similar scenario was unfolding. As Philipsen and the others swung left to go around the outside of Van Moer, I launched towards him knowing that I might have to brake, but that this was my only option if I wanted to win. I knew I couldn't go around the outside of them. It was too far to go. I had to try to make it through on the inside, counting on the fact that the other sprinters don't think like me and would give Van Moer plenty of space as they accelerated past him – more space than they needed to.

They started the sprint, quickly closing in on Van Moer with 200 metres to go. They closed and closed and closed, and for an instant it looked like they wouldn't give him the room I needed. It was tight, really tight. But then the gap opened as they went to the left of the Lotto rider. This was my chance. I started sprinting towards him, taking advantage of the gap he'd left in the air, which was now opening more easily than I'd expected, and I accelerated into it.

I was coming on the inside of Philipsen and had more speed because of the run-up I'd got from Van Moer. I was closing on him, closing, and the line was coming, and I was still closing. Then I was past him.

You're not looking at the finish, but at that big red Vittel banner across the road. It fills your vision. It was coming, but I could sense that no one was coming from behind. No one was coming close. My front wheel hit the line and I just roared. That stage in Fougères was the only one I won in 2015 during what was a hard Tour until then. And I had the same ecstatic release, joy mixed with relief. I'd won!

Without even intending to, I did the same celebration as in 2015, pumping my fists as I roared. For a few moments it felt like it does in films when everything goes quiet and you don't hear the noise all around you. You don't hear anything.

I came to a stop and just started hugging *anyone*. I saw the soigneurs and started hugging them. I think it was Sharky, who massaged me every evening, I hugged first, and after that I turned to find my teammates. People were coming to say congratulations. Michael Matthews had patted me on the back as we crossed the line and said, 'Brilliant, mate!' And I think even Peter Sagan gave me a tap of congratulation, but I only saw that later. Tim Merlier came over to say well done. I feel bad looking back, because I should have been friendlier to all of them, but I just wanted to see the boys. That's all I wanted to do, see the boys. And then came the obligatory tears.

Everything that had happened in the last few years, this year, seemed to lift off me. It was like a weight had gone, and I couldn't stop crying. It felt like, 'I'VE WON A STAGE OF THE TOUR!' As if I'd never done it before. I sat down and just bawled, although I at least had the wits to keep my glasses on because I've got the ugliest crying face.

The team, the boys, had believed in me, and I'd repaid that belief. The huge pull that Julian did, that's belief. That's not doing a job because you're supposed to, that's belief. Morky moving me up at the right moment, that's belief. Tim fighting to get back through to the front, that's belief. Dries pulling, that's belief. It was incredible. I didn't even think of Van Moer, didn't feel sorry for him. It wasn't until I watched it later that I realised how fucking close he was, what an incredible race he'd done.

Our team doctor on the race, Phil, suddenly appeared. He's massive and he picked me up and hugged me. Although he'd supported me for the whole year, the Tour was the first race I'd done with him. He's one of the funniest men you'll ever meet, and he's like our big brother, going around the rooms in the evening, chatting and making everyone laugh. When he picked me up, I just cried into his shoulder. As we went into the changing cabin to get ready for the podium ceremony, ASO's director-general Yann Le Moenner, who's been a good friend for a long time, came in. 'I'm so happy,' he said as he gave me a hug.

Then it was podium time. It wasn't like it used to be, because the health restrictions meant you didn't go out and shake people's hands. But the music for the ceremony was the same: I know the exact note that signals the moment when you start walking out onto the podium. Rather than a trophy, they give you a medal now to mark your stage win, and this was the first one I'd ever got. You get it just before you walk out, wait for the last crescendo in the music, then out you go. There's a guy down at the front with a sign telling you to stand, stop, whatever, but all you can see are the crowds, a sea of people. I went back behind the stage and found out that, as a result of my stage win, I'd inherited the green jersey from Julian. So I zipped myself into that and went out again.

Once I was back behind the stage, I was ushered into the video-conference cabin nearby to speak to the media, who were connected via video link from the pressroom. I really hate being interviewed in there because firstly, you can't read the room, and secondly, it's not intimate enough. As I took my seat, the camera was panning around the journalists waiting to quiz me. I had my back up slightly because I was expecting some criticism or a negative spin being put on things. That was the way it always had been for me; there was always something, either someone being a dickhead or someone else trying to rile me for a soundbite. I've been a dickhead in the past too, but when you're 20 years old, have never had any media training and you're from a small island where everyone tends to say what they think, it's not hard to rub people up the wrong way.

But there was none of it. Everyone seemed genuinely pleased for me. For the first time in my life, everything I heard in that impersonal little cabin was positive and it meant a lot to me. It was warm, and I didn't feel like I was being tripped up. I felt like I was being treated like a human.

From there I went to anti-doping and then into the mixed zone where all the TV media are and where Patrick was already being interviewed. He hugged me and said, 'I've never, ever seen every single one of our staff members crying, never seen it. They've all just been in tears on the bus.'

Then Yann came up to me again. 'Can you come over here? There's a school over here with a statue of you,' he said. I hadn't seen this statue before, didn't even know that it existed. It was a memorial of the last stage finish here in 2015, a metal sculpture of a bike with a photo of me winning. 'Will you sign it for the school?' he asked. It said something about that 2015 win being my 30th Tour victory. So I signed it, we had some photos taken and then I crossed out the '30th' and wrote '31st', adding the words 'Always believe'.

I went back to do the TV interviews and talked a lot about having belief in yourself. I can't claim to have been in a worse position than lots of other people in the last few years, especially since Covid hit. Sports people can get so consumed with our lives in our little bubbles that we become selfish. We've been lucky because we've been able to continue with our lives while so many other people have been dealing with immense turmoil. However, despite being in that safe little bubble, I've been through real hell in recent years. People who were always there for me disappeared. Even Rod, the guy who was my confidant for 20 years, stopped believing in me. But thankfully there were people who were always there, none more so than my wife. Peta's a really strong personality, hugely supportive, and she always believed, much more than me sometimes. When I was like, *Fuck it! I can't do it,* Peta pushed me on as I battled with illness, misdiagnosis, injuries, depression, loss of form.

I know it might sound like bravado, but I honestly feel that if I can come back from setbacks like I've had, anyone can, as long as they've got the right people around and a will to do it. It's doable. I had this overwhelming sense of that. And that's why I wanted to see the boys, because they'd been part of my support network, even if they didn't know it. A lot of them I'd never ridden with, others I had, but all of them and all of the staff I'd worked with had believed in me, and that had enabled me to rediscover the ability I knew I still had and, ultimately, to win in Fougères.

Finally, I fulfilled all of the media commitments and got into a team car with Patrick, with Phil the doctor and Phil our press guy in the back. As Patrick drove us to the hotel, I FaceTimed Peta, and Casper was there with her, absolutely beside himself with excitement. Peta said Casper had burst into tears when I'd won and didn't know why. She'd taken a video of the kids watching the finish, and while she was filming she was going, 'He's not going to do it. He's not going to do it …' and the kids were screaming. It was so nice. Then I called Vasi and he was crying his eyes out. He was up at Livigno at a training camp, with some of the boys at the table, and they all said well done.

We got back to the hotel and I hugged all the mechanics and staff, giving Fitte the biggest hug of all. After everything we'd been through, the shit I'd given him the last time I was on the team, he'd been one of my biggest supporters this year.

By that point I was totally spent from all the emotion, so tired. I did a video interview for the team and then I just went to my room. We were staying in a Campanile, one of those budget places where your door opens onto an exterior walkway rather than a corridor. On the plus side, when we stayed in one of their hotels this year we had our own rooms, instead of sharing like we normally do.

I went in, closed the door and put my bag down. I logged on to my phone and there were more than 700 WhatsApp messages. Seven hundred! I don't know how that many people have got my number. I dropped the phone on my bed, sat down on the floor, still in my green jersey and my podium stuff, and started crying again. I don't know how long I sat there for; I don't even know why I was crying. I didn't feel happy or sad or relieved, just overwhelmed. I might have been there for ten minutes – it could've been half an hour or an hour, I don't know. I just couldn't stop crying. I didn't get in the shower, I just sat there.

Eventually, someone knocked – Sharky, I think – and said, 'Do you want to come for a massage?' So I got in the shower and then went for a massage. It was late by that point and everyone was already at dinner. When I went in, I hugged all of the lads again. They had pretty much finished eating, but they stayed where they were until I'd eaten so that we could share a celebratory drink. Patrick stood up and did a speech, then I got up and said, 'Thank you for that – you did a good job today. It was more than a good job, though. It was belief. So thank you for believing in me, all of you, all of the staff, thank you for believing in me, and more important than the belief, thank you for making me happy. That's the thing that means the most to me – you've made me happy.'

I had one final commitment, a Dutch TV show. They had a video message for me from Fabio, which was super-nice. Then it was bedtime. I called a few people and tried to reply to a few of those 700 messages. The funny thing is that you reply to the last people who contacted you because their message is at the top, they reply back, and you instantly realise there's no way you can get through all of the messages.

I felt happy but somehow not happy, mentally drained, devoid of emotion. I needed to sleep, but somehow it just wouldn't come. One of my final thoughts before I did eventually drift off was, *Just as well we've got a time trial tomorrow …*

STAGE 5

30 June: Changé–Laval Espace Mayenne
time trial, 27.2km

'd set my alarm for the morning because we had to go and recon the time-trial stage, but I hadn't got to sleep until the early hours and was knackered when it went off. I messaged Tom Steels and said, 'Mate, I slept shit last night. Can I miss the recon?' It was OK with him, so a quick reset of the alarm and my head hit the pillow for a further two hours.

We were right by the time-trial course, so I knew I didn't have to stress too much. I got up at about 9.30 and went to breakfast. Everyone was already at the start, so I shovelled down my granola, put my rucksack on my back and pedalled my bike through the melee of team vehicles to our team bus. My green time-trial skinsuit had already been delivered by the race organisers by the time I got there. I always thought that they custom-made it for you, taking all your measurements and cutting it to fit perfectly, but only the yellow jersey gets that treatment. They'd estimated my size and sent across one that they thought would fit snugly.

The next thing on the agenda was the recon. Although I obviously wasn't going to go full gas in the time trial – Vasi's plan was for me to get through it comfortably and save all I could for the Châteauroux stage the following day – I did need to know if there were any tricky corners or other parts where I needed to exercise some caution. It was getting on for 10.30 and my start time was at 12.51, so Fitte told me to jump in the car and he'd drive me round the course. It was only 27 kilometres, so it would only take half an hour or so. Or at least we thought it would.

We did the first bit. There were one or two corners where I needed to be careful, but it wasn't overly technical. Then we hit an unforeseen snag. We caught the publicity caravan, an immensely lengthy and slow-moving convoy of sponsors' vehicles in all kinds of garish shapes and sizes, blasting out dire French pop and advertising jingles, from which hyped-up holiday-job students chuck out all kinds of PR tat. We were only about a third of the way around the course and we now had just a couple of hours before my start time. Fitte went into full panic mode. You can't pass the caravan and you also can't turn around and drive in the wrong direction on the course. The only option we had was to find somewhere we could exit the route and get back to the start.

We looked at the map. 'OK, there's a corner here we can cut through,' said Fitte, pointing to somewhere a couple of kilometres down the road. We got there and it was barriered off. 'Shit! OK, we'll have to go to the next one.' We dropped back in behind the caravan again, restricted to 20km/h. We got to the next side road and it was barriered off as well. On a road stage there'd just be a gendarme and a volunteer or two standing at each junction, but on time-trial courses, which tend to be much shorter and usually require the roads to be closed for a good deal longer, the race organisation can barrier or block just about every one of them.

Fitte was almost in meltdown by now. We got to the next junction and he wound down the window and pleaded with the volunteers:

'We need to get off the course. Please can you let us through?' This one had a truck and some bollards blocking it, so they had to find the driver to move the bollards. Thankfully, they managed to track him down quickly and we got out and back to the start.

By the time we'd weaved around all of the road closures and back into the start area, there were just 40-odd minutes remaining until I started. I had to get my numbers on my skinsuit, get dressed, warm up, then find my way to the start. Out of my tracksuit, I was already in Kermit the frog mode, hopping into the green Lycra and wriggling it up over my bum. Actually, more akin to Miss Piggy than Kermit. *Rrriiippp!* With my lack of grace in this game of dress-up, I'd ripped down the stitching of the chamois, leaving things literally flapping in the wind. Not ideal for a time trial, definitely not ideal for any public decency.

Although none of the young guys do it now, when I first turned pro you always had a sewing kit in your bag. It's remained a staple whenever I pack. I got my sewing kit out and didn't even have time to take my skinsuit off. I'm pretty adept with a needle and thread, largely because my mum owned a haberdashery shop so I learned how to sew when I was a kid.

It took me a few minutes to stitch the skinsuit back together, and once I'd done it I had little more than ten minutes left before I had to go to the start. I jumped on the rollers, did the fastest warm-up in Tour time-trial history and sped off to the start.

I'd spoken to Vasi about how to ride it. He'd said, 'Stay in this zone, between these numbers, and you'll be inside the time cut.' I set off and stuck to his figures, but I felt incredible. I was actually having to back off to stay in his zone. The crowds helped. Although a lot of people were still arriving, I was able to enjoy racing in the green jersey.

The last time I'd done a time trial in green was on the penultimate day of the 2011 Tour, and I can't remember much about it. But this time trial was incredible. The fans were getting behind me, and I loved it.

Once I'd finished, I knew in all likelihood that I was going to retain the green jersey, but I would have to wait four hours to find out. Julian was the only person who could take it off me and he was the penultimate starter. There was a big transfer that night so I decided to kill some time by riding back to the hotel to get a shower. When I got back to the bus, Patrick was there and we watched the rest of the time trial together. Occasionally, one of the guys would come in after his time trial, get a shower and go off to the next hotel. By the time Julian reached the second time check we could see that he wasn't going to win, so I got back into my kit and rode to the podium. I saw Pogačar come through to win the stage, while Cattaneo did a stormer of a ride too, finishing in the top ten, not far behind Kasper Asgreen, who was our big hope.

After I'd done the podium, I did the transfer to our hotel in Le Mans with our mechanic Guido (the one I would later be seen shouting at in a video that went viral during stage 19). I've known him a long time. He was at Telekom when I was there, right at the start of my career, and we've always got on well. He's got the most infectious laugh, a real giggle. I don't remember how it came about – it started that long ago – but when we're talking I'll always end sentences with '*aus Deutschland*'. So, it'd be like, 'Hey, Guido, your telephone's ringing, *aus Deutschland*.' This morphed into me just calling him 'Guido *aus* …' and adding a random German town name, 'Guido *aus Mönchengladbach*' or 'Guido *aus Wuppertal*'. As we drove, I was picking out towns on the map of Germany, Guido snickering at my bad German.

That's why seeing that video saddened me, because we've always had such a good bond. People think I don't have any regard for these guys, but the irony is that if we didn't have that relationship I probably wouldn't have reacted like that.

We called Rolf Aldag on the way because we all used to work together. 'Hi, Rolf, I'm with Guido *aus Berlin* …' Rolf is someone I always call for advice on stuff. He's the straightest man you'd ever meet. Obviously, there was a big controversy when he took over at T-Mobile because he'd doped as a rider on that squad, but I don't think there could have been anyone better to run a clean cycling team. I remember Rolf saying to us, 'Look, it's hypocritical because I've admitted to doping, but if any of you go and ruin this team I'll sue you for everything you've got. I've ridden with drugs, I've ridden without drugs and you can win without drugs now. You can do it.' He would always be completely open with us, and for me, as a kid, it was an amazing way to be. He was always straight about the things he did, the amazing benefits doping could have, but also about how stupid it was. He didn't hide the issue away, which was for the best.

He had the magic touch as a manager and he was the reason Bahrain Victorious were living up to that name this year. He had a similar impact when he joined QuickStep at the same time as I did in 2013. They weren't always this Wolfpack, and it was Rolf who turned them into the team they are now. One key element of his approach was to say that the team needed to look beyond the Belgian talent pool and think more internationally. He'd seen at T-Mobile that if you have a lot of riders from one country, cliques will form. When the T-Mobile team later transformed into Columbia and then HTC, he made a point of making the roster very international, but also packed it with young talent, attracting them by laying out how they could develop. He focused as much on their character and personality as on their strength. We've worked together for almost all of that time, and I've spoken to him regularly all the way through last year and this one. I think he even called Patrick to put in a good word for me before I joined Deceuninck.

When we got to the hotel it was late and everyone was at dinner. I had to go for a massage with Sharky, which is always a good moment in the day because we're always joking with each other. He's got to know the kids while I've been on the massage table because I usually FaceTime them there, as it's the only time in the day I can speak to them before they're in bed.

After massage I went down to dinner and there was no one at the table. *Strange, everyone's outside.* Naturally, I went out to see what the outdoor congress was about. I found all of the riders sitting on a bank at the front of the hotel, looking over the road, with a good number of hotel staff out there as well. There was an unexpected show taking place.

We have two team buses, the big one that always ferries us to starts and from finishes, and a camper that's about the size of a large horsebox. When it's parked up, the sides fold out like an RV so there's quite a big space inside. It's got about six seats and it's usually used at smaller races, such as the Tour of Germany or the Tour of Denmark. At the Grand Tours they can lift the floor up and it's got ice baths that we can use post-stage. It's also useful as a second bus at the end of time trials so you've got somewhere to go and get a shower. In the evenings, the staff have their meetings there to discuss plans for the next day, usually over a few beers. In the old days the riders would have been in there too.

I asked the others what was going on and they pointed across to the driveway into the hotel. It was a steep ramp that rose at a very sharp angle from the road. Our bus driver Nick had turned onto this driveway and the camper had got wedged, in the process blocking the main road on which our hotel was located. The whole Tour convoy, including the caravan vehicles, all trying to get to the next start town, were jammed up, the queue stretching as far as we could see, almost a couple of kilometres back up the road.

Poor old Nick was in shock. He'd inadvertently brought France to a standstill, and there was nothing anyone could do except watch this chaos unfold, which we all gleefully did. In the end, an emergency rescue vehicle managed to get through the gridlock and come to Nick's aid by putting a pneumatic jack underneath the back end of the van, enabling him to move it. The entertainment was over and we trooped back into the hotel for dinner.

That night I was back in with Cattaneo. The pair of us were in a family room that had a double bed and two singles that were more like beds for kids. Our sponsor Latexco provides each of us with one of their mattresses, and each day some of their staff go ahead and set them up in our rooms. They're single mattresses and they'd been put on the kids' beds in our room, which were narrower than usual and meant that a good part of the mattress was in mid-air. You rolled over in the night at your peril. I remember thinking, *We've got a sprint tomorrow and I'm sleeping on this thing …*

As we'd had our own rooms the night before, I'd missed Catta. We had a good conversation that night, him talking about his girlfriend and his dog, me about my family, both of us about the time trial. It was nice having company again. After everything that had happened the day before, it was a good way to end a super-relaxed day, when the only moments of stress had been Fitte fretting in the car and my skinsuit ripping, and I was already seeing the funny side of both incidents. After four full-on days of racing, the time trial had really cleared my mind, which was good because we had to get back to business the next day.

Châteauroux. I'd done this sprint twice and won it twice. I could tell you exactly how it goes for the last five kilometres, the round-abouts and narrowings, but it essentially boils down to one thing: staying at the front will stand you in good stead. It's an old-school Tour de France bunch sprint, a boulevard sprint. If you look back along the course from the finish line, you can see the *flamme rouge*, the one-kilometre-to-go banner. Lovely. You know if you get the lead-out right, you nail it, and if you don't get the lead-out right, you can work your way through. But first we had to get to that point.

The start was savage. We thought it would be two guys who would go, that we'd be able to control it and let it go easy. We rolled out of the start and, *boom!* A couple of guys went. Perfect. Then one more went. And then another went, Thomas De Gendt. Then two more. We started to close them down. DSM appeared to be our allies, but we realised they were playing two cards when Søren Kragh Andersen accelerated off in pursuit of the breakaway. Kasper reacted immediately and went with him.

It wasn't what we'd planned at the start, but it was the ideal scenario because we'd got a guy in a strong break, one that might make it to the finish, and that meant someone else would have to do the legwork to bring it back. Within a kilometre or two they had 40 seconds or so.

But as quickly as things had fallen into place for us, they unravelled again. Arnaud Démare's Groupama teammates swarmed to the front of the peloton, their acceleration causing a touch of panic in the group behind. Those guys don't ride for a sprint normally, and all of a sudden they had the energy of Team Sky back in the day. They put the peloton into one line, and we steamed through small towns, over bridges, up little bumps and down the other side. We were in the Loire region and it probably looked beautiful on TV, the magnificent châteaux, the Vouvray vineyards, the great river never too far away. But I didn't see any of that, just Morky's rear wheel as we clung on near the front, hoping the pace would ease.

Even though we reeled in the break, it didn't. We flew up an unclassified climb, a two-kilometre drag where rider after rider went backwards. At that point any thought of the race being straightforward had vanished. It was being blown to pieces. There were a few jumps on that climb, and we hung on and hung on. Over the top, everyone was on the limit, the whole peloton. It was *à bloc*, the hardest point of the Tour so far. Everyone was so finished that whoever moved at that moment would get into what was sure to be the definitive break. Greg van Avermaet and Roger Kluge had the strength to manage it, two powerhouses. As they went clear we knew we had to keep them on a relatively short leash, so we went to work with Alpecin. Two in the break, just what we'd want. After close to an hour of mayhem, it finally settled down.

There wasn't really a threat of crosswinds, but you know when it's open that the bunch is going to be nervous about them anyway. That almost certainly means it's not going to split because you know the GC guys are going to try to stay at the front. Like I said before, unless you've got someone in blue talking about crosswinds, it's not going to split.

With just two riders away and the contest for the green jersey still very tight, the intermediate sprint had real significance. We were ready to contest it, knowing that the profile in the Tour roadbook didn't reveal how hard it was. We approached it on a descent that ran for about three kilometres to reach a bridge, the road then flicking 90 degrees left and climbing steeply for another 700 to 800 metres to the line.

Bora did a full lead-out to set up Peter Sagan, and it was pretty chaotic coming down to the bridge. Climbing away from it, we were about eight back. Bahrain's Sonny Colbrelli jumped first. Sagan was still on his lead-out guy going up the barriers, and as we came up Morky just held Sagan there, boxing him in. Sagan tried to bash Morky out of the way, but Morky continued to hold him there on the barriers. I couldn't take advantage because I was already on the limit racing uphill. So Colbrelli took the sprint for third at a canter, Morky eased through behind him for fourth, three places ahead of me and four ahead of Sagan.

We crossed the line and Sagan started losing his shit with Morky. I didn't know what he was saying to begin with, but Morky was just being Morky, totally calm, saying, 'What? I didn't do anything wrong.'

Sagan was furious. 'You have to sprint fair. You put me in the barriers,' he shouted.

'I didn't. I just held you on the barriers,' was Morky's unruf-fled reply.

By now I was losing it too. I don't like it when someone goes after one of my boys, and I appreciated it even less that it was Sagan. Everyone tiptoes around Sagan, but I don't mind saying that I don't like him. I don't feel that he has deep-rooted love for the sport like I do.

The final straw was probably his complaint about the barriers. A switch flicked inside me. I turned round and yelled, 'Peter, SHUT THE FUCK UP!'

'How can you say anything to anybody? You?' He started arguing with me and I lashed out again.

'Do you want me to give you this jersey? Do you? Do you want me to just take it off and fucking give it to you? Here, do you want my gloves as well? Do you want my fucking gloves?'

Morky grabbed me and said, 'Cav, stop it. Shut up!'

Sagan was riled and he was panicking. He gets like that when things aren't going his way, gets quite vindictive. And I wasn't having it. Normally people back down, but I've got no problem giving it back to him given our history. But Morky simply said, 'Leave it! Just ride your bike.' Morky had done exactly the right thing. It wasn't the time to waste energy by getting wound up. Châteauroux was little more than 50 kilometres away.

Like two days before, no one came to help as we approached the finish. We almost reeled Van Avermaet and Kluge in with 20 kilometres to go, but the gap started to go out again. We knew this was going to happen because we didn't want to use up too many of our riders, although we wanted to hold the position at the front. We approached Châteauroux on a wide road, the Deceuninck riders in a line holding the left-hand side of the road – perfect! Ineos were close behind us, which meant Luke Rowe was not far behind me, and we always look out for each other. In situations like this, they want to be near the front but not right at the front, so he'll sit behind us and stop people coming up the inside, which benefits both teams.

With ten kilometres to go, the gap was 40 seconds, so Kasper had to come up and start pulling, then Dries. But the gap wasn't coming down. Catta was up there as well, and they were going at a phenomenal speed. I was in about sixth position, just hanging on to my handlebars, once again not paying attention to anything apart from Morky's wheel. That painfully high but sustained pace did exactly what was needed, bringing the two breakaways back within easy range while enabling us to get into the town first. This was vital because it meant we had a clear run into the roundabouts, which we wanted to go through with speed rather than having to accelerate out of them. The road also undulates a little. They're not climbs, but if you haven't got speed you've got to get out of your saddle to get over them, and that takes a bit more out of you in the final sprint.

Going through the roundabouts, I got knocked out of the line, but my only thought was to keep getting back to Morky's wheel. We caught the breakaway with two kilometres to go and Julian hit the front. By that point no one team had enough riders to take it up from us, so Julian could kind of ease back. We didn't need to keep the speed high because we were in control anyway, which meant Julian could save a bit, relax a touch, and go a little further with his lead-out. Then, when we could feel the surge of the riders coming, he went again, we hit the final right-hand corner and he kicked out of it, his job then done.

We still had more than a kilometre to go, and now there was only Ballero, Morky and me. Julian had barely pulled aside when Ballero went – *boom!* 'EASY!' we shouted. I don't know how you can go from that far out at that speed, but he did. He's always fully committed but he doesn't realise how strong he is sometimes. Morky was shouting, 'WOAH! WOAH!' But he kept going and going and going. Then he started to tie up and it was still a little bit too long for Morky to go.

We could see the finish line and were on the left-hand side of the road, just as I had been in 2011 with Mark Renshaw and Matt Goss – I'd been on the right-hand side in 2008. It was pretty like for like. So, like Julian, Morky gave himself an extra 50 metres by easing before he started to wind it up.

I was a little bit in the red from Ballero's acceleration when Morky started to go. I could have gone on his left but we were still 50 metres too far out. I'd have had to go, hang on and be in the red, which would have increased the chances of someone passing me.

At this point Alpecin hit us on the right, and as they did so there was a gap on that side. That now gave me two options. Morky had left a gap on the left because the wind was coming from the right, which was perfect because no one could really follow me. But it would still have meant going from a little bit too far out to sustain my efforts, given how much I was in the red. So I made the split-second decision to give myself 50 more metres by jumping into the gap on the right and using Alpecin.

It was a gamble because I was moving into the middle of the road, where you're opening yourself to being boxed. I might have been able to hang on if I'd gone on the left, but it wasn't worth the risk. Whereas if I could get on the Alpecin lead-out and give myself 50 more metres and then go …

This was all going through my head in a split-second, so I actually went to go left, saw Alpecin, changed my mind at the very last moment because there was a gap there, went into it and got on Philipsen. I took a big breath, then, *Go!* He hit out and I went over him.

With a lot of my sprints, I move slightly in front of riders as I go past them because there's a vortex effect that gives you a little more speed. Just like a following car creates a vortex that you can use to your advantage in a time trial if it gets close enough, if you can get in front of another sprinter you get a vortex off him – it's marginal but enough to create a difference. When I kick past someone, I move over a touch and it gives you just a little extra. I did that and I knew once I'd kicked that I'd won. I even had a little bit of time to think about how I was going to celebrate. *Why don't I do it the same as the last two times?* So I put my hands on my helmet, just like I did in 2008 and 2011.

I wanted to throw back to that first win on my return to the Tour. I think there's real significance in winning there 13 years apart – it's pretty extraordinary – so I wanted to mark it. I guess the celebration was premeditated, but not to the point that I was sure I was going to win. If you'd said to me in the morning, 'If you win today, what celebration will you do?' I would have said that I would do that, but it wasn't like I went out thinking, *I'm going to win today and I'm going to do that.* It was a decision made in the last couple of seconds when I crossed the line. In the old days, when I was at my peak, when I could choose to win, I'd be able to say, 'Today I'll win and I'll do that.' But I wasn't in a position at this Tour de France to be able to do that. I wasn't overly confident in the morning, although I knew I could win. But it wasn't a given that I would win.

Although there's not one Tour stage win that means more to me than any other, Châteauroux is special to me, because it was my first win and I'd already won there twice. Cipo (Mario Cipollini) won there on the Tour's only other visit, so it's got a sprinting pedigree. They've also got a sprinters' Classic there, the Tour de l'Indre. I don't know if it's on the same level as the Champs-Élysées or Bordeaux as a sprinters' finish, but I think it's a prestigious finish.

One thing I'd say about every prestigious race I've won is that they're fixed in my mind as a finish line rather than a place of particular significance. I don't expect that I'll be making personal pilgrimages to Châteauroux or Fougères or wherever in the future.

To me those places are just finish lines. When Peta and I have got the chance to do some husband-and-wife stuff without the kids, we've been to Paris a couple of times. When we're walking up and down the Champs-Élysées I don't really think about the bike race being there. It's two different worlds. In the same way, when I think about Châteauroux, I see that red Vittel banner across the road. I don't see anything else. It's a finish line. If I went any other day I probably wouldn't even recognise it.

There's one caveat to that. When I was in Denmark after the Tour de France, to race the Tour of Denmark, I stayed on for a couple of days with Brian Holm. I did some media on the first day, then Brian and I went for a ride the next day. I told him I wanted to go and look at the finish of the 2011 World Championships that I won. I'd not been back there since. It was strange. I called Peta, and Casper came on and I started crying. I said to him, 'This is where Daddy won the Worlds.' I don't know why I reacted like this because I'd never really got emotional before when I'd been back to a place like that. Of course I've cried buckets when I've won stages, but I'm pretty sure that if I went back to, say, Fougères I wouldn't cry. Perhaps it was seeing Casper, because he knows what it means.

The emotions weren't as strong as with the first win, when it felt like something had been lifted and it was really overwhelming. However – although it sounds a bit crap, I don't know how to say it any other way – it's a fucking stage of the Tour de France. I know how hard it is to win a stage at the Tour, what it takes, and that is why no one of them means more than any of the others, really. The emotions can be different, as I said in Fougères, but the elation is still the same.

I was as elated with this one as I was with any of the others, no more and no less. And if I win one more or fifty more, I'll be as elated every time I win. It's that wall of colour, the red banner. I'm obsessed with it, obsessed with that race. I don't think there's any rider outside France who's got the same amount of respect for that race as I do. When riders choose not to do the Tour, I'm mystified. 'This year I'll go to the Vuelta.' *What?*

I can't comprehend that. It doesn't make sense. It angers me. I find it really insulting to the race and to the sport. I love the race, it's as simple as that. I love it in every way – talking frenziedly with the soigneur about how it went after the finish, waiting for the boys to come through, being whacked by a TV camera across the back of the helmet in the melee. Every fucking part of it!

That elation sustains you for a while – it's what people see on TV or from the side of the road. When you cross the line your adrenaline is pumping so much that it keeps you upright, prevents you from collapsing, which is what you should be doing because the effort expended in a sprint is ridiculous. The muscle damage caused by a sprint can mess you up for two or three days. It's the kind of effort the GC guys can't make, and as a result they don't get that same muscle damage, just as I've never endured the muscle damage that Chris Hoy used to get on the track. I've seen him finish an effort and curl up in the foetal position. In training I've been puking or had to lie down, but not like him.

After a Tour de France sprint you're completely done in. Fans don't really see that amid the elation. But once you get to the little cabin behind the line where you get changed, you collapse into the nearest chair. I hadn't really thought about this until it was pointed out to me by my former agent, Simon Bayliff. He came to the 2012 Giro when I was with Sky. There was a finish on the Adriatic coast where I beat Gossy in the sprint, and Simon came into the tent afterwards and said to me, 'People don't realise how fucked you are after. You just sit there and get wiped down and can't move.' I guess because people don't see that, they just see you winning and celebrating, it does make it look easy. Rest assured it isn't.

I was like that in Châteauroux, physically spent, but I managed to do one thing I'd forgotten to do when I won two days earlier. I got a photo taken with Mathieu van der Poel in the yellow jersey. I hadn't raced with him and guys like Wout van Aert and Remco Evenepoel for the previous three years. But I'd been following them, all of them, and I know that when I've retired in a year or two, I'll be watching them, probably with Casper sitting next to me, as he's a fan too, especially of Van Aert. Some of them are almost young enough to be my kids, like Remco. Watching them race, especially this season, has been an honour. It'll be a privilege in a few years to be able to say that I raced with them, and I like getting photos with them when I get the chance, which I never used to. I didn't give a monkey's about my competitors when I was younger.

I don't like to look too far ahead at the Tour, but when we got to the hotel that evening I knew that Châteauroux would be the last chance I'd have to sprint for a few days. Before that I would have to get through the Alps. The first six days had been hard and I was worried about whether I would get through the mountains. I honestly didn't think I would, although I obviously wanted to go as far as possible. So, as well as winning, I'd had to focus on saving as much energy as I could and also on losing weight without compromising my performance.

I'd never worked with a dietitian before. Every day I had to send my training file to the team's dietitian, Marije Jongedijk, so that she could work out exactly what I needed and what to consume. I was living like a monk: no dessert, not even fruit. Every bit of pasta was weighed out, as was my cereal. Three hours before racing I'd have this bowl of cereal and then she often added a pancake to my regime an hour and a half before the stage began so that my glycogen levels didn't spike. If it was going to be a long and particularly hard day, like the next one was, I wouldn't have protein because I needed more carbohydrate – never mind sustaining the muscle mass, it was more important to get through the day.

It was super-anal, but I couldn't pass up the opportunity. I had to do everything within my power to make sure I couldn't have an excuse, so that I couldn't say, 'I should have done this, or should have done that.' I had to be like a GC rider. I wasn't living, I was just existing, but it was less than a month that could change my life. I'd been given a hugely unexpected and very welcome gift by being able to race at the Tour de France. I couldn't take it for granted.

STAGE 7

2 July: Vierzon–Le Creusot, 249.1km

'd had a night off the protein and on the carbs to prepare me for the longest stage of the race, an old-school Tour de France stage nudging 250 kilometres, the final part of it rippling through the unforgiving Morvan massif, France's smallest mountain zone that lies on the northern edge of the Massif Central. Featuring five climbs in the last 90 kilometres, it was bang on for a breakaway. All we could say for sure was that every team and perhaps two-thirds of the peloton would want to be in it and, as a consequence, it would take a long time for the break to go.

Up until then the breaks had gone relatively easily, apart from the day before. But as we headed out from Vierzon across the flat, heavily wooded countryside of the Berry region, it was full-on from the start. It wasn't snapping, though. A little break would go, get maybe 15 seconds, then get reeled back in again. As groups went then got hoovered back up, Tom Steels calmly relayed information through the radio. 'Guys, you're coming to a roundabout and you need to go on the right. 200 metres later you turn right, then you have a left going into a straight, make sure you're at the front end as it gets narrow …' As he's talking, it's like he's drawing a map in your mind. We weren't actively trying to get riders into a break, but we'd been briefed on which teams we needed to watch and follow. At the same time, you always know that if a group goes clear with more than a certain number of riders in it, you've got to have at least one rider in it.

After about 40 kilometres, soon after leaving the cathedral town of Bourges, we turned onto one of those just-out-of-town French roads that's got two or three lanes either side of a central reservation and is lined by car showrooms, garden centres, furniture stores and, I guarantee it, Buffalo Grill, a burger chain whose red-roofed restaurants are adorned with a huge set of white horns and have a towering totem pole outside. As it dragged up for one or perhaps even two kilometres, we were dodging riders who'd been trying to get in breaks and were coming back like stones through the peloton. At the crest there was a roundabout, and, approaching it, I sensed that the snap was coming.

It sounds off for a sprinter, because it's usually the last scenario we want to find ourselves in, but, humblebrag, I do kind of know how to get in a break. Look back at my final three races of last year: the final stage of Luxembourg – in the break; Gent–Wevelgem – in the break; Scheldeprijs – in the break. I can often get into a break if I want to, it's just that I never want to. You know when it's going to snap. Sometimes you might be wrong, but it's a feeling. You sit and watch how it's going, knowing that when people are getting tired the elastic will snap, and that's the time to go.

I was about 40 back in what was becoming an increasingly stretched line. Guys whose breakaway moves had been thwarted were still coming back, and I looked ahead to see who was up near the front. I had the feeling that it was just about to happen. I could see Kasper a couple of riders ahead of me, and I just started sprint-ing. As we reached the crest, the peloton thinned into one line. I shouted, 'Kaspi!'and just got him onto my wheel. I jumped and he came with me, going around the roundabout. We passed a dozen or so riders as I did a full sprint to help Kasper get onto the back of the group edging away. As I looked up, I could see that riders were now going off the front of the group we'd tacked onto.

I had to help him move further up. He jumped, I went with him, then past, riding a little bit out of the gutter so that he could get a bit of shelter from the slight crosswind. The group was coming closer and closer and closer. I was sure that he would jump past me and close the final metres on his own, but he didn't. So I made another surge and that was enough. We were both there. I glanced back to see who was chasing behind and there was no one, just a gap that got bigger and bigger, started to close again briefly, then stretched once again and we were gone. 'Break on, Kasper and Cav there. Well done, boys,' Tom called into the radio.

Wout van Aert was there, Mathieu van der Poel, Matej Mohorič, Vincenzo Nibali, Søren Kragh Andersen, Magnus Cort, Philippe Gilbert, all these guys. We formed an echelon and it started to turn, each rider rotating through to the front. In that kind of situation it's easier to ride through than it is to try and sit on, so that you contrib-ute to the pace-making rather than simply benefiting from the work other riders are doing; otherwise you end up getting pushed out of the back. It wasn't particularly hard, not like being in an echelon in Qatar or Gent–Wevelgem, where it's tough no matter what position you're in. It was just hard when riding through to the front.

As the gap started to extend, we heard that Tadej Pogačar's UAE team were pulling on the front of the bunch, but they had no chance of reeling us in given the number and calibre of the guys at the front. Sure enough, our lead kept growing. It really was going to be a long day.

I'll admit that for a while I was thinking, *I'm in the green jersey and I don't really want to be here.* But I could also see that it would probably suit me to be at the front once we got into the difficult back end of the stage. I didn't have a cat in hell's chance of going to the finish with the break, but I would be able to take the climbs on the run-in more comfortably than if I'd been in the gruppetto.

While I was up at the front, I had to make myself useful and do all I could to help Kasper chase a stage win. 'Right, anything you need,' I told him. 'If you want me to ride, get bottles, anything, just tell me.' He a super-nice guy but doesn't say much, just grunts one-word answers. Like fellow Dane Morky, he's got a dry sense of humour when he wants to show it, but he's very much to the point. He's also a Trojan when it comes to working, and this was my opportunity to repay the efforts he'd already made on my behalf. It was baking hot and I regularly went back to the car for bottles and ice packs, which Kasper wanted to put on his neck to keep cool. I noticed that almost every time I went back, he'd end up pulling at the front, so I'd end up giving it full beans to get back up to him, ice dripping down my arm and over my bars. I also noticed the commissaires keeping a close eye on what I was up to.

There's one thing that really gets to me at the Tour – it sounds like I'm complaining but it's the honest truth – and it's something that every time I come to a team and work with new directors I have to explain. To put it bluntly, commissaires can be dicks to me. This is why it's so laughable when I hear insinuations that I've held on to a car. It's actually impossible for me to ever get away with holding on to a car. This stage was the only one in this Tour where I got a bottle from the car. I'm that scared of even taking a bottle from the team car that I get my teammates to do it for me.

The insinuations about me benefiting from sticky bottles are ridiculous, firstly because I'm a fucking good bike rider and I can climb when I want to climb, so I don't need to get an illicit boost of that kind if I'm getting a bidon from the team car. There have been occasions when I've been dropped on my own and the commissaire has stayed with me while the two-dozen guys who were dropped before me were all back in the cars. Then they'd go flying past me and I was still on my own. It's happened countless times. I'm sure there'll be plenty of people who think that I'm just griping and have nothing to back this up with. But I've got hours of video footage that highlights this discrimination towards me, all of it saved up just in case I ever have to go back to the UCI. Rolf Aldag has lots of it. I'd always ask him to video it because I might need it some day.

This bias all stems from when I won the green jersey in 2011. My closest rival that year was Movistar's José Joaquín Rojas, and he told the media that I'd been hanging on to cars. That's when the scrutiny began. His team director went to Brian after the race and said, 'Sorry about that, we were just doing it to fuck with his head!'

That day there were guys in the break who were stopping to take a piss and then using the cars to come back. I never stop for a piss. It's not worth the hassle – and, on the upside, it enables me to get out of anti-doping quicker than most because I rarely have any problem providing a sample. Feed zones are another area where I've got to be on my guard. I'll start off by saying I think we should get rid of them. There's no need for feed zones – there are more crashes in them than anywhere else. When we get to a feed zone, I just go left and stay left until we exit it, avoiding all of the likely chaos on the right.

The feed zone on this stage was on a little hill. You know gaps are always going to open in a feed zone when you're in a big group or the peloton. The guys at the front grab their musettes easily and keep on riding, but they have to slow a bit, the next rider has to slow a bit more, and so on, in the same way that cars jam up on the motorway after the front one brakes. The knock-on effect of that slowing is that the riders at the back lose ground while they're pocketing their stuff. I was one of those towards the rear as we went through the feed, and usually you'd just use a team car to get back on. But the commissaires had barraged the road so that wasn't possible.

We were halfway through a 250-kilometre stage, on the flat, with the climbs still ahead. There were four or five of us who'd lost ground because of the feed, not because we were struggling. I was with Ineos's Dylan van Baarle, for heaven's sake, one of the most powerful riders in the bunch. They were strong guys and they're not getting dropped. Normally, when you're getting your stuff in your pockets you don't panic, because you know that you'll get back without any hassle. On this occasion, though, it didn't look like we were going to get back, and it was only because I was there.

It was stupid, but it didn't matter to me because Kasper was our only hope of winning the stage and he was still at the front. It really made no difference to me whether I was in the break or not. So I told the other guys I couldn't ride. They understood that there was no point in me chasing. We'd been through the intermediate sprint, where I'd taken the points after Kasper had led me out. They could see that I'd got all I possibly could from being in the break, so they started riding and I sat on their wheels.

It was farcical really, and it became even more so. EF's Ruben Guerreiro was one of the other riders dropped, and he wasn't riding through either because his teammate Magnus Cort was still at the front, but the others started kicking off about this. They started swapping off, going hard, still asking Guerreiro to come through. But then he started to drop back with me on his wheel, trying to force me to come around and tow him back up to the others. So I waited until we were 50 metres back, then accelerated past him and went back up to them. Then I looked behind and the cars had been allowed to come past him, and he was in the cars. I turned to the motorbike commissaire and shouted, 'Show some consistency.' Then the cars had to back off and we never saw him again. I felt quite guilty, because I wasn't complaining about him, I was complaining about their application of the rules. In fact, I felt pretty bad about it. I wasn't bothered whether he was there or not; I was just bothered about the discrimination against me, because I've got a chip on my shoulder about it – and with good reason.

Not long after, we got to the hills and my plan was simple – get over the first couple with the group, then drift slowly back, riding the final three more difficult ones with groups that were behind. The attacks began as soon as we reached the first third-category hill, but I hung on OK. I even went back to the front and started pulling again for Kasper, as a couple of riders had got away, including Mohorič. Then we got to this little drag, not even a hill, and everyone started attacking. That was me done with about 50 kilometres to go.

We were about ten kilometres from the first of the steep final climbs. I wanted to get to it before the bunch reeled me in, ride most of the way up on my own, then get pulled over the top and stay with that group till the following climb, then repeat the process again on climb four, and again on climb five, eventually ending up with the gruppetto, but having ridden the climbs much slower than

I would have done if I'd been in the gruppetto from the off. In order for the first part of the plan to work, I started riding as aero as possible, a commissaire tracking all the time, of course. Just before I got to the climb, I started hearing the radio in my ear. When that happens you know they're pretty close. I started up it OK, then reached a steep section and the bunch was on me. I went straight through it like a fucking rock.

As they reached the top, however, they eased off. It levelled briefly and I could see I wasn't too far behind, but there was nothing to gain from making an effort to chase. After a short descent, I got caught by the second big group and rode to the penultimate climb with them, which was perfect. The Signal d'Uchon was the steepest of the day. I thought they'd go easy, but their pace was just a little bit too hot. I could have hung on, but with 50-odd guys still behind I rode up at my own tempo, dropped to the foot of the final climb and waited for another group to sweep me up. But no one ever did. I finished the Tour's longest stage on my own, but with 25 guys still behind me. I felt I'd managed my effort well, but the Alps would likely prove a more severe judge.

STAGE 8

3 July: Oyonnax–Le Grand-Bornand, 150.8km

I was nervous before this stage, my unease partly stoked by memories of my first Tour de France in 2007. My T-Mobile teammate Linus Gerdemann won the stage into Le Grand-Bornand and took the yellow jersey, but it was my last full day on that race. I'll never forget the last climb, the Col de la Colombière, and how horrible it was. I remember riding up the climb before it with Axel Merckx, another T-Mobile teammate, next to me, and my vision blacking out because I was going that deep. Although I managed to finish, that was the end of my Tour debut. My fear was that my comeback Tour might end in the same way.

An examination of the profile only increased my concern. Five climbs lay ahead, the final three of them first-category, the last of them once again the Colombière. We also started with an uncategorised five-kilometre climb right from the gun. That was a guarantee that, as soon as Christian Prudhomme waved his flag at kilometre zero, it was going to go nuts.

It was raining too, but it wasn't all bad. Being in the green jersey does make you a target, but it also has its benefits. It meant that I got to line up on the front row alongside race leader Mathieu van der Poel and the previous day's stage winner Matej Mohorič, who was in the polka-dot mountains jersey. In that situation I always fight for the bumper of the race director's car. '*Bonjour, Christian. Ca va?*'

I'd also got a bit of confidence from my sensations on the climbs the day before, and the team had said that Morky and Tim would stay with me, shepherding me towards the finish. For most of the year I hadn't had anyone waiting for me whenever I was dropped on the climbs, which had also been the case the year before, at Bahrain. In fact, it wasn't since I was riding with Bernie Eisel at Dimension Data in 2019 that I'd been able to count on that kind of support. I'd got used to being isolated in the mountains – and to being nervous about the prospect of it.

All the analysis that's done within the team of Strava records and other data means that you actually know what your power is and what you can sustain for 10 minutes, 12 minutes, and so on, although you can't really look at your readings in the tumult of a stage start because you've got to look where you're going. But you can keep an eye on it if you start to slip back. If that happened, I knew exactly what I'd have to do to get over this first climb without being dropped, and it was going to have to be one of my best 15-minute powers of the year, probably even of my life.

We started off, and right away I was thinking, *Fuck, here we go …* Thomas De Gendt went haring off and everyone started after him. Guys were diving past and cutting in front of me, but I couldn't let myself get angry and start mouthing off at them because it would have got me out of sync with my breathing and messed with the tempo I was trying to keep to.

I started off holding what I could until I began to feel it bite, then I looked at my power meter, aware that I was dropping further and further back in the pack. I was beginning to feel edgy again, but I heard in the radio, 'Good job, guys. There are riders getting dropped everywhere.' I was OK. I was still in the bunch. But for how much longer?

Guys were still coming past me, and then a gap opened up in front of me and I couldn't hold the power I was doing. Panic was just starting to rise, and then the next thing I knew Tim came past grinning, although it wasn't a grin of happiness. He slid in front of me and started to set a tempo. He's so big it's like drafting behind a truck. I couldn't feel any wind at all, and my panic instantly died away too. He held that power while I looked at his wheel. When I began to struggle a little I'd just tell him, 'Easy!' and he'd knock a little bit off, 10 or 15 watts. 'Harder!' told him to step up that amount.

We started collecting riders as we got towards the top of that opening climb, then picked up a few more as we dropped down into a long valley that ran along the southern edge of the Jura Mountains. It was a big old group and it immediately started working really well together. Then we were joined by a dozen or so guys from behind, including Arnaud Démare and all of his Groupama clan. They'd made a great effort to get back up to us, because we were shifting.

Their arrival made the gruppetto massive, and everyone contributed to the pace-making to the point that we were absolutely flying. We rode a decent tempo on the first two smaller climbs, then you had 50 guys going through and off, which is when riders take it in turns to advance through a pace line till they reach the front, then ease and drop to the back to continue the chain-like motion that keeps a group's pace constant and high. The strange thing was, the gap between us and the front of the race just kept going up. At one point we heard that Wout Poels was out on his own ahead of the peloton, and he was pulling away from 50 guys all working together. We could hear on the radio, 'Gruppetto at five minutes … six minutes … seven minutes …' And it was like, *How the fuck is this possible?* We didn't rest up for one second – we didn't even want to rest up because we needed as much time in hand as possible before we got to the Col de Romme and the Colombière.

By the time we got to the foot of the Romme we were 16 minutes behind the leaders. Most of the sprinters were there, but there were some big GC names too, notably Roglič and G, who were both struggling with injuries after crashing on stage three. It was pissing with rain as we started up the road hacked out of the cliff face, rising at 10 per cent right from the very bottom. In a group that size there are always some who forget that we're all in it together. Some are nervous about the time limit, others are just dick swingers and want to do their own thing.

Before the stage, the coaches and directors work out what power we need to ride on the climbs to lose a minute a kilometre or what-ever they think is necessary to get inside the time limit, which is imposed on every rider. This limit is based on a percentage of the winner's time and is designed to ensure you can't ride along, chatting to your mates as if you're on a Sunday club run. It's quite scientific, but as we climbed the Romme we knew we'd be cutting it fine if we held to the pre-set numbers, so we had to ride a little bit harder. It's not a long climb as Alpine passes go, at just under nine kilometres, but it averages 9 per cent, which meant I was out of my in-the-sad-dle comfort zone for long stretches. About three or four kilometres from the top, I was empty and the lads waited for me. Other riders in our big group were starting to get antsy about the time limit, but the lads said, 'Stay at this pace, we'll get back on the descent.' We were only cutting off around five watts, but it was enough that it was sustainable for me without blowing.

I hadn't been to altitude since rejoining the team. I hadn't trained at altitude, and that made all the difference when we reached the high mountains. As soon as I get to a height of about 1,500 metres I struggle, I always have. There's a massive difference in my power output. When I train at altitude, I climb so much better, although I'd qualify that by saying it's not that I climb better, it's just that I'm better at higher altitude. That acclimatisation is what I get out of altitude training rather than any significant boost in performance. But I've always felt that 1,500 metres is a kind of ceiling for me, although perhaps it's just in my head. While I was swinging on the Romme, which tops out at 1,300 metres, I already had the Colombière looming in the back of my mind. It's more than 300 metres higher.

Beyond the top of the Col de Romme, there's a short false flat, then a four-kilometre descent which brings you into the Colombière about halfway up the pass, with about seven kilometres to the summit, so at least we weren't coming all the way up from the bottom. Once we were climbing again, the guys went at a slightly quicker pace. Some of the riders around us were stressing about the time limit, but we kept pointing out that there was a 15-kilometre descent into the finish. People also seem to forget that you don't need to be five minutes inside the time limit – just one is enough.

There's always that same narrative on the TV as well: 'Will they or won't they make it?' I'm often the focus of that, and in this case it was understandable because I was in green. But there were 90 guys there, half of the peloton. Of course we were going to make it. People start stressing about the fact that it is going to be close, but of course it's going to be close. We want it to be close.

As on the Romme, I got dropped before the top but we got back into the gruppetto on the descent. It's quite twisty to start with, but lower down you can start riding through and off, making up a little bit of time, then there is a sharp left-hand just over a kilometre out and it kicks up all the way to the line. We were in our own world then, just focusing on making it, but I wasn't panicking. We crossed the line with two minutes to spare.

I went into the tent at the finish with Tadej Pogačar and Dylan Teuns. I had no real idea what had happened, although I could see Tadej was now in yellow. I was just talking to them about the day and how it had gone for them. Listening to them, it struck me – as it often has in the past – that the guys in the gruppetto are in our own, very different race. It just blows our minds, because we couldn't have done anything else at all to get closer to them. It's like they're competing in a different sport to us.

I'm not insinuating anything at all by that; I'm just underlining how good they are. They race very differently, and being reminded of that on the first day in the mountains put the fear of God into me. It hadn't been a particularly hard mountain day, and that evening I couldn't help thinking, *There's no fucking way I'm getting to Paris, because tomorrow we're going to Tignes.* It had been on a very similar stage in 2018 that I'd been eliminated from the Tour de France for the only time in my career for failing to make the time cut. I was absolutely shitting myself. I was ready to do everything I could to stay in the race, but I was probably going home.

STAGE 9

4 July: Cluses–Tignes, 144.9km

The day began with the news that Mathieu van der Poel was leaving the race to prepare for the Olympics and Primož Roglič wouldn't be starting the stage to Tignes due to the injuries he'd been carrying for the previous few days. I felt for him, as he'd clearly done an awful lot to get himself into the right shape to win the Tour. He's a nice guy and, like the other big names, I'm a fan of his. I'm genuinely in awe of what they do.

What I particularly like about Roglič is that he knows he's still learning, and he's always keen to extend his knowledge, to fill the gaps that are there because he came into the sport so late. I remember when he won the first edition of the UAE Tour in 2019. On the penultimate stage that finished up Jebel Jais, the highest mountain in the UAE, there was a big crosswind and someone was pulling, trying to split it. I think there'd been a crash or something. Roglič was in the leader's jersey and he came up to me and said, 'Sorry for my ignorance, but can I ask you, why is this team pulling?' I can't remember what I told him – I might even have been as mystified as he was – but it was interesting because he was in the leader's jersey but still humble enough to realise that he might be able to get some useful advice, to learn a bit more. He wasn't just looking at his power meter and working out the best time to go, he wanted to learn about what was going on. That one incident told me a lot about him.

I always speak to him, say congratulations, 'It's your day today,' stuff like that. But I look at guys like him and often feel that they get the life sucked out of them. They're not able to express their true personality because they live on these regimes that are incredibly difficult to deal with from a psychological point of view. That's why cycling is going to be in the dark ages commercially. If it doesn't attract these people, it turns them into these people.

There were a lot of stages in the Tour where I was nervous, and for different reasons, but this felt like the first major hurdle, one of those days when you know your survival in the race is on the line right from the start. It would only take one thing to go wrong – a crash, an unexpected hunger flat, perhaps even a dramatic change in the weather – for our expectations and calculations about the time limit to be thrown out. It was quite a short stage, so it was likely that the riders contesting victory would be riding flat out for the duration. Of the five climbs, all were second-category or harder, while four went above 1,500 metres, the last one in Tignes rising to more than 2,000.

The opening 15 kilometres or so from Cluses were flat. Breaks were trying to go, but it wasn't happening. That meant it was sure to be faster and harder on the first climb, the Côte de Domancy, renowned as the place where Bernard Hinault shredded his rivals at the Worlds in 1980. It's steep and definitely not the type of climb I'd have fancied tackling 20 times like they did that day. Physically and physiologically, I can sit and pedal on a climb, but when it's steep and you have to get out of the saddle, I always struggle. I've got short levers and I use short cranks, so I can't get over and torque it out. If you've ever seen a duck running, I'm more akin to that than the fluid circles pedalled by the guys with better-proportioned limbs. So anything above 7–8 per cent starts to make my pedal revolutions feel more square than circular, and 10 per cent is just horrible for me – I can't do it.

I was towards the front going in to it, so that I could have sliding room on it. I set a tempo above what I'd be able to do for the day, above threshold. Straight away, Tim was in front of me, Morky was there too, and Dries was with us because he was never going to make it to the front. It was three kilometres to the top, and once we were there Dries got on the front and set a good tempo on the false flat that followed, which allowed me to sit in the big ring as it dragged on.

Once again, the sprinters who'd been dropped before us on the climb came back in the cars and got back to us with what seemed like ease. Their arrival did at least take some of the pressure off our guys, though. As the gradient eased and then flattened out, we started to swap off. As I've mentioned, one of the things that stood out for me this year was the cohesion within the gruppetto, which was the best I've seen for many years. There were enough sprint teams to ensure there were plenty of riders there for that job, and everyone just got on and rode. Nevertheless, we lost a lot of ground to the front group on the undulations that led to the foot of the Col des Saisies, even though we were going fucking hard and fast. I couldn't understand it. The pouring rain was likely one cause, as it made it sketchy at roundabouts and bends where you were forced to slow down a lot and then sprint away, using energy that you'd pay for later.

We calculate our wattage on losing a minute per kilometre on the climbs, but obviously on a stage like this you have to lose less because you're not gaining anything on any flats or descents, so it was like 40 seconds a kilometre, which is a fair bit more power. It's an all-in effort that requires a significantly bigger power output than a decade ago. Back then, the gruppetto would be able to ride in the high 200s, or at least that's what I would have done at my weight. Whereas now, on a normal day you'd be talking about riding at 330 watts, and on that day to Tignes it was 350 or 360 when we could, which is my lactic threshold and isn't normally sustainable for a day.

Our calculations were thrown out by other factors too. For a start, it wasn't possible to make anything back on the descents, which were narrow and quite technical. On a Tourmalet-style descent, where the bends are nice, wide and flowing, the motorbike can stay far enough ahead that the front group doesn't gain anything, so as a good descender you can make up time in the gruppetto. But on these little technical descents, you lose time because on the hairpins, the riders at the front run up on the motorbikes in the corners and subsequently get a nice pull away from them. Back in the gruppetto, we've got to do all of the accelerating ourselves. What's more, once we'd got to the Saisies, there were no valleys in between the climbs where you could make up time either, so we were doubly screwed.

The Saisies signalled the start of the day's serious climbing, although it's not too steep. A long descent followed into the next uphill test. I've had to look back at my roadbook to check its name, because I'd blotted it out of my mind, it was so awful. The Col du Pré didn't start off too fiercely, but after half a dozen kilometres it changed like Jekyll to Hyde. It went from 3 per cent one moment to 10 per cent the next, like that driveway where Nick had got the bus stuck at the hotel in Le Mans. No chance of an emergency rescue this time, though.

Tim, Morky and Dries formed a triangle, with me in the middle, and started riding. Dries took a raincoat from the car for me at one point but I didn't want it. Nothing, not even getting a jacket on and zipped up, was going to prevent me, even briefly, from doing the watts I needed.

The pace was horrible. Whenever I felt myself just going over the limit, I'd say, 'Guys! Guys!' to get them to back it off a touch. As soon as I got my breath back and my heart rate level, they'd lift the tempo again. It was like a nightmarish interval session, and as we got higher and hit 1,500 metres, the stop-go rhythm became more pronounced. I think surging like that, producing a burst of acceleration rather than speeding up gradually and consistently, pissed a lot of the other guys off, because they'd be shouting, 'Woah!' But we knew we couldn't wait and look after anyone else. We just had to do our own thing. As we got near the top, the group had thinned out. Bouhanni was dropped, Démare was dropped; we kept our own pace. Just short of the top, the gradient relented and we pushed on a little quicker, and then nailed the little descent that goes down to the lake that lies between the Pré and Cormet de Roselend passes. We chopped off around the lake like it was the last two kilometres of the stage, opening up a massive gap on the guys we'd dropped.

I remembered from 2018 that the Roselend isn't that long or steep, and I said to the guys, 'Let's try and get as far up here, like it's our finish line.' As we rode up there, I had flashbacks to three years earlier, when I'd been alone. My Dimension Data teammates Julien Vermote and Jay Thomson had been with me, but I'd told them to go back to the gruppetto because I was fucked. I knew I was out. This time I was going better than I had been back then, even though I was six kilos heavier. I had the power I needed and that spurred me on.

Next up was the climb to Tignes, which is just long – really long. Though there are one or two kickers on it as it rises for close to 25 kilometres, it's more of a mental than a physical test. You can't surge up it; you have to ride a tempo that you can hold for more than an hour. If we nailed it, we knew that by the time we got most of the way up, the winner would have finished and we'd able to work out the time limit and re-evaluate everything then if we needed to. In the meantime there was no possibility of any respite.

The guys had been getting gels for me from the car before we started to climb again, and I was smashing them down, even caffeine gels. Mostly, though, they just stayed in their triangle formation around me, with Tim always at the apex. It was beautiful because it meant that I didn't see the wind no matter which direction it came from. The tempo was all I needed to concern myself with. Every time Tim got out of the saddle to go, I'd say, 'Stop surging!' And Tim would be like, 'What?' I didn't realise at first, but he didn't understand what I meant. He didn't know the word 'surge'. It then became a thing between us, so when we send each other voicemails we always end them with, 'Stop surging!'

When we got about halfway up I was too spent to say even that. Morky started talking for me. When he saw me starting to move in the saddle, he'd be like, 'Tim, easy!' I became mute, my gaze fixed on the wheel in front. I was fucking hurting, right at my limit, on the verge of blowing because my glycogen had gone. It wasn't about making an effort now; it was just a question of suffering, about how much I could endure the hurt: not that sudden pain that you feel when someone punches you, but the agony of it being drawn out. It's physiological torture, the competitive equivalent of someone pulling your fingernails out very slowly.

But having the guys around gave me belief. They slowed down when I needed them to, Morky talked for me, somehow able to read how I was. There was no need for encouragement, which can sometimes feel a bit patronising. They didn't say anything. They got me gels, brought stuff, carried stuff, kept the wind off, they were doing a job. They were fucking brilliant.

As we were getting close, some of the other guys in the group started attacking, which caused a bit of panic about the time limit. It was getting tight. In the team car behind, Fitte relayed the news that the first rider had finished in Tignes – we of course had no idea it was Ben O'Connor – and that the cut-off was 37 minutes and 20 seconds. As I struggled up the final kicker to the dam that lies just below Tignes, we could sense it was going to be close. Just after we got on the final stretch up to the town, Fitte gave the order to 'go', although we didn't pick up who he was directing it to. It created confusion. Dries didn't know whether he was supposed to try to save himself, Morky just stayed where he was, while Tim thought Fitte was saying, 'Fuck it, abandon ship, whoever can should just get in the time limit!' so he went off like a bullet. He must have got the Strava for the kilometre just before you get to the avalanche tunnels approaching Tignes, while Morky yelled after him, 'Tim, where the fuck are you going?' He did the sprint of his life then had to stop and wait for us.

We still thought it was going to be touch and go, but we didn't realise that the last couple of kilometres are flat. We were thinking we might just make the cut by a few seconds, then we were cruising and we knew we were OK. We crossed the line filthy and wet, but with 90 seconds to spare. I was crying when I crossed the line, just like when I won the stage in Fougères. We were all hugging like it was a victory. What we'd been through that day had been absolutely epic. We'd been over the limit on so many occasions, and it was a case of just suffering. We got through on willpower and team-work, as much as on ability. I realised that it had been a long time since I'd had a unit stay with me like that. I'd always had Bernie Eisel or someone, but having an actual unit, half a team waiting and wanting to wait, doing everything they could for me, and without seeing any sign in their faces that they were pissed off with me, made all the difference.

The team's support behind the scenes was vital that day too. Our dietitian, Marije, had planned out what I needed to eat and when, and although I was empty when I reached Tignes, I wasn't underfu-elled. The strategy she put in place was spot on. It was having to ride 5–10 per cent harder on the climbs that left me running on fumes. Also, although I had decent legs compared to the last time I'd done some of those climbs in 2018, they didn't feel as good as they had the day before, heading for Le Grand-Bornand.

I was fortunate in the end that there's not too much out-of-the-saddle climbing on the road to Tignes. It was just that one in the middle, the Col du Pré, which was really horrible. I hated it. But even there, the remembrance of 2018 and how much better I was going compared to that day was a real driving factor, as was knowing that the little climb after the lake wasn't steep and you could big ring it and almost use it as a finish climb, with a long descent to follow. Reflecting on it later, I also realised that not abandoning in 2018, even though I knew I wasn't going to finish inside the time limit, also played in my favour. I knew those climbs. Even though I'd only done them once, that's usually been enough for me to remember the key characteristics of a climb, and that was a big benefit. Knowing that we could go pretty hard on the Cormet de Roselend, over my limit, and that we could make it over the top before I blew made a big difference.

As soon as I got changed into dry kit at the finish, I had to go straight to the podium. They were rushing me: Thierry Gouvenou was tapping on his watch as I got my stuff on. I was freezing. It was the only day when I had to wear a woolly hat because it was so cold, but I didn't have an undervest or arm warmers on. The team doctor had had a fit in the car because I didn't put a vest on, and he was worried I would get sick.

When I got back on the bus, the boys were there getting changed. I went to the bag where the soigneur had put my kit and took out my jersey. It was dirty and still had the numbers on it. I said to Tim, 'I hope this means something to you. For me, this means as much as any win.' And he was like, 'No, really?' We'd been through so much that day, and he was the driving force that got us through, which is why I gave him the jersey. From then on, every day I'd give the jersey with the numbers still on to one of the riders, still unwashed, to show my appreciation for what they'd done for me.

I had a beer with the boys at the table that night. The atmosphere was really good. It wasn't like we were celebrating a win, but I felt we created a bond that day. All of the Grand Tours have that kind of impact, but the Tour especially because every one of your senses is heightened to such an unparalleled extent. Every part of the emotional rollercoaster, the turbulence and joy, brings you closer, because everything is on the limit at that race. I felt that same bond with Fitte too. His belief in me made such a difference, and the pride that he got from our performances was so evident. It was so different to the last time we worked together, when we didn't really get on. We'd got to the first rest day, which was the next day, and it'd been successful so far. It felt like an accomplishment.

We had our own rooms in Tignes. When I went up to mine and called Peta, I told her I didn't have the energy left to chat. I needed to go to sleep. And that was it for 11 hours. I was a bit nervous because at altitude you don't really sleep well, but I didn't have any problems that night. With kids you get used to six, maybe seven hours, if that. When I go to a race I'm always thinking, *I can get a good eight hours' sleep now.* I'm usually an eight-hours-on-the-dot guy. Sleeping for that length of time is unheard of for me, which underlines how wrecked I was.

The next day, a recovery ride was scheduled, and we also had to go up into the top part of Tignes and get a Covid test. So we got prepared to go training, thinking we were going to ride up. But when we went out, we discovered that Specialized had brought in a load of ebikes, and they were an absolute joy. They'd been set up individually for us, and we rode up to the resort on them with Specialized doing some video stuff. We knew they hadn't brought them just to make life easier for us, but it was the most welcome marketing opportunity we could have possibly hoped for. I don't think I could have ridden mine any easier; I bet I expended about the same amount of energy as I would have done in a car.

Once we'd done the test, some of the lads went for an extra little loop, but I rode down to the bus and got a handful of wine gums. Then I went back to my room and lay on the bed for the rest of the day, only getting up for massage, lunch and dinner, plus a little bit of media. I spent quite a bit of time that day going through the press coverage of the race. When I had depression, I had strategies in place to enable me to avoid what was being said about me in the press and online. There was one point when I never read anything because I didn't give a shit. Then when I got sick I had to stop myself reading anything negative at all, because it affected me so much. My main coping strategy then was to keep trying to maintain a positive outlook on stuff and avoid negativity in any form. There would even be times when Peta would talk about something that was nothing to do with cycling, and I'd have to say, 'I can't talk about it. That's what I have to do now.' She was so good at helping me get through that period.

However, reading the coverage of the Tour this year, there was nothing that really pissed me off at all. For the first time in my career, everything was overwhelmingly positive. The reaction from fans was really nice too. Obviously the interaction with them was different because there weren't any people outside the buses and you always used to be able to gauge how you were doing by the size of the crowd outside. Despite the distance that was imposed because of the health situation, it still felt like such an upbeat experience, an emotionally positive thing.

When you win and people cheer and point at you, you know it's because you're just a big name. But this felt different; I felt supported. Before, I might not have given a fuck, but after everything that's happened I'm not afraid to admit that it was really nice to be loved, really nice. I believe I'm a nicer person than I used to be, and it feels like people are with me now, like they are supporting me the person rather than Mark Cavendish the sporting star. I think 99 per cent of the people standing at the side of the road at the Tour never thought I'd be back at the race. But they also knew that my being back there wasn't just about winning like I had done before. There was a whole story that went into being able to win again, the kind of comeback story that sports fans always love.

STAGE 10

6 July: Albertville–Valence, 190.7km

The French talk about the mountains being the judges of the peace at the Tour de France, and the Alps had fully lived up to that billing. A sense of order had been imposed, most obviously in the contest for the yellow jersey, where Tadej Pogačar was now firmly in control. The atmosphere was different too, the tension that had been palpable on every previous morning of the race less apparent as we all signed on and made our way to the start on the riverside in Albertville.

As you'd expect of any city that's hosted the Winter Olympics, it's overlooked by high peaks. But the broad Isère valley runs away to the south-west, and this was the route we were set to follow, heading away from the mountains to Valence. This felt like the first transition stage, a day when the race was in between key battlegrounds and there wasn't quite as much at stake – for the GC guys at least.

Valence is becoming something of a sprinters' town. André Greipel won there in 2015, Peter Sagan three years later, although the town's name didn't really resonate with me until we were on the bus heading for the start. I looked at the details of the finish in the roadbook and recognised the map for some reason – déjà vu perhaps. I googled it and that 2015 stage started to come back to me. There'd been a climb early on, the peloton had gone at it full-on, and a group of about 30 of us ended up just off the back. Usually we'd have got back on, but that day we didn't and instead spent the whole day chopping off to make the time limit. Although I hadn't sprinted at that finish, I could picture it from watching it later on.

There's always a likelihood that it's going to be windy in Rhône valley stage towns like Valence, and that was factored into the team meeting as we discussed how to lead out. There were two likely scenarios. The first was that there would be no wind and it would end in a sprint. The road into the finish was wide, with a series of roundabouts. Tom told us where we needed to be in front and to take control. The other option was that it would be windy. On this team we don't have to fret too much about what to do in the wind, because you know there'll be blue jerseys all over the front if it is blowy.

The atmosphere was super-relaxed as we rolled out. A lot of the guys were still chatting when we got through kilometre zero. I wasn't even paying attention to what was happening in front, and I didn't see two riders go clear as soon as the start flag was waved. Having just two to chase was perfect for us, and we started to control.

The only significant obstacle of the day was an uncategorised climb about 40-odd kilometres from the finish. It wasn't too steep or long, although it wasn't as if I was going to just flow over it while chatting to the guy next to me. We'd talked about it in the briefing and knew for sure that BikeExchange would want to try to rip it up on there, hoping they could drop me and some of the other sprinters so that Michael Matthews – Bling to his mates – would have a shot at the win and the green jersey. That's the plan they always have.

I've called them out a fair bit on this tactic, which seems to be more about trying to beat someone else rather than looking for the win, if that makes sense. I think they burn too many candles to be in a position to really help Bling when he needs it, and I told him that during the stage as we all sat in behind Tim, who was pulling the bunch along behind the break.

'Listen, mate,' I said. 'I know you guys are gonna go full-on on that climb, but you're gonna use all of your matches there when you've got a chance of winning. I'm not getting dropped on that climb. I'm telling you, I won't get dropped there. I reckon you'd be better saving your guys for the sprint. You'd get a better shot.'

'I've gotta try something,' he responded.

'Do what you want, but you're not dropping me on that climb.'

The climb offered an opportunity to BikeExchange and some of the other teams because it plateaued at the top and was quite exposed. It meant that you not only had to stay with the peloton, but also make it over the climb in a good position just in case it split. We'd said in the briefing that we all had to be there at the bottom because it went quite narrow, or at least narrow enough that once you'd got your position, you'd be able to hold it because it would be difficult for anyone to move up from behind.

As we approached it, we sat at the front, Tim still in the vanguard. We didn't really do a lead-out into it. We were just strong enough and, thanks to two bunch sprint wins, confident enough to make sure we stayed in the right position and hit the climb on the front row. Lo and behold, BikeExchange went off like a train …

For a few moments it was chaotic. Morky stayed with me, while Julian and Ballero chased the move. In situations like that, if you say to them, 'Stay at the front till the top of the climb,' they do precisely that and go full bore up it. Whereas Morky and I are a bit more calculating in our effort, thinking, *OK, it flattens a bit towards the top and that's the portion that's crucial, so that's the time to move up.* We just kept to our pace and made sure we stayed sheltered.

That might make it sound easy, but it absolutely wasn't. It was pretty gnarly. I don't want to go that hard out of choice, but, like I'd said, we weren't going to get dropped. As it began to flatten out, Luke Rowe came up next to me. 'Six hundred metres, mate.' We always look after each other, and little touches like that show the human side to what's going on.

Over the top, it dipped then kicked up again and the terrain opened up. I was about twentieth wheel, thinking, *Perfect.* I could feel the wind had picked up a bit, and then I saw Sonny Colbrelli puncture and go back. We'll never attack if something like that happens to a rival, but there's always likely to be someone who will, and I sensed it might kick off. The speed went up, the wind making it very nervous, riders battling for position as teams tried to stay together. At moments like this, there's loads of shouting going on – not insults or anything like that, just riders' names. Someone would lose their team, shout and you'd just let them through, respect shown both ways. Occasionally, if someone won't move or doesn't hear me, I'll shout again: 'Are you going to let me through or are we going to have to fight?' Or I start counting down, 'Three, two ...' One of those usually does the trick.

We crested the top of the next little rise then began to descend, not steeply but at a ferocious speed. It was one of those moments when, if you were to sit up and think about what you were doing at that point, you'd go, 'We're all fucking idiots!' We were fighting for position, racing at 70-odd kilometres an hour with the wind buffeting us … But when you're in it, you're just looking at the gaps, not at other riders, just looking where you need to be, where your team is, thinking, *I just missed them and I need to get back. OK, they're going to move there, I'll get around, then I can just wait,* or, *I need to just push now in the wind to get back to them* …

While all this was going on, we could hear Tom Steels in our ear, giving us simple instructions. 'In a kilometre, you've got a left-hand corner.' You picture it and think, *Where's the wind coming from? Now it's crosshead, it should be crosstail out there* … Tom's always dead calm. You almost don't even need to concentrate on what he's saying: it's subconsciously going in as you're working out what you're doing, like when you're following the GPS in your car. There's the odd time when you're not sure, but mostly you can work out what's happening and what's likely to happen just ahead, rather than needing to be told.

With the break by then reeled in, we got inside the last 30 kilometres, still running gently downhill. The peloton kept bunching together because no one was willing to take it on that far from the finish, but everyone wanted to be near the front. Then it would stretch out through corners, bunch up again on a wide road, stretch on a narrow one. If you stay at the front you're not aware of the carnage that's going on behind, and it wasn't till we saw it later on TV that we realised just how frenetic it had been.

You still get little insights into the chaos, though. We got swamped on one wide section of road, for instance, and went back 20 to 30 riders. We could see a corner coming up in the distance and needed to be further up because the front guys would go through it faster. Instantly, Dries appeared, just like he did with Julian on the first day, gave us a nod to get on his wheel and flew up the outside of the peloton so that we were first into it. We could have fought for a kilometre to achieve the same result, but if you know what you're doing or if you come from Belgium and are innately gifted with that kind of skill, you don't need to get involved in that stress.

Coming out of that right-hander, we were on a narrow road and had to ride in an echelon to stay up at the front. When you're watching on TV they'll generally greet the sight of an echelon by saying you're trying to split the bunch, but sometimes you're not, and in this case we weren't. It's just more comfortable to ride in an echelon for a bit and hold your position rather than sitting in the gutter, because then you're in the shelter on the way back down the line, protected from the wind by the other riders. If everyone wants to commit, then the echelon can go away, but no one really wanted to because we were about to reach the main road into Valence.

The run-in was long and straight, with a couple of roundabouts where you had to go on the left, then one where you had to go right, and a final one to the right 400 metres from the line. We had everyone there. The peloton had been trimmed in half, so you know that's going to make it less frenetic, while some teams like BikeExchange had used almost everyone on the run-in and weren't going to come.

From my perspective, sitting at the front behind a line of blue jerseys, we were the only ones who had the whole team there. Catta and Kasper pulled us into the final kilometres. They were really shifting, but it wasn't like it had been when we were going into Châteauroux and still desperately trying to catch the breakaway. They were using that speed to control the peloton rather than being balls-out to catch someone. We were showing that we were the strongest team and it meant we could go longer with the lead-out.

I was sitting there thinking, *There's only one team leading out here.* It went like clockwork into the last kilometre.

After Châteauroux, where Ballero had gone off too hard, Morky had explained to him what he needed to do: 'We've got this last little roundabout where we go on the right side, then it's a right-hander. Ballero, don't kick when you get on the front coming into the roundabout. No one's going to come as you hit the roundabout, no one's going to bother you. We need you to come out of the corner hard if you can, but the key thing is just to get us into the corner.'

It played exactly like that. The first riders peeled off, *boom, boom, boom,* Ballero went into the corner, led through it, gave all he had left, then Morky came around him as easy as you like and began to ramp it up. The wind was coming from the right, so I had to go up the left, where he would leave just enough space for me.

As Ballero pulled over to the right, Morky went a bit faster, bit faster, bit faster … I was waiting to feel someone go. I didn't want to go too early, because if someone else did move we wanted them to be in the wind on the right.

He got faster and faster and faster. I lay off him just a little, and then, at 175 to go, as I sensed that he wasn't going to go any quicker, but before he slowed down, I went, *boom,* on his left. Wout van Aert followed me and Jasper Philipsen tried to come, but the positions we were in then were how we finished.

I think of all my victories at the 2021 Tour, that's the one where I really didn't have to do anything. I was delivered perfectly that day. If you were writing a story in a cycling magazine about how to do a lead-out, you'd use that stage as your template. There was nothing you'd change about it. Everybody was spot on, they did their job exactly right, there were no variables.

However, things didn't run anything like as smoothly once I'd done the podium ceremony, fulfilled my media commitments and then made my way to anti-doping, which was located in a Portakabin adjacent to the finish. It's a pretty routine process, especially when you've done as many as I have – one after each of my 150-odd wins, every time I've had a jersey, plus out-of-competition controls. I wouldn't be surprised if I'd done more than a thousand of them. I don't mind being tested most of the time, because it means you're winning. OK, they sometimes come at six in the morning for a random control, and that's not ideal, but if we don't do that people are going to cheat, aren't they? I'm happy to let the testers get on with their job.

There were two UCI officials working in the anti-doping cabin, and I'd had the same guy after both of my previous wins. The Tour must have been one of the first races where they'd started using iPads instead of paper, to make the procedure quicker and more efficient – less form-filling and all that, and probably more hygienic too. But this guy was struggling to get to grips with the new technology. He kept pressing the tablet as if there were buttons on it and didn't seem to grasp the fact that it had a touchscreen. It didn't save us any time at all.

I followed the standard routine – went to the urinal in the corner and weed into the pot they'd given me, while being observed through the glass side panel. I turned to place the pot on the table and realised the UCI tester had his tablet and papers spread on it, so I put it on the edge of the sink where you've got to wash your hands before starting the control. I turned again to get some paper towels to put under the pot when he'd cleared the table, and just then someone closed the door of the cabin. The whole thing shook and the pot toppled and fell on the floor, to the accompaniment of my plaintive yell of, 'Nooo!' There was piss everywhere.

It wasn't anybody's fault, but it meant that I now had an empty bladder and still had to produce another sample. 'Do you want me to go and get some beers?' asked Dr Phil, and off he went. Beer is said to be the best thing to drink if you need help peeing, and riders will often neck one when they're struggling to produce a sample. It's the quickest way, apparently, though don't ask me if there's any science to back that up.

Dr Phil soon reappeared with the required beer, which I glugged down. It instantly went to my head. Physically drained, a little dehydrated and now unused to alcohol thanks to my strict dietary regime, I was in proper one-beer wonderland. I wasn't falling over but I could feel it as I sat there waiting and waiting, for the best part of an hour, to finally complete the control.

There was a nice vibe when I eventually got to the hotel that evening, triggered by our fourth stage win rather than any alcohol excess, although we did stick to tradition and toast the victory. The win had also boosted my lead in the points competition to 59, and for the first time we started to think about the possibility of winning the green jersey, which would likely mean a change of strategy on the sprint stages that lay ahead. First, though, we had to safely negotiate the first ever double ascent of Mont Ventoux …

This was the stage that had been the focus of most of the pre-race hype because of the unprecedented double ascent of Mont Ventoux. It's a mythical peak, especially to cyclists. Tree-covered on its lower slopes, but bare higher up, where the heat in the lunar landscape can be blindingly oppressive, it has an infamous reputation, stemming largely from the death of Tom Simpson, Britain's first cycling superstar, who died a kilometre below the summit during the 1967 Tour. It's perhaps better known now, though, for Chris Froome's *Forrest Gump* impression in 2016, after a crash into a race motorcycle left him with a broken bike and his rivals pedalling away into the distance. Put in that situation, I would probably have punched someone, but Froomey made the courageous decision to run up the 10 per cent gradient in his cleated shoes.

While I wouldn't say that I was looking forward to climbing Ventoux twice, the stage didn't instil the same degree of trepidation as the day to Tignes and a couple that still lay ahead in the Pyrenees. The fact that it was close to 200 kilometres long, featured a good deal of riding in between the climbs where the gruppetto should be able to make up some ground, and went up the 'easy' side of the Giant of Provence, from Sault, provided us with good reason to think that we wouldn't be flirting with the time limit once again.

Consequently, when the stage got underway in Sorgues, we weren't that stressed. Our plan was to try to stay with the peloton over the two fourth-category climbs in the opening 40 kilometres, hopefully picking up some useful points at the intermediate in between them, and then to hold on for as long as we could up the first-category Col de la Liguière, just before half-distance. We thought that we'd then be fine riding our own tempo to the finish. According to our calculations, we were likely to have a decent buffer of time to play with.

That was the theory, anyway. But the speed at which they set off that day meant it was a fucking war, attacks going and coming back constantly in the opening 30 kilometres on the flat, Julian in the thick of them. When we got to the little climbs, they were harder than we expected, steeper than the profile suggested. I didn't see or hear any mention of 16 per cent until we got to them. If the bunch had rolled steadily up them, we'd have been OK, but guys were attacking them like it was a one-day race. As we rode up the first one there were riders going backwards already. I actually felt good on that one, but there were already too many riders off the front to think about contesting the intermediate sprint.

The second climb came right after. It was narrow and then suddenly went steep, bunching the peloton up and almost forcing us to a stop. As the riders ahead moved through the pinch point, we had to accelerate to follow, and suddenly there was nothing in my legs. From that moment I was on the limit, hanging on, hoping there'd be a let-up in the peloton because two or three groups had gone clear ahead of it. Ineos had other ideas, though, sending Luke

Rowe to the front in an all-guns-blazing attempt to blow the peloton and the GC battle apart.

When we hit another little climb about 50 kilometres in, I just started sliding back. I was drowning in lactic acid. Tim and Morky were with me, and we'd briefly seen Ballero, who'd tried to go in a move early on, then blown and gone straight through the bunch. He was in a worse state than I was, out the arse behind, and we couldn't send guys back for him because they had to be around me. The only other rider with us was Jasper Philipsen, who'd been left to fend for himself by his Alpecin team. Initially, he wouldn't pull with us three Deceunincks, so I stopped working too, and a sense of panic started to grow. We weren't long into the stage and we hadn't the slightest chance of finishing inside the time cut unless the peloton's frantic tempo eased. United by a sense of desperation, the four of us started swapping off, and we got our reward when we managed to claw our way back up to an easing bunch just before we reached the first-category Liguière.

The heat was so intense by then, the surface of the road was melting. As we started up the climb I felt like I was riding the Tour of Britain, heavy roads where you can't get over your bottom bracket and every pedal stroke's an effort. You could almost hear the road sucking your wheel into it, each push on the pedals producing a small, Velcro-like ripping sound on the tarry surface. Strangely, though, I felt OK again. Being dropped and riding at our own pace towards the climb seemed to have done me a favour. As we climbed, guys who'd hung on to the peloton were now going backwards, while we were holding a pretty nice rhythm, setting our sights on the hairpin ahead, then the next one, dropping back a few positions on each until I told the guys to ease up and stick to our tempo.

Although we were drifting slowly back, we were still going well enough to capture the odd guy who'd been dropped after us, most of whom would sit in with us. We caught Sonny Colbrelli, then Luke Rowe, who was swinging because of the work he'd done for Ineos. 'Just stay with us, mate, and carry on riding tempo,' I told him. But when I turned around a few moments later, I realised that even our pace was too much for him. Sadly, that was the last we saw of him. I spoke to him that night and he said he'd been completely empty.

From the Liguière, we were soon onto the Ventoux for the first time, climbing from Sault. It's the longest route to the top, but by far the most straightforward, the gradient around 4–5 per cent for the most part, then almost levelling out as the road approaches Chalet Reynard, where it joins the traditional Tour route that grinds up from Bédoin. We were going at a decent pace, Sonny staying with us for a while but in some difficulty, throwing up after going so deep to stay with the peloton earlier on. 'I vomit, I vomit …' he repeated, before he dropped back. We didn't see him for a while, then the next thing we knew Sonny came back up to us on the flat bit just before Chalet Reynard. He was barely with us, though, before he attacked and went up the road. He managed to get up to the next group, which was bigger than ours and meant that he wouldn't have to ride as much and could save a bit for the days ahead.

At Chalet Reynard, where the Sault road emerges from the trees and onto the open mountainside, the telecom masts at the top of the Ventoux were visible for the first time. Looking back a few moments later, I could see a rider in the cars. Seeing this, I was going nuts at the commissaire, who was as usual sitting next to us, over-revving his bike and apparently happy to let the riders all around us do whatever they wanted. 'Look! Look!' I yelled to the commissaire again. I'd been puking, I'd been swinging, I wasn't talking; the guys with me were suffering, we were hot, our jerseys open, under constant surveillance, yet a couple of hundred metres away ... It's bloody ridiculous. I can't even get a bottle for myself, because if I did there'd be a photo of me taking it and everyone would be shouting, 'Sticky bottle!'

Approaching the top of the climb, we reached Tom Simpson's memorial. Every time I pass it I throw a hat or pay some other tribute. Sometimes when I've been in the gruppetto I've even stopped briefly, because we usually finish at the top. But with another lap of the Ventoux to complete, I took my helmet off as a mark of respect. A couple of guys in the group with us wondered what I was up to. When you tell them the story they all know it, but only vaguely, whereas ten years ago every rider in the bunch would have known about Tom's memorial on the Ventoux. Now all that romanticism, the stories about the sport, are getting lost, changing the demographic of people getting into cycling. One-handed wheelies? Yeah, cool.

As we crested the top and started down the descent, Fitte came on the radio: 'Guys, don't take risks. Push, but don't go over the limit.' The thing is, when you're my age, you don't enjoy descending any more. When you've done it that many times in the gruppetto and put your life in danger, descending becomes as tiring as climbing – you're on the limit, you have to sprint out of every corner ... I'd never done this descent, because every time we'd done the Ventoux before we'd finished at the top. But it was the first descent I enjoyed in the race. You didn't have to sprint out of any of the corners, it just flowed the whole way.

I'd always thought the most flowing descent was the one off the Tourmalet, but this was the best I've ever done. It reminded me about something a good few years ago, when I used to give it absolutely fucking everything on descents: I got asked to do this challenge for *Top Gear*. The idea behind it was that if your fuel ran out on a mountain, which would be the quickest way to get back down. They took the engine out of a car, so it was almost like a soapbox, and they wanted to put it on a descent and time it against me. I told them, 'I don't think you understand. Even if it had an engine, it wouldn't get anywhere near me,' so the idea ended up getting canned. Even though it never happened, I'd always thought that if they were ever going to do anything like that – a car versus a cyclist – the Tourmalet would be ideal. But that day changed my mind. The descent off the Ventoux was the most amazing ever.

My speed topped out at a maximum of 101km/h, but we were just in a small group, and I've no doubt at all that the peloton would have been going much quicker with a bigger group. Our average speed was 77.5km/h, which illustrates how beautifully it flowed.

We dropped into Malaucène then started to circle the western side of the mountain, the road rolling up and down a bit. There was quite a big gruppetto by then, almost everyone contributing fully to it, and we were quickly around to the second ascent of the Ventoux coming out of Bédoin. While undoubtedly one of the most renowned climbs in the sport, it's always grim, a real slog. It runs almost straight, it's unrelenting, the heat is stifling under the trees. The best thing I could say about it was that we didn't have to push ourselves to the limit on the way up because we were almost certain to make the time cut. If we'd been up against it, it could well have been like Tignes all over again.

As we were passing Tom's memorial for the second time, I knew we had loads of time to spare, so I dropped back to Fitte in the team car to get a cap to leave as a tribute. I wanted to stop and take it up the steps to the stone marker, but Morky wasn't having it. 'You're not fucking stopping,' he insisted. I tried to explain, but he was adamant and I completely understood why. They were riding for me, waiting for me: you can't risk anything. So as we passed, I threw it and someone went, 'Get it!'

Fuck! I thought, but as I turned around I could see that the guy had picked it up and put it on the memorial for me, and I shouted thanks.

Of course, I never knew Tom Simpson, but he's always meant a lot to me for two good reasons. Firstly, he was not only a pioneer in British cycling, but he also showed you could be a superstar of the sport if you were from Britain and, as a result, you always knew that kind of status was achievable. Secondly, his death changed world sport for ever. It marked the start of anti-doping. There are some people who simply brand him a cheat because he'd taken amphetamines, and a little part of me is like that. Ultimately, though, we owe our lives to him. His death underlined the fact that being a cyclist isn't the be all and end all; it's not win at all costs. While anti-doping has to be predominantly about stopping cheating and encouraging fair play, it saves lives too.

We were close to the memorial when Wout van Aert won the stage down in Malaucène, and we were told the time cut would be at 47 minutes. We were well inside that and went super-easy for the last kilometre or so to the top, then we enjoyed the second rush down the Ventoux. As we neared the finish, we could hear the compere hyping up the 'Will they? Won't they?' question. It came up again in the post-stage interviews: 'You were only inside it by seven minutes …' But the truth is that I was pissed we were inside by that much. We could have eased off a bit more. But we'd got through another difficult day in the mountains, and that was the only thing that mattered.

Although Julian was disappointed that the stage win had eluded him, I knew there would be one happy Cavendish back home in Essex. Casper's a huge Wout van Aert fan and he'd be beside himself. It's beautiful how guys like Wout, Julian and Mathieu van der Poel race, a breath of fresh air. Racing's been strangled and we all know why, but they win because they take chances, they're willing to risk, and obviously they are great natural talents. They use the science to back up their training and then they just go out and race.

At the same time, though, I think a lot of courses are designed now for that type of rider. Climbs are being put into races for the sake of it, and those guys can get over them. While sprinters are seen as still getting a lot of opportunities, I don't think we do, really. Races that were once the domain of sprinters are changing, with organisers saying they're making them 'harder'. Why are they harder? A climb doesn't make something harder, it just stops sprinters. A race isn't easy because a sprinter wins it. All climbs do is eliminate the number of potential winners, so these guys who can do everything end up shining. Don't get me wrong, it's great to see this open racing, but I think if I turned pro now, given my physiology, I wouldn't get to the finish of most races.

Nîmes is another town that a sprinter likes to have on their *palmarès*. I won there in 2008, Alexander Kristoff did in 2014 and Caleb was the winner on the Tour's last visit in 2019. But it's always a complicated finish because the run-in to the city is shit. It makes new towns like Harlow or Milton Keynes, with all their roundabouts and road furniture, seem uncluttered. There's so much stuff to deal with that the presentation Tom did in the briefing felt as long as the stage. The last five or six kilometres ran steadily downhill, switching left and right constantly, with roundabouts, road furniture, pavings. It was like a road planner's wet dream. What's more, on stages in this region you've also got to factor in the wind down the Rhône valley. It's always likely to catch you out, because it gusts so strongly and bounces around; it doesn't necessarily flow, so you can end up getting thrown about, like you might do on a coast road.

It was another stage that was going to go one of two ways. It was either going to be super-easy and we'd just roll in for a sprint, or it was going to be on all day. It'd never be in between. It was really blowy at the start in Saint-Paul-Trois-Châteaux, but we knew what to expect. 'It could split at the beginning, because it's windy, but it will come back together. Just make sure you're there,' Tom told us.

Sure enough, once we got underway a couple of teams tried to force it right from the off and it split immediately. Two kilometres later it came back together, because they commit, then they're not sure, and then they stop riding. We were near the front, tracking the moves. It was one of those days when we were expecting Tadej Pogačar's UAE team to impose a bit of order at the head of the peloton, but you could never be too sure whether they'd turn up. We'd ask them to help us by being up there at the front, saying, for instance, 'It narrows at kilometre six, so if you're up there we can block the road,' and Davide Formolo would be like, '*Si, si, si!*' Rafał Majka would tell us, 'Yeah, we'll be there …' Then at kilometre six you wouldn't see them. They did get better when Tadej was in yellow, but they could still be erratic.

The attacks continued to go as the route turned and twisted. One moment we'd be riding into a bit of a headwind, then it would come from the side, and after another change of direction it would be cross-tail. About 30 kilometres in, as we were approaching the hills running down the western side of the Rhône valley, we could see that people were starting to tire. As we turned onto a 1.5-kilometre climb, rising at maybe 4 per cent, you could sense the moment had arrived and the break was about to go.

Someone went and I followed them, then a couple more came across, another couple more, then Julian bridged up and by the time we were at the top of this little climb there were 14 guys clear at the front. I spent three or four seconds deciding what to do. *If I'm here, this isn't going. I'm in the green jersey, the likes of Alpecin are going to pull it back.* We had Julian in there who was a good bet for victory, so I sat up and slipped back to the peloton. As I watched them ride away along the valley ahead I was happy I wasn't in there. It was a big old break with lots of strong guys, and it was fair to assume that one of them would go clear on the undulating roads running into Nîmes. I hoped it would be Julian.

No one was interested in pulling the break back and then holding it for the whole of a flat day in blazing heat, with the wind always likely to be a complicating factor. As a result, it was a pretty straightforward stage, although as the break's lead stretched to 15 minutes, we had to be aware of the time cut, which is always quite tight on short, flat stages like this. We were expecting it to be around 18 minutes, which wouldn't catch out the bunch. But that meant staying with the pack as it accelerated up the final rise coming into Nîmes, the GC teams testing each other out just to see what might happen, while the rest of us are doing all we can to hang on, knowing that if we are dropped and have to ride in alone, the time cut might become a big issue.

As we grimly hung on going up the climb, I turned to Morky and muttered, 'Thank fuck I'm not in the break.' I wouldn't have got a sniff of the stage win, which went in the end to Bora man mountain Nils Politt.

We still had something to ride for, however. With 13 riders off the front, there were points available for fourteenth and fifteenth places at the intermediate sprint and the finish. Before the intermediate, Michael Matthews came up to me and said, 'Do you want to have a pact so that we don't sprint today?' A couple of points here and there wouldn't make much difference to the green jersey competition and I said I was up for it, but added that I wanted him to make sure everyone was on board because I'd had a bad experience in a similar situation during the 2009 Tour.

I'd been battling with Thor Hushovd for green that year. Back then, there used to be three intermediate sprints, and one of the inflatable arches deflated one day and caught Thor out. I didn't go for the points because I didn't see it as fair game. Then, literally 15 kilometres later, there was a crash and I was behind it, and he took the fucking points. There were just a handful of points between us in Paris, as he took green. So I said to Bling, 'You've got to make sure everyone buys into it. I don't care if we sprint or not.'

There was no issue at the intermediate. We just rolled through it. As we were dropping down into Nîmes, the peloton still a bit stretched out after that final little climb on the outskirts, I was near the back, dodging, dodging, dodging, trying to stay out of trouble. Bling and Sonny Colbrelli, my two closest rivals for green, were there as well. With two kilometres to go there were no lead-outs, we were just riding in, and I was thinking I was quite happy that there hadn't been a bunch sprint because I was tired and it was hot and windy. There are always going to be days when you might be a bit disappointed that the opportunity to sprint has passed by, but it can affect the end game, and you've got to be aware of that.

As we neared the finish, I thought, *I'm just going to go to the front to keep an eye on things.* That day, it was easy to move up, and as we came towards the right-hand corner that turned into the final straight, I was sitting behind Ballero. Then, *Woosh!* Alpecin came past with three guys leading Philipsen out. I jumped right on his wheel as we went into the roundabout 400 metres out and swung to the right. As he opened up his sprint, I sprinted too.

I really like Jasper. He's a super bike rider and like all young Belgians he loves the sport. But seeing him sprint when I thought we'd agreed not to got my back up a bit. I drew alongside him, eased off and looked at him, then kicked again and won the sprint for fourteenth place.

When I crossed the line I thought, *Cav, you fucking dickhead!* That's something I would have done in the past, but I would have done it for a completely different reason, as a dick swing, basically. In this instance it was more like, *For fuck's sake, what are you doing?* But it would still look the same as a dick-swinging move, especially with glasses on.

I really had to give myself a talking-to afterwards, which is something I would never have thought of doing in the past: *Don't do that shit. It's not nice.* Perhaps I was getting cocky as a result of being able to win, but whatever it was down to I didn't like it. Whether it's because of everything that's happened or the fact that I'm 36 years old, I made a point of telling myself to wind my neck in, to stay grounded, and it felt nice being able to do that.

STAGE 13

9 July: Nîmes–Carcassonne, 219.9km

I didn't want to end this Tour on 33 wins, and I knew this stage was an opportunity. If I could win one more then everyone would shut up for ever about the record, wouldn't they? Take a quick look at the profile and you'd probably say that this stage was a good bet for a bunch sprint. There was, after all, just one categorised climb. Yet a glance down the list of previous winners in Carcassonne would reveal not a single renowned Tour sprinter among the names.

Magnus Cort was the last winner there in 2018, and the canny Dane typifies the type of punchy, opportunistic all-rounder who thrives on the narrow, twisty, grippy and windy roads in this part of France. We talked a lot about the wind in the briefing. It was going to be a factor all day and would undoubtedly complicate our attempts to control the race, especially in the final 30 kilometres or so, which were very open.

I was just as worried about the finish, though. The final kilometre was about 3–4 per cent uphill and I wasn't overly confident for it. A kilometre at 4 per cent doesn't sound much, but at the speed you're travelling into a finish, I knew it would take me close to my limit in terms of the power I could sustain. I admitted I was a bit concerned about it, and the other guys told me, 'You'll be fine! You'll be able to deal with it.' That encouraged me, but even so, I knew that if I made even one tiny error in the final, I'd be fucked.

As we began what was, at 220 kilometres, the second-longest stage of the race, it was very hot and windy. The start was super-twisty, running through a string of towns where narrow sections forced the peloton into one line. Several breaks went and were brought back again, but we were always there as a unit at the front, knowing full well that it would be down to us to control. Once again, UAE were nowhere to be seen, but why would they ride on the front that day knowing that we'd pull it back?

Our plan for the break was like the one we had the day before: if five guys were in the break then we'd let them go, but if there were more than that we'd need to start thinking about one of our guys being in it. It took a good while for the break to go because so many riders wanted to be in it, but after 30 kilometres or so three guys went clear. After a few attempts to bridge had come to nothing, we set to work, with Tim on the front.

It was relatively flat, but it was suffocatingly hot, a horrible heat in which you feel like you're steadily being cooked. You can feel a sweaty, salty residue coagulating on your skin, your hands slip around in your track mitts. When you drink, you don't care whether the liquid goes in your mouth or over your face. We were getting ice bags and drinks at regular intervals from our soigneurs who were dotted along the course, as is the trend nowadays. The ice would go straight down the back of the jersey in an attempt to keep cool.

In these conditions it's easy to get dehydrated because you need to drink so much. At the same time, you don't feel that hungry because it's so hot and you can forget to eat. But Tom kept prompting us on the radio, reminding us to keep to the feeding strategy that was in place. So you chew your way through bars that are sticky and hard to get down. You can't help but feel a little miserable at moments like this, when it's the end of the second week, you're tired and pretty much every other race in the calendar would have been done and dusted. The roadbook tells you it's stage 13, but you've honestly got no idea about how many you've done. It feels relentless.

The intermediate sprint arrived just before halfway. It was on a little rise, and with only three in the break there were some useful points to go for. We knew it went left, right, over a small bridge and then kicked up. On the radio they told us, 'You've got a slight descent before it, so you can run up into the intermediate.'

We were waiting for this small descent to get a run-in, and the next thing it goes left, right and then up, and we were still six or seven back, wondering, *Where's that fucking descent?* Colbrelli, Matthews and Philipsen were moving already, so Morky began to chase and go around them, but I couldn't hold his wheel as they approached the line. I'd only lost four or five points, which I wasn't too fussed about. What concerned me far more was that I didn't feel great. That knocked me quite a bit. It wasn't exactly a great omen if I did get the chance to sprint up the hill into Carcassonne.

Beyond the intermediate, it kept dragging up, and then we started to hit the rollers that continued almost all the way into the finish. We were told that one of these small hills had a narrow descent, with some gravel on it, and we expected there'd be a fight to secure position near the front going over the top of it. We decided to pre-empt that by getting to the front and leading on to it. The first part of that tactic worked fine, then, in the place you'd least expect it, Philippe Gilbert shot past, moving so quickly that you couldn't even sense his attack was coming. From where I usually am, about seven back in the line, you see someone go and you can shout a warning to the guys ahead of you. But he went with such speed that I didn't even have time to react. Then a couple more went after him and Tim started going backwards because he'd been pulling all day. *For fuck's sake, here we go …*

We went over the top of the little climb, hit the descent and, *Crughh!* I could just hear crashing at the back, loud enough to tell me that a fair number of guys had gone down. But that was the last thought I could give it as it started to roll incessantly. It was like being in the first 30 kilometres again before the break had gone. It was fucking on.

While it wasn't going to split, you've got to be in there, pushing. It's not like on a climb when you fill up with lactic acid and you know you're going to get popped. You've just got to suffer and stay in there. You've just got to fucking hurt. It remained like that for about 20 kilometres, the break caught in the midst of the surge, then it kind of calmed down again. It was another one of those moments when everyone wanted to be at the front, but no one was keen on pulling.

Julian and Dries were with me, but I was in the wind a lot because you couldn't avoid it on such a narrow road. Morky kept saying, 'Sit back! Sit back!' And I was telling him, 'No, I need to stay here.' I didn't want to be baulked up on people's back wheels when the road started going up on the last big roller before Carcassonne. I wanted to be able to do my pedalling.

As we started to come over that final hill, Julian started pulling to get into the descent first and I went over the limit to follow him. We made it, but as we sped down the other side I hit a hole and, *Crack!* My saddle snapped.

I was so pissed because I'd given so much effort to get to the descent first. My next thought was, *Should I try to finish with a broken saddle?* because I knew it was going to split in the next few kilometres, when we entered open countryside where a crosswind was likely. I shouted, 'Saddle's snapped! Saddle's snapped!' into the radio.

'Don't stress, we've got three kilometres before it gets open,' Tom replied calmly.

Don't fucking stress? We were coming into the last 30 kilometres of the stage.

'Stop! Stop! Stop!' he told me with more urgency.

I stopped, changed bike, got back on. Dries was waiting for me. He towed me back up to the peloton, then up the side of it, and at that moment the wind hit. We got there with maybe 15 metres to spare. If we hadn't that would probably have been game over for the day.

Dries kept moving me up, and as we got near the front, some teams were trying to split it in the crosswind. The peloton did kind of split, and the odd time it was easier to rotate through and ensure you stayed near the front. But once again nobody was totally committed to it and the split never happened. Instead, it was just ON, and it didn't really let up till the finish.

Coming into the last ten kilometres, it started to bunch back up again. We were in a good spot, all together close to the front, well set for the final run-in. But I began to notice that one or two other teams were starting to really get physical on me, Alpecin especially. Guys like Jonas Rickaert were coming underneath me in the corners or leaning on me. *They're trying to fuck me now,* I thought. I hate that kind of tactic. They were just trying to get me angry, get me off the wheel, get me in the wind, fuck up our unit. Yes, that's a legitimate tactic and there's nothing to stop anyone from doing it, but why not just try to win the race rather than devoting your effort to making someone else lose?

There was another unexpected distraction, too. We started slipping out in the corners with about five kilometres to go. 'I think I've punctured,' I said into the radio.

'You haven't – it's the road, it's the road,' Morky told me. The surface was melting.

Coming into Carcassonne, I was getting chopped in every corner. I'd have to go back around and back on, then we'd get it dialled again. With three kilometres to go, it went sharp left, curved to the right, then it went wider and we instantly took the opportunity to move to the front.

Catta and Kasper had taken it on early, and they just went. The last couple of kilometres were the biggest blur of any sprint I can remember. Normally I can visualise how sprints have unfolded in quite a lot of detail, but I can't picture the two-kilometre banner in Carcassonne. I just remember it was a straight road, then we turned right with 1,200 metres to go, then it kept curving left the whole way to the line.

I had my gaze fixed on Morky's wheel. I didn't see the barriers, didn't see the banners. As we came into the town centre, we reached the right-hander and once again someone came underneath us and I lost Morky's wheel. I quickly managed to find my way back to him again.

With a kilometre to go, it started going up, and I looked for another gear but realised I didn't have one. I was already in my 54x11, so I went down a gear, only to find it was too easy, then went back up again and started churning it. We got to the final left-hander, 700 out, and Rickaert was bashing me, while other people were coming, and at that instant Ballero hit out so hard that he got a gap. As he accelerated away I was still on Morky's wheel, then Bouhanni knocked me off it. I could see Ballero up the road and I was thinking, *He could get this and I don't want to go.*

Just as I moved back around onto Morky's wheel, Movistar's Iván García Cortina jumped. He almost got to Ballero. Then Morky surged, using García Cortina's slipstream to pick up pace. It was now so blurred I didn't know what the fuck was going on. I was so far in the red that I couldn't think properly.

As Morky went, the others started slowing down. He kept going on. He passed García Cortina, and then I started passing him, kept my speed going, and going, and going, and, *Boom!* I crossed the line. Win number 34.

I was completely fucked. I couldn't raise my hands off the bars, just about managing a one-handed celebration. I couldn't understand what had just gone off, but I'd fucking done it. Everyone would now shut up.

I braked and was desperate to get off my bike. It's not often that I'm like that, but I was finished. I had nothing left. I was gasping for air, my legs were wobbly, my head was banging.

And then the boys arrived, and I was revived. Morky picked me up, Ballero hugged me. '*Abbiamo fatto la storia!*' I said to him. We've made history. It was incredible, an absolutely joyous moment.

It was only then that I noticed Tim hadn't come in. 'Where the fuck is he?' I was asking as I got shuffled off to the podium. When the ceremony and the flash interviews were over, the doc told me, 'He's had a bad crash. He's on his way, he's riding, but he's a mess.'

Our press guy, Phil, led me down to the mixed zone, and one of the first faces I saw there was my long-time teammate and close friend Bernie Eisel, who's now a TV reporter for Eurosport. I wanted to give Bernie a hug because he'd been there for most of those 34 wins, but I could see he was in two minds about it, so I was too. Then Brad Wiggins, who was also there for Eurosport, appeared. 'Fuck professionalism, this is a big thing,' he said as he hugged me.

I looked at Bernie and I wanted to enjoy that moment with him too. Thinking back now, I still feel guilty about it, because I was worried that it might reflect badly on him in some way because he was quite new to the role. I didn't want him to feel embarrassed or awkward, or at least put him in a position where he might have felt that way. But it's eaten me up a little bit. I was celebrating all these wins and he was part of most of them. I just wanted to remind him of that.

When we got in the car, they were talking about Tim, who'd been the last rider to finish, just a couple of minutes inside the time cut. Apparently, he'd gone off the road and hit a pole on the verge. There'd been some concerns that he was concussed, but he'd been given the OK to continue and had ended up spending almost the whole day riding on his own, first at the front of the peloton and ultimately for more than 50 kilometres at the back. He'd been on his own through all those ups and downs where we'd been battling for position in a peloton that was really shifting. The effort it must have cost him. When he crossed the line he'd collapsed.

I wanted to go and see him as soon as we got to the hotel, but the doc told me, 'Get yourself in the ice bath, you're cooked.' The other guys had done their 15-minute plunge and some of the directors were already on the bus, ready to start the meeting to discuss the next day's stage, as I stripped off and lowered myself into one of the three ice baths, which are shaped a bit like a tyre lever, wide where you sit and tapering in towards the end. I sat there, almost literally freezing my nuts off, chatting to Peta and the kids.

After my first two wins, Fitte had said to me, 'If you get to 34, I'll go in the ice bath.' I'd shot back, 'If I get to 34, you go in the ice bath naked.' He said he would. As my 15 minutes ended, I got out of the bath shivering and shrivelled, and Fitte came into the truck. 'Fitte, get your kit off,' I yelled at him. To his credit, he didn't protest. He undressed straight away and sat in the ice bath. Fitte didn't quite fit in, though, which made it even funnier for the rest of us in the truck.

Phil had some more press lined up for me to do, but I insisted on seeing Tim first. I went in and he was lying in a darkened room, all banged up. The other lads were coming in to see if he was all right. I told him, 'If you feel bad then don't start tomorrow.'

'OK,' he said.

Then it was time to speak to the press once again. There were, of course, lots of questions about equalling Eddy Merckx's record. All I can say about Eddy is that I think he's as pissed off with it as I am. You can't make a comparison between us as racers. It's no more than a comparison of a number – a number that's actually pretty arbitrary. On the one hand, a lot of his wins were half-stages (also known as split stages, when a Tour day featured two or even three mini-stages over short distances) and time trials, so in terms of massed start stages, I'd got the record a long time ago. On the other hand, he won across all terrains, and I couldn't do anything like he did. You have to put these things into proper perspective, and I think Brad did that really well in his podcast after my first win in Fougères. I'm paraphrasing, but he essentially said, 'When you see all the shit that goes on in bunch sprints, all the crashes, Cav's got through that shit

30-odd times. That's what makes it so phenomenal.' I'd never really thought about it like that, but he's right.

By the time I'd finished the media commitments the lads were already eating dinner, and the atmosphere was great when I got there. It was like the first day again. Everyone had forgotten how tired we were, and we were laughing and joking. Julian was on particularly good form and it's never dull when he's like that. We had a glass of wine to toast the win, and as we were finishing, Tim came in. He was wearing a pair of these fucking pearlescent see-through sunglasses because he wasn't feeling great. You know when you're coughing and trying not to laugh? I knew I shouldn't laugh, because he was doing the right thing for him by wearing sunglasses, but he just looked like he was doing a cabaret someplace. No one laughed and I was just trying not to, but it was hurting my stomach, trying not to piss myself laughing. I couldn't help it. He wouldn't have found it funny if I'd laughed. He wasn't doing it for a joke. But it was so funny when he sat down and ate his dinner looking like that.

During dinner I said sorry to Morky for coming around him at the finish, and I think he was a bit taken aback. 'We're here for you,' he told me. 'Second on a Tour de France stage as a lead-out man when your sprinter wins is the best you can do.'

Whether he just didn't let on that he was disappointed, I don't know, but it seemed like it didn't matter one bit to him and hadn't even crossed his mind. I think he was expecting me to go by him. His job is to get as close to the line as possible going as fast as he possibly can, and he did it perfectly in that instance as he does so often. It showed who he is and why he excels at that job, why he's paid such good money to do it. There are undoubtedly a lot of sprinters who would have much longer and more profitable careers if they realised they were lead-out men too. Sprinting's not simply about being fast; you've got to be able to deal with the pressure of being expected to win, of delivering the prize after all your teammates have gone all in for you. Carrying that weight has a tendency of sapping the speed from the legs of a lot of sprinters.

Morky just wanted to make us win, and ultimately I understand that. That's why I always make a point of ensuring people realise that it's a team effort. It's not just about me. I'm standing on their shoulders. Like I promised Morky before the Tour, 'You'll never, ever get as much praise as you will when I win, not from anyone.' Every one of those 34 wins also belongs to the guys like Bernie, Morky and Tim.

STAGE 14

10 July: Carcassonne–Quillan, 183.7km

Fair play. For me, this is one of the fundamentals of bike racing. It's a bloody hard sport, so why mess other people around or be disrespectful? It really winds me up when I feel like I'm being picked out for unfair treatment, or if I see other riders not getting the respect they deserve. I'd seen plenty of instances of both on the Tour, but this stage took the fucking biscuit.

It was the first of five in the Pyrenees, although this one only ventured into the foothills. There were a couple of little climbs early on, long enough that if you weren't on it you could be gone and never come back all day. But I felt all right when we got to them, and even though the peloton started to fragment, I managed to hold a good position, quite near the front. The biggest of the hills was about 50 kilometres in, a third-category. I hung on over the top, but a big old group of guys was dropped.

The break was only 15 or 20 seconds ahead of the bunch at that point, and the pace was full-on, so I was surprised to see that group behind get back on. I got the hump at that, because I was sure that they'd been in the cars and not been barraged. That might seem petty, but I knew that I'd get dropped when we got to the bigger climbs halfway into the stage, and if those guys had still been behind, the gruppetto would have been bigger and we could have shared the work around a bit more, saving ourselves a bit for the harder mountain days ahead.

I didn't have much time to dwell on that, though, as the intermediate was fast approaching. As is often the case, it was at the top of a little hill. I was sitting quite far back in the bunch with Morky. We went by five kilometres to go, three kilometres to go, and Morky wasn't moving up. 'Stay here, stay here,' he told me, and in the end we didn't get any points at the sprint.

I said to him, 'What the fuck? We've just lost a load of points there.'

And he was like, 'Trust me, save your energy. Fuck that one. It's about picking our days now.' I knew he was probably right, but I could have got some easy points there and I was a bit pissed about it.

The first significant climb of the stage came soon after, up towards the Château de Montségur. As we got onto it, there were guys getting dropped again, including Tim, who had managed to start that morning. But Morky, Dries and I wanted to hang on just a little bit longer with the bunch. We pushed at a slightly harder tempo than we'd have liked to, climbing well.

As we got to the top, Fitte came on the radio: 'Guys, Tim's three minutes behind you.' We weren't that far behind the peloton and we knew that the time cut was likely to be very generous, so we decided to wait for him. This didn't mean knocking off our speed entirely. We kept riding down the descent and on the flat sections that followed, then went easier on the climbs because they were where Tim would be able to push a faster pace and close the gap.

When we reached the next climb, the Col de la Croix des Morts, the longest of the stage, we were in a small group, and as we knocked the pace back a bit I explained to the others in it, 'Guys, we're waiting for Tim.' Fitte was counting down the gap between us and him: 'Two and a half minutes … two minutes … one minute …' Then Jonas Rickaert started pushing it on. Like Pavlov's dogs, as soon as the other guys saw Rickaert accelerating, they started to chase after him. If someone was going to ride, they were going to do that rather than wait for someone. They wanted to be going forwards. But I was pissed because Rickaert was being a dick.

I rode up to him and said, 'One of your best friends is getting dropped and you're pushing on. Come on, man …'

He shouted back, 'I didn't know Tim was dropped.'

'Fuck off that you don't know he was dropped,' I yelled back.

He wasn't happy, but he did ease off. Soon after, Tim caught us and we rode on, still going fairly easy on the climbs, the group collaborating well in between them, in absolutely no danger at all of flirting with the time cut.

Once we'd got over the top of the final climb, it was 17 kilometres downhill into the finish. We knew that the time cut was going to be around 45 minutes and we were at about 20 minutes or so. We were only likely to lose another minute into the finish, so we were still going to be 20 minutes inside the time limit. If I'd walked to the finish, I would have probably just about made it.

We'd got a little way down the descent when my front wheel kind of went away on me a bit going around a corner. When the road straightened I got out of the saddle and it was spongy. Puncture.

I radioed the car, Fitte came, the wheel was changed, I got back on, and Fitte went in front of me to get me back up to the gruppetto, which had about 20 guys in it. He'd just started to accelerate when there were two or three sharp blasts on a horn right next to us. It was one of the motorbike commissaires. I was like, 'What the fuck's going on?'

Fitte slowed down and got in behind me because we couldn't take any risks at all. In my ear I heard him say, 'Guys, they've barraged Cav. Just wait.' So the whole gruppetto sat up and waited for me.

I was livid. 'You, come here!' I shouted across to the commissaire. 'Why are you barraging me?'

'It's not possible …' he told me.

I said, 'Grow the fuck up. We're going to make the cut by 20 minutes. You're just being a dick. Listen, you stop with me at the finish. We'll go to the chief com. Or we'll go to Christian Prudhomme, whatever you want, after the finish, and we'll discuss this situation. It's bullshit. Bullshit!'

As we got across the line at the finish, I saw Christian Prudhomme and told the commissaire to stop. I started telling Christian what had just happened. I said to the guy, 'Mate, look at the time cut. There was no need to be a dick.' Christian was trying to calm things down. 'OK, we speak,' he said. But I wasn't finished yet and had another go at the guy.

Here's the thing. In that situation I'm not cheating. It's one thing if the race is on and you get a pull from the team car, but it wasn't because a group had got across to us not long before. What's more, if you puncture you're entitled to get back to your previous position. You don't get an advantage by doing this behind the car because you expend far more energy getting back to the group that you were in before than you would have done if you had stayed in the group. You don't ride at 200 watts behind the car, but 400.

'We could have fucking stopped for a picnic and made it, just let me get back to the fucking group,' I told the guy. Then I saw Nacer Bouhanni coming in and that triggered me again. 'He was on his own with fucking 60 kilometres to go and he's finished 10 minutes behind us. And you're trying to barrage me on a puncture with fucking 7 kilometres to go in a stage where we're 20 minutes down …' I was raging.

Incidents like that feel personal, discriminatory. I've had stuff like this happening to me all through my career and I've come to expect it, although that doesn't mean I'll just accept it. I understand that it's the job of the commissaires to ensure a fair race, but a fundamental part of ensuring that is by being consistent with decisions and rulings, and not trying to disadvantage someone who's doing well.

STAGE 15

This was a stage in three parts. Act one began with me on the rollers before the start. I'm never really into this, and it was the only time in the Tour that I warmed up like this before a stage, simply because I was so nervous about the climb that we went up right from the gun. It wasn't categorised because it wasn't all that steep, just 3–4 per cent for the most part. But it was a good 600 metres higher than the start town of Céret, and you could pretty much guarantee that the pace would be ballistic from the off because so many riders would be looking to get in the break. If you got dropped from the bunch on that climb, you'd really struggle to get back on in the gradually ascending valley beyond it, where the peloton would be sitting on the motorbike. If they'd carried on racing up that valley, you'd be out.

Once again, I was lucky that I was in a jersey and could start on the front row. The fight in the neutral zone was like the run-in to a bunch sprint. When we reached kilometre zero I managed to stay at the front for the first couple of kilometres, then slid back. The climb was actually two passes in one, so I got a bit of a breather as the road briefly dipped in between them.

The peloton concertinaed on that second climb. The pace would go up and I'd slide back, then it'd slow because a break had gone and we'd bunch up again. Each time, though, I'd lose another ten spots or so, the back of the peloton beckoning more and more as we neared the top. When I got there, I was the fifth-last man in a much-reduced bunch. 'Has anyone been dropped, Tom?' I asked in the radio. I'd been at my limit, and he told me quite a few hadn't been able to hold the pace, which gave me a little bit of motivation.

Most of them got back quickly, though, as the pace slowed almost to a stop as we went over the crest and onto a really technical descent. If they'd have raced down there, there'd have been crashes everywhere – everywhere! Thankfully, everyone went down it pretty comfortably and sensibly.

That was the first act done. The second began when we turned left at the foot of the descent to reach the main road that rose for 50 kilometres to Mont-Louis, a first-category summit. Although the climb only extended to 8 kilometres, the 40 or so that led up to it were all uphill, only very slightly to begin with, but the gradient gradually picking up a bit all of the way towards it. I'm fine when I'm on a hill that you ride fast up. But it's the slogs like this one that are my Achilles heel, when it's just 3 per cent for kilometre after kilometre and you're on the threshold the whole time. It's horrible for me when it's like that. I can't do it. My glycogen stores dwindle rapidly and I can't sustain the effort, even if I'm in the group. It all comes down to the fact that my body is meant for short bursts, not long hauls like that. I was concerned about the effect the altitude might have, too. All four of the climbs beyond the top end of the valley were above my psychological threshold of 1,500 metres, the Port d'Envalira 900 metres above it!

As we started up the valley, UAE took control behind the break, which had more than 30 riders in it. Michael Matthews was in there and he cleaned up at the intermediate, taking the maximum of 20 points, but there was nothing we could do about it. All that mattered to us was that we were in the bunch, sitting on the wheels, edging ever closer to Mont-Louis. We were sitting quite far back initially, and I asked the guys to move further up so that I had some sliding room if it kicked up or I began to suffer for a minute. This would mean that I'd be able to ease up for a minute but we wouldn't drop out of the back of the bunch.

It was baking again. Dries, Kasper and Ballero were taking it in turns to shuttle back to the team car and get bottles. By the time you'd finished one, someone would be going back for the next. I'd not taken much food with me to get over that first climb, in order to shave off every bit of weight I could going up the valley, so Dries went and got that for me too, and kept it all in his pockets until I needed a gel or a bar or whatever. Asking for these was the only time I spoke the whole way. I was suffering, but driven on by my determination to get as far up the climb as possible with the group.

When we hit the first part of the Mont-Louis climb proper, the change in gradient was almost imperceptible. The peloton quickened as we went into the first switchbacks. We swung one way, then back again. All of a sudden, we were into a block headwind, which would stay with us over most of the climbs that day. Right away, the peloton bunched up, which meant I could hang in there. 'Use this headwind!' I was telling myself. 'Use it to get as far as possible.'

Eventually, nearing the top, there was a little surge, from Ineos I think, and I kind of squeaked, 'Guys! Guys!' Morky, Tim and Dries dropped back with me to a more comfortable pace, maybe 340 or 350 watts, so that we were moving out of the back slowly, slowly.

Inevitably, we got barraged, but we held the peloton at around 100 to 200 metres, motorbikes next to us revving, a commissaire keeping an eye, a TV bike broadcasting my suffering. I turned to the motorbike and asked, 'Why are you videoing us? Why don't you go and video the French guys who are hanging on the cars behind?' I'd looked down a few moments before and seen another team hanging on to their car. There were others doing it too, just a couple of hundred metres further back behind the barrage that was being enforced behind us. Another case of one law for some, I guess...

We reached the top of the climb at Mont-Louis, but the road kept going steadily up towards Font-Romeu – easier than before, though. There was a feed zone, which took some speed off the peloton, and we managed to get back up to it. We'd got much further with the bunch than I'd thought we'd manage, and by doing so we already knew that we were almost certain to finish within the time limit. We just had to ride our own tempo from that point on.

Going down what was not a very steep descent into a headwind, we had to keep pedalling to stay with the peloton, which meant I didn't really get a lay-off. But that came when we hit the next climb of the Col de Puymorens. It started to kick off at the front of the peloton, and that was our signal to drop off and find our own tempo; a lot of other guys made the same decision, creating a decent-sized gruppetto.

After the short descent from the Puymorens, the road dragged up again to the Andorran border. It was kind of windy, so we were swapping off on the flatter parts. But as we got into Pas de la Case and its shopping complexes, the wind started to pick up and soon became so fierce that Dries, Tim and Morky couldn't stay in their triangle formation around me. We all ended up sitting in a line behind Dries as he led the way up the last couple of kilometres to the Envalira, the final hairpins taking us past what might be the most bizarrely located go-kart track in France.

From the top, there's a massive descent into Andorra, and when the wind's blowing like that, if you're not in the slipstream, you can lose time faster than you can while climbing. We struggled to cope with it, the group splitting apart going around every corner, forcing us to wait for each other, costing us time as we got back together. It was just as well we had plenty to play with. It eased, though, as we lost altitude, and the going got easier. As we neared the main towns in Andorra, the crowds started to grow, and featured familiar faces at times. There was a heckling mullet in an Aussie rules football shirt – Shane Archbold. My C Team accomplice for the year, Archie's one of the dozens of pros who've set up home in Andorra.

Act three of this stage began at the bottom of the long descent as we swung onto the final climb, the Col de Beixalis. It was less than seven kilometres long, but its middle section was by far the steepest bit of road we'd had to tackle all day, averaging 11 per cent for a couple of kilometres. We were in no danger of missing the time cut, as we could afford to lose 15 or 20 minutes, so more than two minutes a kilometre, and I was set on taking it easy.

'Guys, don't try. We'll ride our own pace,' I said as we started to climb. The rest of the group didn't hang about to wait for us, but we stuck together. The route was packed with people, with lots of Basques waving their flags. We were going so slow I could also pick out a few more people that I knew. I saw the Moto GP riders Aleix Espargaró and Jack Miller, who also live in Andorra, and fellow pro

and Essex resident Alex Dowsett with his baby. Fans had painted lines on the road to see how far you could wheelie; Max Walscheid gave them what they wanted, while I rolled my eyes. Grow up, will you …

I was doing fine one moment, then suddenly, completely out of nowhere, I just went lights out. Maybe I hadn't eaten enough, because I wasn't at all worried about whether or not I would make the time cut; maybe it was the heat, the altitude – I don't know. But I started to swing. I was never going to be in trouble of not making into the finish in time, but I hadn't expected to suffer so badly up there. My overriding thought was, *Thank fuck it's the rest day tomorrow*. We'd been going slow already and I had to tell the guys, 'Please, not so quick.' We were at a snail's pace, but I couldn't go any harder.

By that point it barely mattered, though. After the fast descent back into Andorra's main valley, we were the last four riders to finish, but still a good nine minutes inside the cut. We'd have taken that if it had been offered to us in Céret six hours earlier.

Jack Miller came up to see me that night at the hotel. He's a good mate and big into his cycling. He had to go on the bus with the doctor and have a Covid test before he was allowed in, then he came and joined us for dinner. Catta and Ballero knew who he was because he rides for Ducati and they like motorbikes. Tim didn't have any idea, though.

'Sorry. Who are you?' he said. It wasn't a dig: he didn't know Jack from Adam. 'What do you do?'

'I race motorbikes.'

'Ah, I don't really watch motorbikes.'

Jack's wicked. He's in his twenties, grew up on a farm in Australia and doesn't take life too seriously. He's the most humble guy you'd ever meet. We sat there talking about bikes and motorbikes. We agreed to meet up again the next morning and have him along on our short rest-day ride, up the valley to the foot of the road that leads to the resort of Arcalis, where we'd finished in the Tour in 2009.

After Jack headed off, Catta and I watched the England against Italy Euro 2020 final in our room, Ballero's screams of delight echoing down the corridor. I'm not a massive football fan but I was a bit upset when England lost. Overall, though, I had nothing to complain about. Two weeks of the Tour were complete and I had 24 hours to rest up for the final hurdles in the Pyrenees.

STAGE 16

13 July: Pas de la Case–Saint-Gaudens, 169km

This was the most straightforward mountain stage of the whole Tour for me. It was cool, the climbs didn't go that high, there was never really any chance of the time cut being an issue, and I felt good all day.

The start was at Pas de la Case, the little town just inside Andorra where French tourists come and buy their duty-free and fill up with cheap petrol. It was close to freezing when we got there, the cloud so low down that you couldn't see in front of the bus. We got wrapped up and went out to sign on, and it was weird. It didn't really feel like the Tour. Even though it was different at the starts this year because of the Covid restrictions, this still felt like an unusually quiet start. There wasn't really anyone there. It was quite eerie with all the mist blowing about as well.

There was a long neutral zone down the mountain back into France, 20 kilometres or so. We all had loads of layers on because of the cold and drizzle. I put on a green rain jacket and arm warmers, but didn't bother with leg warmers. I hate them when it's wet. I feel like they do more harm than good. I'd rather just put a bit of embrocation on my legs.

Heading down that neutral zone, you had to stay near the front because it was a bit slippery and there was always a chance of a crash, and if you got caught up in it or behind it you might end up fighting for position. When we got to the start line, we all stopped so that we could take some of our layers off. I even took my jacket off because I knew it was going to be full-on right from the start. Fitte was fussing a bit about it, telling me to put on an undervest and a gilet instead, but I don't like being bulky like that when I'm racing.

Then we started. We knew what to expect on our team because Kasper had had a massive gear fitted on his bike, and almost instantly he flew away from the peloton and got a big gap very quickly. There was real panic behind as we hit the valley before the first climb, the second-category Col de Port. I could remember the Port from the 2009 Tour and was confident that I'd be OK on it. There's quite a steep section near the bottom, so you've got to get through the first couple of kilometres, but after that it's not so bad. If you get into a rhythm you can spin a little gear up there, and I reckoned I could do that well enough to stay in the peloton most of the way up. That was the plan, anyway.

When we reached it, guys were getting shelled on the first ramps, more than would normally get dropped before me. But even though it was hard, I hung on for those first couple of kilometres then settled into it with the guys all around me. About halfway up, we started to slide back, but we kept to our tempo. We were doing a higher wattage than we'd ride in the gruppetto, but we thought if we kept to that we could get back up to the peloton on the descent and then get most of the way up the next climb, the Col de la Core, with them.

We weren't too far behind when we started down the Col de Port, but the descent was horrible. The road snakes down through

TOUR DE FORCE | 243

the trees and it was greasy and quite treacherous, so you just couldn't take any risks on it, and we couldn't get back to the peloton as easily as we'd expected. On the plus side, we were in a really big gruppetto, maybe 30 or 40 guys in it. We were on the front down all the Port, then we hit the valley and started to ride, trying to get the other riders to come through and collaborate with us. The problem was that half of them hadn't been in the gruppetto before and thought they could use us to get a free ride. Also, some of them didn't understand why you would want to get back up to the bunch. They didn't get that if we all put in a big effort in the valley we would end up back in the peloton and being pulled up the following climb.

We managed to get back into the peloton before the Col de la Core, and then it dawned on some of the guys in the gruppetto why that effort we'd made in the valley had been worthwhile. We rolled up most of the climb in the group, putting out the same watts that we would have been riding at in the gruppetto, but we weren't losing a minute a kilometre in the process.

We were quite close to the top when it kicked off again at the front of the group and we lost ground again, but by then we knew that we would never be in trouble of missing the time cut. We had a nice little gruppetto from the Core onwards and just rode into the finish from there. It was absolutely pissing down on that final part, but I didn't mind that. I always seem to go better when it's wet like that and there's more oxygen in the air. I was soaked but happy at the line. Just two more mountain stages to go…

STAGE 17

14 July: Muret–Saint-Lary-Soulan (Col du Portet), 178.4km

I ended this stage with just about every rider and staff member in the Tour convoy cursing me. In my defence, the situation that led to complaints raining in to the Tour organisation about me receiving preferential treatment from the French police was completely out of my control and down to one over-zealous gendarme who was apparently delighted to be looking after the rider in the green jersey.

The end of any stage with a summit finish heralds the start of another contest – the battle to get off the mountain. This can take far longer than anyone expects, especially if there's only one way out like there was on this one from the Col du Portet. The Pyrenees are always trickier in this respect. The valleys are tighter, the roads narrower, the bottlenecks more frequent. To get around this, the Tour organisation and the French police have introduced an evacuation system in recent years. Within a few minutes of the broom wagon reaching the finish behind the last rider on the road, all of the team and race organisation vehicles form a convoy behind police outriders and get an escort off the mountain, into the valley and, more often than not, to the nearest junction on the autoroute, so that they're not too late getting to their hotels.

The convoy starts to rumble even before the podium ceremony has kicked off, which means the stage winner and the riders in the different jerseys are often the last to leave and, as a consequence, to dinner and bed each evening. But no one seemed to have informed the gendarme who was escorting us that this was how things worked. He was wicked. I got in the car with the soigneurs, and right from the get-go he was whistling everyone out of the way, which they always do to the general public. But he was taking it even further, gesticulating for other team cars and buses to pull over as we approached.

Normally when that happens, the race vehicles will pull over, let the police motorbike and the vehicle with it go by, then jump in behind it, creating a new convoy. But this guy wasn't having any of that. He'd stop, kick off at them and order them back into line. People would still try to get in and he'd shout, '*Non!*' and order them back. Then off we'd go again. At one point we had two gendarmes: one would tell the cars coming the other way to get in, while the other kept it clear behind. It was like a police escort for royalty. We were absolutely flooring it, going past everyone like a Formula 1 car.

He ended up taking us past the whole race and all the way to the autoroute. When we finally stopped and pulled over, I took the green jersey I'd got on the podium, signed it and gave it to him. Apparently, as all the other Tour traffic streamed by a bit later, they saw him standing at the roadside waving the green jersey around.

That evening, the group chat for the team directors and race organisation was full of messages from people sounding off. 'It's not fair that one rider gets a police escort and everyone else has got to sit in the traffic. Blah, blah, blah …' I mean, come on now, grow up. Keep a bit of perspective. It made a change for me to be first into the hotel rather than the last, and I kind of felt like I deserved it after the day I'd endured on the bike.

I was nervous about this stage, not because I was afraid of the time cut, but more due to the prospect of the suffering that lay ahead for me on the long road from Muret to the summit finish on the Portet. The stage was effectively a repeat of 2018's short 65-kilometre stage to the same finish, but with 115 kilometres of mostly flat road to Bagnères-de-Luchon tacked on the front end of it.

This first section provided us with a bit of a tactical conundrum. We would have to ride it full gas in order to ensure the time limit wouldn't be an issue and also control it so the right break ended up going away. In other words, we had to treat the opening bit to Luchon almost like a sprint stage. What's more, it was Bastille Day, so just about every home rider would have *fourmis dans les jambes*, as the French say – ants in their legs. They'd all want to be in there, giving the locals something to crow about. And there was one more thing, too. Sonny Colbrelli and Michael Matthews had finished second and third at Saint-Gaudens the day before and were way closer to me in the points classification. Bling was only 37 behind, so we couldn't let them get in the break and take the points at the intermediate going into Luchon.

So we had to be very careful about who we allowed to escape. We couldn't let too big a break go, because if it managed to get a long way ahead of the peloton by Luchon, that would complicate our chances of making the time cut. Why? If there's a break of 20 guys who aren't a threat on GC but among them are a few riders who can climb well, a Nairo Quintana or Woet Poels, for instance, we couldn't allow them to get to Luchon ten minutes ahead of us, because we'd only lose a lot more time to them beyond that point.

As a result of all that, Tom's pre-stage briefing was even more detailed than usual. The plan for the day was to ride on the front from the off, only allowing a maximum of five guys to go clear – in short, a break that we could control if we needed to, assuming Tadej Pogačar's UAE team weren't interested in closing it down. They might be, but we couldn't count on them.

We all started at the front as the peloton headed out on narrow roads. Attacks kept going and then coming back. A break went and it was pretty strong, but the guys in it weren't good enough climbers to be able to pull that much out of us on the final climb. It was manageable. Then UAE surprised us by starting to pull, and, oh my life, they were going quick. We were nearing the end of the Tour and it was grim trying to hang on.

We got to Luchon with the break very much in range, the peloton together and all of us still in it. Tom's plan was coming together perfectly, and the intermediate sprint didn't change that too much. Bling edged me out for sixth place behind the break, but moved just a single point closer to me. Now for the climbs …

The Peyresourde isn't my least favourite climb in the Pyrenees, but it's a strong second after the Tourmalet. I despise it. It's relentlessly hard. There's one brief section near the bottom where the gradient eases a little, but after that it's 8 per cent pretty much all the way, just a touch out of my comfort zone. But I had a plan for it. I was a bit nervous about the fact that I had to do this full-effort sprint and then try to recover in two kilometres before the climb started, so once I was through the sprint I just carried on riding ahead of the peloton.

Rod used to get us to do these efforts where we'd do a sprint before a climb and then try to recover at threshold on the climb itself. We'd do loads of them. It teaches your body to recover at a higher wattage. Would it work as well after I'd just sprinted against Colbrelli and Bling with the green jersey on the line? I was about to find out.

I stayed at an unusually high wattage after the sprint and kept it going through the roundabout just beyond, the two right turns that followed and then the left onto the first steep ramp of the Peyresourde. A couple of guys passed me, but I was third onto it, kept my pace going until that short easing in the grade as you reach the sweeping left-hand corner where the road from the Port de Balès comes in from the right. As it kicked up again, I steadily eased back to the watts I wanted to keep to. We kept the tempo quite high, like we'd done on Col de Port the day before, higher than we'd been doing all Tour in the gruppetto. We weren't calculating on losing a minute per kilometre to the yellow jersey group as we'd planned going into the Alps, but about 40 seconds because we were riding that well. There were some guys working in there with us who we weren't used to seeing, like Froomey and Ineos mountain domestique Michał Kwiatkowski, and they knew if they stayed with us they'd get through and have a relatively easy day.

This was actually the first time I had been up the Peyresourde and thought, *That wasn't as hard as I'd expected it to be.* It had always felt steeper to me. We got over it all right, went down the descent, then hit the Col d'Azet and rode our gruppetto tempo again. We got over it without any real difficulty, went down the other side and then almost straight onto the final climb of the Col du Portet. We led up the first bit at our tempo again, then a few other riders started to come to the front and ride just a bit too hard. This got Tim and Ballero's backs up a bit, seeing these guys dick-swinging, and they started going with them until Morky brought them back into line. 'Guys, forget them. We're on the last climb now. Forget them,' he said. He was right. We had one more mountain stage to come, tougher than this one, but we could almost see Paris now. We were almost home and dry. Now for the Tourmalet …

STAGE 18

The Col du Tourmalet is my worst climb, without any doubt. I've never had a good experience on it. I hate it, absolutely loathe it. People think I hate all climbs, but I actually quite enjoy a lot of them; it's just that I'm not very good at climbing, relatively speaking. But the Tourmalet, I just hate it, hate everything about it, always feel shit on it. I don't like how it grades, and even though it's kind of flat at the bottom, I can't just sit and pedal there. I should be able to do the little flat bit at the bottom, but I never can. I'm always fucked before we get there because you almost always drag up the valley to get there.

Thanks in part to my pal the gendarme, I got a nice early night in our hotel, which you'd probably describe as grand but fading. It's the place where the team always stays when the race is in Pau, and Catta and I had been given a suite. Well, they called it a suite, but it was just a room with two double beds and a kitchenette.

I've no idea how long I'd been asleep when, *WAW! WAW! WAW!* The fire alarm went off. I got up and went to see what all the palaver was outside. Just as I opened the door, Carole Maes, the daughter of Luc Maes, the owner of our sponsor Latexco, came out of the room opposite. 'Where's your dad?' I asked her. I love Luc, he's so sound. I've known him for years and he's one of those sponsors who just does it for the passion. I always have a drink with him when I'm in Belgium. In all of the confusion, Carole couldn't hear me. 'Carole, is your dad all right?' I shouted.

'He's in that room,' she replied, pointing. 'He'll be all right, he won't even wake up.' It was just chaos, as if there really was a fire in the hotel, which it was already clear there wasn't.

People were running up and down the corridor. Fitte was dashing around but not really doing anything. Ricardo, the team's technical director, was trying to sort stuff out in the way that he does, like there's a process to everything. After five or ten minutes the alarm stopped, so everyone went back to bed. Ten minutes later, though, it went off again, and this time it was on for more than an hour.

The pandemonium was all anyone was talking about at breakfast. There were so many stories. I'd only seen what was happening on our floor, but there'd been plenty going on elsewhere too. It came up again in the briefing. Every day in the team meeting, Tom would always have a funny picture of some kind that was designed to release the tension before the stage. He'd often ask the team's photographer to Photoshop them. One day, when we had a long transfer, he put up a picture of a load of people packed like sardines on a bus with our faces superimposed on them. On this morning the photo was of a smoke-filled room with Ricardo's face superimposed on the body of a Calvin Klein model, just hanging out. We were crying when we saw it – so funny.

Tom had also printed off a picture of Fitte dressed as the Pope that had been taken a few years ago at a fancy-dress party. He'd put it above the urinal in the bus, and every day, when I went for a piss before the stage, it made me chuckle. It was one of those little things that make being on this team so gratifying. They're super-serious when they need to be, but everyone loves to have a laugh. I'm sure every other team would say the same, but it was only coming back to Deceuninck that made me realise how special the atmosphere is here.

There were two critical points for us that day: the intermediate sprint, which was located just beyond the second of two fourth-category climbs; and the Tourmalet, of course. We predicted – and everyone knew – that BikeExchange would go full gas on the second of those climbs before the sprint. It was about two kilometres, quite steep, but I wasn't going to get dropped on it. I was a bit insulted that they thought that might happen. Whether they attacked or not, I felt insulted even by having the assumption that they'd do it, but they have to try everything, I guess. All we had to do in response was to follow them in the sprint.

There were a couple of little kickers from the start, and Julian went away going up one of them. Because it was narrow, it was a bit chaotic in the bunch for quite a while, as it was difficult for riders to find the space to counterattack behind Julian, but lots of guys were clearly keen to try to bridge up to him. Michael Matthews and Colbrelli were active too, so we had to be on them and pull them back when they did move. Three more guys did manage to chase after Julian, and then it settled until, lo and behold, BikeExchange began to line up for the intermediate.

Tim stayed with me from the bottom of the climb, where we slid back twenty or so places. We got to the top in about fortieth position and then used the descent to move back up. After that, it was five kilometres to the sprint. We were slotted in behind BikeExchange, as Bling realised when he turned around and I was grinning straight back at him. I was just supposed to sit on him, and Morky was sitting behind me. If Bling, my closest rival in the points competition, moved, I had to go with him.

However, with a kilometre to go before the sprint, Morky came alongside me. 'Fuck 'em – let's just beat them!' he said. As they started to lead out, Morky got me on his wheel and went past them like they were standing still. He'd gone from quite a long way out, which meant I had to hit out from longer than usual as well, but I held on to win the sprint from the bunch, with Morky next across the line, so we gained an extra point on Bling, who was third. It was the psychological blow more than the points that mattered, though.

We sat up and waited for the bunch, but just before it caught us, *Wooosshhhh!* Thomas De Gendt went by like a rocket. If there's one thing that sows panic through a peloton it's Thomas De Gendt attacking. I was in the red after the sprint, and the bunch ignited. We'd just reached the point where the road starts to drag up the valley towards the foot of the Tourmalet, and it was *on* for maybe ten kilometres. I was absolutely swinging for the duration. They finally eased off when they caught Thomas, but I couldn't recover. I'd depleted every glycogen store I had. I'd blown for the first time in the Tour, and we hadn't even hit the two mountains.

As the road kept dragging up, I was suffering big time. The peloton wasn't even going that hard. We went through the feed zone and, just before you turn right to start the Tourmalet, I couldn't hold on any more. As the pass starts, the road rolls up and down a bit, reaching maybe 5 per cent at most, and we were off the back. I would have been fuming at me, but the guys didn't say a word. They all knew that I was on the limit after the sprint, but being dropped that early meant they would have to work much more than they'd expected. They didn't bat an eyelid, though. They just eased back to take up position in front of me and started rotating, sharing the work between them.

We held the peloton at 20 seconds until the climb actually started. Then the gap began to yawn. Having been so good the day before, I now couldn't push what we needed to push. Simply put, I was fucked. 'Guys, slow down, I can't do it,' I whimpered.

'Come on, Cav, come on. Last day, uh? Come on!' They formed a circle around me, kept the wind off, gave me bottles and gels, taking them back from me when I'd taken a swig or was left with just an empty wrapper.

Like I said, I fucking hate the Tourmalet. I've done it enough times to know exactly which kilometre we were at, where it was going to get particularly hard. The only bit that surprised me was the very last few hundred metres, which were steeper than I remembered. Or was I just going worse than I had done in the past?

After the final hairpin to the right, I crawled up to the crest. Our soigneur was there with bottles, and as I went to grab one he saw the green jersey and pulled it away, thinking I was from another team. 'What are you fucking doing?' I screamed. He panicked and ran after me to give me the bottle. It was Filip Sercu, who wasn't on the team when I'd last been with QuickStep. He didn't speak to me again for the rest of the Tour, but when you're in that much oxygen debt, you are totally irrational. You've got no idea what's going on.

One thing I had noticed halfway up the Tourmalet was that there appeared to be something wrong with my bike. When I got out of the saddle, I kept looking down, thinking I'd got a puncture. There was some kind of weird movement there. As we went into the first hairpin on the descent, I felt the bike skipping out and it spooked me. I told the guys I thought I'd punctured and they said to leave it, that it was just the road. I sussed out pretty quickly once again that I hadn't punctured, but I told the guys that there was definitely something wrong.

'Can you ride it?' Tim asked me.

'Yeah!'

'Keep going – we haven't got enough time to change it.'

We carried on. Normally, I fly down the Tourmalet. Bernie and I used to pick up three or four minutes coming down it, but we had to go slower than normal because I couldn't corner confidently.

We sped down into Luz-Saint-Sauveur, through the town and out the far side on to the climb to Luz Ardiden. The lead group was nearing the finish, and we knew as we started up it that we were safe, especially as it's not hard at all near the top. I'd also recovered by then because I'd taken a lot of gels in. Although we still had to press on, we had quite a lot of time we could lose if there was any problem.

As we climbed, we could hear snatches of Tom talking to Catta on the radio about the race that was going on ahead, which added to the feel-good atmosphere we had on the climb. Catta had been given a GC role because he was just outside the top ten – and that was after doing so much for us. We later worked out that if you took away the time he'd lost working for Julian in the first few days and then in the sprints for me, he would have been right up in the top ten. Hearing him being allowed to do his own thing and fighting for a position on GC was super-nice.

The whole way up to Luz Ardiden we took in what was going on around us and savoured the experience rather than suffering. We still had to push, but it was the first time there'd been no urgency. I could reflect a little at last. This was such a good group. They did almost everything for me – carried my bottles, my food, my jacket, kept me out of the wind. They believed, they cared, they protected me. No one had complained, no one had moaned, no one had made me feel like I was hurting them by making them work harder. Those days were more special than the wins. It showed the strength of our unit, the camaraderie. We'd been through a lot and I was able to really appreciate what they had done on that climb. I was so proud.

On the radio, Fitte was telling us, 'Well done, guys. Just a few kilometres left. We've nearly finished the Tour.' It was an important moment for us because we'd got through the mountains and could turn our attention back to sprinting. We crossed the line and hugged each other. The Tourmalet had bitten me yet again, but we'd got through it. The fact that fortune was with us was underlined when the same gendarme arrived to chaperone us down from the mountain. He was a bit more circumspect, though. Clearly someone had had a word.

STAGE 19

The principal talking point of this stage as far as I was concerned took place before I'd even got on a bike that morning, or more precisely at the moment I was just about to ride mine down to speak to the media before signing on. There had been some kind of issue with it when I'd ridden up and, more noticeably, down the Tourmalet the day before. After that stage had finished, I went to the mechanics and said that there was something wrong with my headset. I didn't know precisely what – maybe some water had got into it and was affecting the smoothness of the steering – but it didn't feel right. I asked them to sort the issue out.

I didn't have a good feeling about that day almost from the start. When Tom did the team meeting he made it clear that the focus would now switch from the mountains to the points title. 'We're switching our focus to green; we have to sacrifice stage wins for it,' he said. I hadn't been consulted about this and, to be fair, you don't argue anyway. Although it was my green jersey and they were supporting it fully, it's not really in my nature not to want to win. I don't want to be cautious. My philosophy is always, *Let's just go for it.* I'm not a gambling man at all, but if I went into a casino I'd put all of my chips on black or red. I wouldn't spread them out across the table. I'd be all in. That's how I am.

I wouldn't say I was pissed off or angry with the decision, just deflated. It felt like there was no plan for the day. We had to go through the final in case there was a sprint, but we weren't going to control it for a sprint. If another team wanted to, fine, but we weren't going to be helping out. But I still couldn't help feeling, *We're QuickStep and I'm a sprinter, so* … But I kept that quiet.

This did, however, add to the feeling of unease I had. It's hard to explain how or why this develops. Sometimes there's something in your gut that tells you it's not going to be a good day. It might not be anything in particular, nothing that you can obviously put your finger on, but you get it now and again as a bike rider. Maybe it also stems from the fact that my head probably plays a bigger role in my performance than my body. Maybe I'm a bit more susceptible to it, the sensation that's something's off. I'd actually tweeted before the third stage about not having a good feeling, and I hadn't been wrong about it that day.

There'd been other days too when I'd felt unsettled. The stage to Nîmes was another one, although on that occasion there was a specific reason behind it. When you're leading one of the jersey competitions at the Tour, each morning you get a bag from ASO, green in my case, containing all the kit you're likely to require for that stage. They're good at working out what you'll need depending on the weather conditions and the type of terrain. You get a new jersey each day, usually a long-sleeved version if the forecast's not the best, plus arm warmers and perhaps a vest. If it's hot, there might only be a thin jersey in there. Then on sprint days, you get a skinsuit. They started putting the skinsuit in for the green jersey – and only for the green – a few years ago, when riders started wearing skinsuits full-time. Before that, you felt like you were at a disadvantage if you were in the green jersey and you didn't get a skinsuit.

That morning in Saint-Paul-Trois-Châteaux, there wasn't a skin-suit in my bag and it blew my mind. I had a freak-out because it was something out of my control, something I couldn't factor in to my planning for the stage. I'm so dialled in on doing what I can to be prepared that stuff like that flicks me. I don't run around screaming – I used to, but I don't do that any more. I was just telling people on the bus that it needed to be sorted, and quickly. Someone dashed off to see ASO and came back to say there was no skinsuit. I only had two and hadn't brought one with me because I'd expected to get a new one. I'd worn one into Valence a couple of days before and then given it to Morky to show my appreciation after I'd won that day.

It turned out that not only did they not have any that day, they didn't have any at all because they hadn't ordered any new ones for the 2021 Tour. They'd made them last year and Sam didn't end up wearing them very much. I think he wore one on the Champs-Élysées, but that was it. Sagan never wears one either. So they were just using up the ones that had been left over from last year.

When we started the stage to Nîmes, there was talk that we weren't going for a sprint that day because I wasn't wearing a skin-suit. During the stage itself, Wout van Aert came up to me after the break had gone away and said, 'We knew you weren't going to sprint today.'

'Why's that?'

'Because you didn't have a skinsuit on.'

'But, mate, they haven't got any skinsuits,' I told him. 'I would have worn one if they had.'

Oddly, that morning in Mourenx there was a skinsuit in my ASO bag of kit because they'd ordered a couple more during the mountain stages. Nevertheless, a bit like in Nîmes, I had a strange feeling that things weren't going to be right.

I had to get ready five or ten minutes before everyone so I could do some media before signing on. I got off the bus, went to my bike and, as I picked it up, the headset didn't turn. Guido was the nearest mechanic. As I mentioned before, I was at Telekom with Guido, I've known him for years and I love him. I said, calmly to start with, 'Guido, feel this, my headset's not been fixed.'

'Oh, yeah, we didn't change it. We checked it.'

'But I asked last night for it to be changed,' I said.

'We couldn't do it. I'll go and get your spare bike.'

That's another thing. Your spare bikes never feel the same – they never do – and I just cracked. I wasn't pissed off that there was an issue with my headset; it was the fact that I'd already said something about it and nothing had been done. It just threw me.

'For fuck's sake, sort it out!' I yelled at Guido, and went back on the bus to try and get composed again. By the time I got off the bus again, Guido had brought the spare bike and we were fine. There was no issue. He knows what I'm like. Only later did it become apparent that someone in the crowd had filmed me sounding off at him.

I don't need to be told that you shouldn't shout at someone, anyone. But we'd worked together so long that he knew it would be instantly forgotten, that it wasn't a personal thing. I was pissed at the situation. It was me getting angry about my bike not working, not being pissed at him. You've got to know the context to understand what was going on, the fact that we've known each other for so long. I know I shouldn't be like that anyway, with anyone, but I am. I've always been like that and I always will be because of the stress that's on me. We were going for green, everyone was fucking tired and, to top it off, I had the feeling that something was off that day.

I went and signed on and saw Eddy Merckx at the start. ASO had invited him to the race because it had been in Mourenx that he'd won arguably his most famous Tour victory, in 1969 after a solo attack over the Aubisque and Tourmalet. We had a bit of a chat, and Eddy told me, 'I so hope you win today.' Unfortunately, there was little chance of that happening.

We'd only just got underway, not even a kilometre into the stage, and were going up a short climb. There were riders trying to break clear, and I was near the front, eighth wheel, when there was a crash right in front of me, a close call. I just had to pull my foot out and then get going again. The break went quite soon after that and, as we weren't riding, the gap started to go out very quickly because no one else was ready to take it up. UAE and Alpecin eventually started setting the pace and asked if we could help them. 'No,' we had to tell them. 'We're not pulling today.'

The road continued to roll a little bit. We were in maybe fiftieth position when, all of a sudden, there was another crash. I braked and stopped before the crash, hoping that everyone behind me had been as quick to react. *BANG!* They weren't. I got hit from behind and went flying. I got up off the deck and was pretty unscathed, but my shoe was ripped. The strap had kind of broken, so it wouldn't tighten, but it could have been much worse. I hadn't crashed all Tour, and within a few minutes I'd just missed one and then been on the ground after another. All this was confirming the feeling of unease that I had.

Not long after we'd been through the intermediate, where Michael Matthews got three points back on me, people started to accelerate going through a town, and I knew I had to keep vigilant. There was an attack and Ballero went with it. It was so narrow and twisty through the streets that nobody behind the front rank of riders really realised this group had gone away. For maybe five minutes afterwards, no one in the peloton really knew what to do. Then it kicked off like we were at the beginning of a race. There were attacks going all over the place.

This ran completely against the standard script for racing. Although it's not written down that when a break goes, a team needs to control it and then pull it back for a sprint, that's how cycling's evolved. It's the most efficient way of racing. Riders who know that their only chance of winning is to be in a break take that option, and then the sprint teams pull them back. After a few years when nobody ever wanted to go in a break because someone, often my HTC teammates, would control them so well, riders now know they've got a realistic chance in a break again, so the standard template for racing has resumed.

Not on this stage, though. Almost without warning, it was like that script had been ripped up and tossed away. It was completely gung-ho. Lots of teams hadn't won a stage up to that point and they were throwing everything at it. Riders were attacking, while the break was a minute or so in front, absolutely tearing along. UAE came to the front and the peloton was in one line; BikeExchange and Israel were pulling too. It made me realise that lots of teams react to stuff and aren't proactive. Why had they waited so long to race like this? Why were they reacting when there were already two different breaks up the road? It seemed to me like they were pissing in the wind. Quite soon, they decided that too and they eased up. That was effectively the day done for us. We rode easy into the finish, where, with a time trial to come the next day, we really did seem very close to Paris.

I did the podium and still wasn't in the best mood. It got worse when Peta messaged me as I was on the way to the hotel to say that there was stuff on social media about me kicking off at Guido. She told me to beware. When we got back to the hotel, the first thing I did was go to see the mechanics. I said to Guido, 'Mate, I'm so sorry. I'm so sorry I talked to you like that this morning.'

'It's fine,' he said. 'I've known you for 15 years. It's fine.'

Then we went in the truck. The mechanic in there explained why he hadn't changed the headset, and I told him that next time it needed to be changed if I asked for it to be done. It was all very amicable. It's a relentless, thankless job sometimes as a mechanic. Early mornings, long, cramped days in the back of a team car, and late nights sorting 21 bikes, three per rider, for the forthcoming stage. Stood in noisy car parks in all weather conditions.

When I eventually saw the video soon after, there wasn't really that much to it. But once things like that are on social, they get a life of their own. Of course, none of the back history between Guido and me is there, hardly anyone outside the team knew about the issues that had wound me up or the fact that I'd already spoken to Guido about it. I spoke to our press guy, Phil, and he was in favour of just leaving it. I told him that I knew it wasn't big and that doing a post about it would make it even bigger, but I wanted to do it anyway just to nip it in the bud with the bandwagon brigade. So I posted something and then people started piling in. 'You shouldn't have done that!' 'You should have apologised!' And so it went on. But I knew all that. Do they think I'm a monster? It ends up being a case of you having to appease social media. It didn't matter that we'd sorted it all out internally, that it didn't amount to much for us. You have to appease people you've never met. Like I said, it was one of those days.

STAGE 20

The plan was simple for the final time trial. Get around safely and save everything I possibly could for Paris. I knew that it was going to be a long day for me. I was one of the early starters but would have to wait around for a good while after the finish for the podium ceremony. I'd decided on a way I could fill a good deal of the time, though.

When the jersey winners get to the end of the race, most of them, like Sam, for instance, order 30 replica jerseys from ASO and give them out to the team to show their appreciation. But I wanted to express my gratitude a little differently. I'd been keeping all of the extra green jerseys and other bits of kit that you get each day as a Tour competition leader in a bag. We'd been in this bubble as a team for almost 30 days now, and I wanted everyone who'd been within that bubble to have a real green jersey. So I put the bag in the camper and told Ricardo I wanted to spend the afternoon with him writing out a personal message to each member of the staff, and then hand them over at dinner that night.

As had been the case for the first time trial at Laval, I planned to do a reconnaissance of the course, but ended up having to abandon it.

That morning, I got a set of new shoes from Specialized, and when I went out to do the recon with the boys I took an Allen key with me to properly set up the shoes and cleats. I wasn't with the others for long. Right from the get-go I was stopping every 500 metres to adjust them and couldn't get it right. After about half an hour I'd only done three kilometres of the course and was still in the outskirts of Libourne. I didn't get out into the vineyards at all. I gave up and went back.

Eventually, I got the shoes kind of right and started to prepare for my time trial. It was about as chilled as a Tour TT gets. I put my numbers on my skinsuit, warmed up and set off on the course with Fitte following me in the team car. I wanted to go even easier than I had in the first one at Laval. I had the Champs-Élysées the next day and Vasi had said, 'Really, don't go harder than I've told you to go.' He gave me a target in terms of watts to sit on and I stuck to it, just riding round, taking every corner easy. I felt so relaxed that I noticed how stunning the time trial was. It was hot, there were huge numbers of fans out on the roads, and the vineyards looked amazing. I was able to take it all in. I was literally on a ride.

After I finished, I spoke to a few people in the media mixed zone and went back to the camper, where my long wait began. I had a shower then a massage from Sharky. The lads started coming in, then going out again, while I sat there signing all of the jerseys.

For a while, it did look like I might have some company in the team car to the hotel after the stage, as Catta and Kasper went close to the win. Kasper was in the hot seat for a long while and we had really high hopes for him, but Wout van Aert just dashed them.

As the final riders were going off, I got changed for the podium ceremony. I rolled down there and saw Wout in the hot seat. The TV cameraman wanted me to go in and say congratulations, but I wasn't keen. 'It weell be nice for ze television,' he said. But I said no. It was Wout's moment, and I don't really like it when people gate-crash at times like that.

I did congratulate him later when I saw him at the podium. 'Nice one, storming ride,' I said, and he replied, 'It was just a warm-up for tomorrow.' We both laughed but I was thinking, *Not a fucking chance!*

Christian Prudhomme came to see me before the podium presentation. 'Thank you so much. This Tour has been amazing,' he told me. I chatted with Tadej Pogačar too. After the Carcassonne finish, I sat with him as we waited for the doping control and asked him if he would swap one of his yellow-jersey lions for one of my Skoda green-jersey wolves so that I could give it to my youngest, Casper (these stuffed toys are given to the jersey wearers each day on the podium). He was happy to do the exchange, but I said we should wait till the end because I didn't want to jinx either of us. We did manage one swap that day, of our podium jerseys, which we signed for each other. I wrote something like, 'To Tadej, it's an honour to ride with you'. His read, 'To Mark, thank you'. That was pretty special because he's probably going to win the Tour for something like the next ten years.

After the podium we had a long drive up to Poitiers, where the teams were all staying. It was just me and Sharky in the car because we'd been the only ones left at the finish. By the time we got there the lads had all eaten. I had dinner and then went round the staff, who were still having theirs, and gave out the green jerseys. 'Listen, guys,' I told them, 'I could wait until Paris, but tomorrow night I'm going to be pissed drunk or just pissed off. So whichever one it is, I'm better off giving them to you tonight.'

STAGE 21

We had to get up early so that we could finish the trip up to Paris, where I knew Peta and the kids were already set up in the team's hotel. So it was back on the bus for the last time. It's decked out with a Bang and Olufsen surround-sound system with a big screen at the front, and everyone was up for watching a movie. We wanted something upbeat and action-packed to get us in the right mood, and there's nothing better than *Top Gun* for that. We watched it all the way to Paris, everyone quoting the lines and eating the carefully prepared pre-race lunch.

That gave us all a lift, and there was better to come. We were on the outskirts of Paris when Peta called to say that she and the kids had an opportunity to see me before the start. She knows that I don't usually like being contacted in the hours before a big race, and tends to leave me to focus. But she knew this was a different situation to normal, because I hadn't seen them for a month. She said she'd understand if I wanted to leave it till later, but I was all for it.

The bus pulled into a petrol station soon after, and I could see Peta and the kids waiting for us. I don't think she'd told the kids that I was going to be there. When the door of the bus opened and they saw me, they leapt on me. I was totally made up. I'm normally so stressed on the morning of the Champs-Élysées stage, but it was a bit of reality, a chance to be out of the bubble for one moment, even if it was right on the very last day. We only had a few minutes before our little treat was over. Then it was game mode.

The Champs-Élysées stage is weird if you're a sprinter or part of a sprint team. While most of the peloton see it as a lap of honour, albeit a really hard one, we obviously have to keep our focus. You're not just rolling in having completed the Tour. This is the Super Bowl for us, the biggest stage for sprinters of any season. It's the reason you battle to get to Paris. You don't do it to get five ProCyclingStats ranking points for finishing. It's the most iconic sprint in cycling.

We had to talk about the finish a fair bit because they changed it this year. It used to be 300 metres up the Champs-Élysées as you swing onto it from Place de la Concorde, but it had been moved another 400 metres up the avenue as a result of changes to the road layout, and that altered the whole dynamic of the sprint. What made this sprint such a great test before was that you had to nail everything, especially that final corner, which was crucial. It was a little too far out to go all the way to the line from there. Equally, it was a little too close to be able to take a breather after the corner and then go. One thing remained the same, though: you established your position before the tunnel that's at the bottom of the circuit after you come down the Champs-Élysées and through Place de la Concorde.

When we discussed it, Morky said that we needed an extra guy coming into the finish: not just one in front of me, but two as we came through that final right-hander. 'At 700 metres, ease off through the corner, take a breath, just wait until you feel them next to you and then go,' he told Ballero.

I'd decided to throw absolutely everything at it. I put on my time-trial skinsuit that has no pockets and zips up at the back, making it more aerodynamic. I had overshoes on for the same reason. Morky was going to carry my food for me and would stay next to me for the duration, giving me gels when I needed them. Wearing the skinsuit meant that I couldn't stop for a piss, so I had to squeeze one out before we went to the start.

The media, meanwhile, had decided that I didn't sprint in Libourne because I was saving myself for the ultimate fairy tale of breaking the record on the Champs-Élysées. But in my head I'd got the record. I'd matched Eddy, so why couldn't they shut up about it now? I felt a pressure that I didn't want. This was the Champs-Élysées, for heaven's sake. Nothing else mattered.

It's a one-off stage that begins as a procession. Photos are taken of the jersey winners and everyone's talking, so it's easy to lose concentration and hit a traffic island or something like that. But I was totally switched on. I didn't speak to many people, I was just doing my own thing, saving myself, saving myself, saving myself, as it's so easy to forget that you have to conserve energy. As you enter the centre of Paris, the tempo starts to pick up. Guys suddenly want to be near the front but not right at the front, and other guys are trying to be in front of them, and the tempo just builds and builds. As the peloton approaches the entry point to the circuit, it feels like you're coming into a bunch sprint because of the speed and nervousness.

As we hit the Champs the attacks started right off, but I was confident that they would all be reeled in, despite some qualms among my teammates that a break might be able to stay away. That barely ever happens, and I was sure it wouldn't on this occasion.

There are too many sprint teams that have waited so long for this opportunity; they're not going to let it pass by.

I sat near the back with Morky, not knowing if our guys were controlling and with little idea of what they were doing at the front, but always confident that they'd be keeping any breaks within range. The two of us moved up for the intermediate, which was located at the top of the Champs-Élysées, soon after the start of the third of eight laps on the circuit. I couldn't really lose the green now unless I crashed, but I still wanted to take all the points I could behind the three riders who were half a minute or so ahead of the bunch. BikeExchange went to lead out Michael Matthews, and Morky intimidated him a bit, sandwiching him behind his lead-out man, while I came around Morky to take fourth place without much of an effort. Morky was quick enough to claim fifth. Then we returned to the back of the bunch until the final two laps.

Coming around the Arc de Triomphe at the top end of the Champs-Élysées for the last time, we went around the outside and ended up close to the front. Ballero then accelerated and moved Morky and me right to the front, where Julian was pulling. *What's he pulling for?* I thought. *We don't need him to be pulling now.* Then Kasper started pulling. It was going to go downhill fast anyway, and we'd said that we needed to stay together at this point, but they'd ended up on the front too early. I hoped that they were going to be there when we hit Place de la Concorde, going down towards the tunnel. But they were done before we got there.

Fuck, we're down! I was thinking. As we hit Place de la Concorde, my chain came off for a split second and I lost Morky's wheel. I got it back on and moved back onto him, only to get switched when we turned left off the Place de la Concorde to go down into the tunnel. I can't even remember who did it, but they came across me so aggressively that I almost crashed. I lost Morky again too.

Flying into the tunnel, Ballero was up at the front, Morky was a few places behind him and I was a few behind Morky. Not ideal, but I didn't panic. I stayed in the line and then used the width in the tunnel to move up, still as cool as you like. I got back on Morky as we came out of the tunnel and immediately swung left on Rue de Rivoli. This was one of the sections that had been changed and was much narrower than before, but Morky managed to move me up on the outside.

There were teams fighting and bodies everywhere as we went left again into Place de la Concorde for the final time. We'd wanted Ballero to lead across here and through the last corner, but he was done, used up earlier than we'd wanted. Morky now had to do the lead-out on his own, coming up the right-hand side of the bunch.

This was the one place we didn't want to be coming into the last corner, which goes to the right. It means you're going to be on the inside and you're likely to get baulked by riders who are taking a smoother line. The best line is to go out wide and swing in because you carry more speed through the corner as you come in tight on it, which means that the guys that are trying to come underneath on the inside have to go on the brakes, give way in effect. As Jumbo hit out on the left to take that wide line and lead out Wout van Aert for the sprint, I could see Wout's Belgian national champion's jersey coming by me and realised there was a slight gap on his wheel. The next instant, I was in it. They had two guys left, lead-out man Mike Teunissen and Wout. Perfect.

We hit right around the corner, still perfect, drifting across to the barriers on the left-hand side of the Champs-Élysées. Then Teunissen began to accelerate. At that moment Alpecin's Jonas Rickaert, Jasper Philipsen's lead-out man, came alongside me. He didn't try to pass me; he just held me there. Like a bird in a cage, I was trapped.

With 600 metres still to go, I thought I was fucked. Rickaert's sole objective was to stop me from sprinting. I knew it there and then, and there was nothing I could do about it. My only hope was that Wout would move to the right as he opened up his sprint so that I could find a gap on the inside of him along the barriers. There was a bit of a space, and when I was 20 years old I might have gone through whatever gap was there, but I knew I couldn't do it without the risk of crashing.

With 300 to go, Rickaert swung off and Philipsen came onto my right shoulder. Seconds later, Teunissen swung off, clearing the way for Wout to sprint. As Teunissen lost speed and came back down the line, Philipsen had to go right to avoid him, on his outside, and start his sprint, and in that moment a window opened for me in front of the slowing Teunissen.

The only problem was that I couldn't get into it. Because I'd been hoping for a gap to open along the barriers, I had my front wheel on the left side of Wout's rear wheel. When I saw the space open on his right-hand side, I couldn't switch across into it because our wheels were overlapping on his inside. I now realised that I was in a hopeless situation. When Philipsen swung back in again to go elbow to elbow with Wout, the window of opportunity closed. I just had to sit there and watch the two Belgians sprint it out, stuck on Wout's wheel until we crossed the finish line. There was nothing I could do, absolutely nothing. I was fuming. I hadn't even sprinted. I hadn't even tried to sprint.

After we crossed the line I was silent. I should have been cele-brating the green and four stage wins, but I'd just lost. My dismay had nothing to do with not getting a thirty-fifth Tour victory or anything like that. I'd missed out on the biggest sprint stage of them all. My mind was already starting to whirr with analysis and the possible permutations of the sprint. If it had happened because I wasn't good enough, I could have accepted it. I'd have felt the same if I'd messed up, but I don't think I did.

I hate a 'what if?' scenario, but this one played on my mind instantly and stuck with me for days. What if I'd stayed on Morky? He'd delivered me pretty much every time before that and I trust him more than anyone. But I think I've been in the game long enough to assess situations and not be afraid to take whatever decision I think is best, and leaving him coming onto the Champs-Élysées was a better option. I also tried to go through what Morky might have done and I honestly don't know. Maybe I wouldn't have been in that position, but I'll never know.

I also reflected a lot on Alpecin's tactics. When I saw Rickaert after the finish I stared at him. It wasn't that I wanted to fight him, because he didn't do anything wrong. I wasn't necessarily pissed off with him for blocking me in – that's a tactic, and I don't expect to be given any gifts – but I'm not very good at understanding people who don't think like me. I don't deal well with that. It blows my mind. I was left thinking, *Why would you do that? Why would you not just go for the win?*

I would have expected Rickaert to keep pushing rather than sit next to me, either to keep Philipsen moving forwards or to block Wout in against the barriers. Wout was, after all, the sprinter in front of me with a lead-out man in front of him. So wouldn't it make sense to do it to him? If Rickaert had done that, I would have been blocked as well, so Philipsen would have had an even better shot at the win.

Obviously, Rickaert had it in his head that Morky would be leading me into the final and he was ready to trap me with that tactic. However, I had another sprinter than Morky in front of me. If I'd have gone in with Rickaert's plan, I'd have just shifted it up one, regardless of whether it's me, Wout, Matthews or whoever else was second in line. You'd do it to the guy who was on his lead-out man, Wout in this case. You could even stop his lead-out man trying to come back out, making it even more difficult for him. But he was so focused on fucking me over that he forgot that there was still a sprinter ahead. What Rickaert did was right in theory, but he ended up focusing on the person – me – rather than on the situation. When you're in a match sprint on the track, you focus on your rival in that way, but if you do that in a bunch sprint where ten riders are going for the win, someone else is going to beat you almost every time.

I just sat quietly after the finish. Julian came and put his arm around me. Then Peta brought the kids out and I was happy to see them. We made our way to the podium, where I congratulated Tadej on his Tour win and we swapped cuddly toys with each other as we'd agreed in Carcassonne, my wolf for his lion. Then I was called up to be presented with the green jersey. After winning it in 2011, it was something I'd never targeted since 2012, when I was with Sky. Then along came Peter Sagan, a rider who was always a threat in bunch sprints and could win intermediates even if there were mountains before them. It meant green was never attainable. I hadn't targeted it this year, because the Tour happened so late for me. When we'd started in Brest, the thought of finishing in Paris hadn't entered my head, not with the Alps and Pyrenees in between. But ten years on from my first points title, I'd got the green jersey again.

I took the kids up on the podium with me and it was beautiful. They were all as good as gold, and the photos … I can't stop looking at the photos, looking at their faces. After being in that bubble for so long, having my family with me put everything in perspective straight away. I felt like the luckiest man in the world. I'll remember that moment for ever and hopefully they'll treasure it too.

Then I was called up to the podium again alongside the other jersey winners, which was Tadej, because he'd won all of the other three. He's this young kid who's still very much in the early part of his career despite already having two Tour de France titles to his credit, while I'm at the other end of mine. The new king and the king of the comeback, a fairy-tale story for both of us.

I'd been certain I would win in Paris and had been toying with the idea of announcing my retirement from racing if I won on the Champs-Élysées. I pictured myself saying that I'd achieved everything that I possibly could and far more, then a mic drop. Career over.

Securing my legacy was the primary reason that I carried on racing this year. I knew I still had it in me, just as I knew that every year I kept racing and didn't win was damaging that legacy. I knew that there were exceptional circumstances that had kept me from showing I could still win on the biggest cycling stage there is. Even before the season started, I knew I could win a bike race again, and as it went on and a seemingly impossible return to the Tour presented itself, I knew I could win there too.

So where does that leave me? I guess I'd say unsure of what the future holds, but very happy as I look forward to it. I've shown that I'm getting better again and I still love riding my bike. If I'd stopped the previous year, I'd have been bitter about cycling for ever. I'd have been one of those old guys who slags cyclists off, bitter about the sport, about the people in the sport, miserable. I didn't enjoy it any more. But, after this season, I've fallen in love with cycling again. Topping it all, for the first time in five years I've had success in the race that means more to me than any other, the race that has given me the life I have. It had been so long since I'd savoured what the Tour means to me that I'd almost forgotten its significance, why you put the sacrifices in. You win races, but when you win at the Tour it's different. Absolutely nothing comes close to it.

Do I stop now? Don't tell me, because I'm sick to the back teeth of people doing that. Instead, just think about what you'd do in my position. It's not easy, is it? Maybe one more year …?

ACKNOWLEDGEMENTS

Peta, Delilah, Frey, Casper and Finn, you're the people that see me at my lowest, who see me at my highest, and who see me as the real me. It can't be easy living with me, but you give me more than cycling ever could: love and support, a sense of reality when I'm off the bike, a reminder of what's fundamentally important in my life.

My team – to Patrick for giving me the opportunity, to Ricardo, Fitte, Tom and the rest of the directors for believing in me, and particularly to Brian, one of my best friends, who pulled for me when I needed it.

To Vasi – what can I say? You've done every pedal revolution with me and put your heart into absolutely everything. It's more than a job for you and I cherish the close relationship that's been born as a consequence of that, the fact that we're now friends and confidants.

My gratitude also goes to Shane Sutton and Rolf Aldag, for always checking in on me during the bad years, for always being there for me.

To everyone at Deceuninck-QuickStep, some of you are mentioned, some of you aren't but all of you have welcomed me back to the family in a manner that has absolutely blown me away. Thanks to Martijn Adema, Franck Alaphilippe, Julian Alaphilippe, João Almeida, Shane Archbold, Kasper Asgreen, Andrea Bagioli, Davide Ballerini, Sam Bennett, Davide Bramati, Mattia Cattaneo, Rémi Cavagna, Josef Černý, Joeri Clauwaert, Dirk Clarysse, Stephanie Clerckx, Geert Coeman, Nicolas Coosemans, Toon

Cruyt, Peter De Coninck, Tim Declercq, Dries Devenyns, Remco Evenepoel, Pauline Farazijn, Ian Garrison, David Geeroms, Yankee Germano, Álvaro Hodeg, Mikkel Honoré, Alexandru Hovcu, José Ibarguren, Fabio Jakobsen, Philip Jansen, Marije Jongedijk, Iljo Keisse, James Knox, Yves Lampaert, Dominique Landuyt, Kenny Latomme, Klaas Lodewyck, Phil Lowe, Fausto Masnada, Michael Mørkøv, Jason Osborne, Marc Patry, Anthony Pauwels, Koen Pelgrim, Jo Planckaert, Frederick Pollentier, Rudy Pollet, Franck Potier, Kurt Roose, Guido Scheeren, Florian Sénéchal, Filip Sercu, Pieter Serry, Stijn Steels, Jannik Steimle, Zdenek Štybar, Alessandro Tegner, Dirk Tyteca, Geert van Bondt, Bert van Lerberghe, Kurt van Roosbroeck, Joris van Roy, Rik van Slycke, Anthony Vandrepotte, Stijn Vandenberghe, James Vanlandschoot, Yvan Vanmol, Mauri Vansevenant, Cedric Verbeken, Patricia Vercamer, Julie Verrept, Lounes Verschaeve, Michaël Verschaeve, Kevin Verstaen, Steven Vrancken and Manu Wemel.

To Jesper Højer at Meatless Farm for his support and friendship, and to the brands who stood by me as a person when things were bad – Oakley, Monster, Richard Mille.

My thanks also to Andrew Goodfellow, Claire Collins and everyone at Ebury Publishing, and to my literary agent David Luxton, my agent Duncan Ross and everyone at Wasserman for making this book happen, and in such rapid time.

To Peter Cossins and Daniel Friebe, who took on a greater task than me going to the Tour de France. The hours were long, the deadlines were tight, but your persistence and desire were unfathomable and this book would not have been anywhere close to possible without that. Thank you, guys.